The Privileges of Independence

Early America
History, Context, Culture

Jack P. Greene and J. R. Pole
SERIES EDITORS

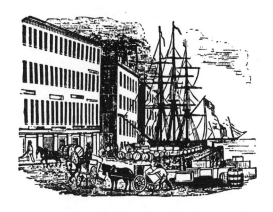

The Privileges
of Independence

*Neomercantilism and
the American Revolution*

JOHN E. CROWLEY

THE JOHNS HOPKINS UNIVERSITY PRESS

BALTIMORE & LONDON

Portions of chapter 4 appeared as "Neo-mercantilism and *The Wealth of Nations*," *Historical Journal* 33 (1990): 339–60, and are reprinted by permission.
Portions of chapter 6 appeared as "Commerce and the Philadelphia Constitution: Neo-Mercantilism in Federalist and Anti-Federalist Political Economy," *History of Political Thought* 13 (1992): 73–97, and are reprinted by permission.

The Johns Hopkins University Press
2715 North Charles Street
Baltimore, Maryland 21218–4319
The Johns Hopkins Press Ltd., London

Library of Congress Cataloging-in-Publication Data
Crowley, John E., 1943–
The privileges of independence : neomercantilism and the American Revolution / John E. Crowley.
p.   cm. — (Early America)
Includes bibliographical references and index.
ISBN 0-8018-4667-6 (hc : acid-free paper)
1. United States—Politics and government—1775–1783.   2. United States—History—Revolution, 1775–1783—Economic aspects.   3. Mercantile system—United States—History—18th century.   4. Mercantile system—Great Britain—History—18th century.   5. Great Britain—Colonies—America—Commerce.   6. United States—Commerce—Great Britain.   7. Great Britain—Commerce—United States.   8. United States—Commerce—History—18th century.
I. Title.   II. Series.
E215.1.C75   1993
973.3′1—dc20   93-3563

A catalog record for this book is available
from the British Library.

FOR MY PARENTS

John Denis Crowley
Mary Elizabeth Crowley

He who considers these provinces as states distinct from the *British Empire*, has very slender notions of *justice*, or of their *interests*. We are but parts of a *whole*; and therefore there must exist a power somewhere, to preside, and preserve the connection in due order.

JOHN DICKINSON
Letters from a Farmer in Pennsylvania, 1767

Nothing can be more weak than the idea of courting commerce. America will have from us what she cannot get cheaper and better elsewhere; and what we want from her, she will sell to us, as cheap as she will to others.

LORD SHEFFIELD
*Observations on the Commerce of
the American States,* 1783

To allow trade to regulate itself is not, therefore, to be admitted as a maxim universally sound.

JAMES MADISON
Congressional debate, 1794

CONTENTS

W AS IT ONLY coincidental that the American republic and Adam Smith's classic work of liberal political economy appeared in the same year, 1776? Could the Revolution have included economic liberalism—the legitimation of economic self-interests and the acceptance of their outcomes in the market—among its principles? Because American nationality depended on independence from a commercial empire, I originally thought that a central question of this book would be Smith's influence on American thinking about commercial relations between Britain and the United States after an imperial monopoly no longer provided economic links. However, it turned out that a book about the influence of Smith on the political economy of the American revolutionary generation would be very short.

As an inevitable result of the imperial crisis and its revolutionary outcome, Anglo-American political economists had to come to terms with the shift from a de jure to a de facto commercial dependence of the American states on Great Britain.[1] This book deals transatlantically with a series of issues during this transition. The series begins with the revision during the 1750s of conventional wisdom on colonial commerce and foreign trade. Next are comparisons of British and American reevaluations of colonial commerce during the imperial crisis. The series concludes with a contrast of the British rationale for postwar commercial policy with that prevailing in the United States.

The commercial outcome of the War of American Independence required just the sort of reappraisal of Anglo-American political economy that Smith had urged as a rationale to avoid it in the first place. Until the 1760s "commerce," virtually identical with foreign and colonial trade, enjoyed unquestioned privilege as a topic in public economic discourse. Most economic literature either dealt explicitly with foreign trade (including the colonies) or else oriented discussion of the domestic economy to a critical concern with the balance of trade.[2] To criticize this conceptual privilege, Smith used the metaphor of an "invisible hand" beneficently guiding selfishness in the market. The metaphor did not refer to the generic pursuit of individual economic interests. It occurred in a chapter about "restraints upon the importation from foreign countries of such goods as can be produced at home," and it applied specifically to the market for *investments*. Smith intended to show the profitability—and therefore the social benefit—of investing in the domestic economy rather than in overseas trade.

> As every individual, therefore, endeavours as much as he can both to employ his capital in the support of domestick industry, and so to direct that industry that its produce may be of the greatest value; every individual necessarily labours to render the annual revenue of the society as great as he can. He generally, indeed, neither intends to promote the publick interest, nor knows how much he is promoting it. By preferring the support of domestick to that of foreign industry, he intends only his own security; and by directing that industry in such a manner as its produce may be of the greatest value, he intends only his own gain, and he is in this, as in many other cases, led by an invisible hand to promote an end which was no part of the intention.[3]

Smith's argument deliberately overturned conventional wisdom in order to reassure British readers that there was nothing wrong, patriotically or economically, with investing in domestic trade rather than foreign. He timed publication of *The Wealth of Nations* in order to show the British government that military coercion to maintain economic empire was counterproductive. He criticized the ideal of economic empire, not just the tactics of coercion. After the failure of those tactics and the loss of the thirteen colonies, British politicians and bureaucrats took the lessons of Smith and adopted his political economy to shape British commercial policy between the American Revolution and the French revolutionary wars.

Americans learned few lessons from revisionist ideas in political economy. Straight through the imperial crisis, Revolution, and the establishment of national government, American politicians used a predominantly prerevolutionary, mercantilist political economy to understand their commercial circumstances and to devise policies for them. Foreign trade remained the priority, an emphasis that encouraged the analysis of trade in political terms and the use of governmental power to regulate economic interests for fiscal and strategic purposes.[4] Individuals' unhampered response to the market's imperatives of supply and demand did not define the freedom of commerce sought by the leading republican mercantilists, Thomas Jefferson and James Madison. Their analyses of American commercial opportunities usually dealt with diplomatic questions of reciprocal commercial privileges, not relative market advantages. Mercantilist thought provided them ways to give more precise, and positive, analysis of market activities than classical republicanism could provide; at the same time, mercantilist thought could forestall a complete identification of liberty with economic self-interest by providing the hypothetical possibility that regulation of the market need not compromise freedom and might indeed serve a public interest. Americans' "liberalism" varied according to the *relative* autonomy they would give markets in shaping commercial policy, and to the precision with which they calculated relations of supply and demand.

"Mercantilism" did not exist as a conceptual entity in political economy until Smith created it with his discussion of the "mercantile system" in book 4 of *The Wealth of Nations*. (It bears noting that Smith actually labeled it "The *Commercial*, or Mercantile System"—which underlines the mercantilist identification of overseas trade with commerce in general.) Smith demonstrated the linkages among a number of interdependent priorities and assumptions, both explicit and implicit, reiterated in discussions of economic behavior and policy throughout the postfeudal era—for example, the location overseas of optimal commercial opportunity, the international character of competition for those advantages, the strategic importance of a national monopoly of the carrying trade, the critical need for a favorable balance of trade, the inherent marketability of exported manufactures, the use of negative and positive regulations (such as tariffs, bounties, and drawbacks) to achieve these structures in market activities, and the need for colonies as captive markets and monopolized suppliers.

"Political economy" here means what it meant in the eighteenth century: ideas about the role of government "to enrich both the people and the sovereign."[5] It dealt with policy. Consequently, this book focuses on the issues of commercial *policy*, and as such it makes no apology for the elite bias in its documentation. The letters, pamphlets, books, essays, government reports, and congressional debate cited here are those of people directly engaged in debating, setting, and executing policy. The book studies the arguments for individual positions rather than accumulate snippets in order to show popular attitudes on a topic. This strategy interprets the political economy of commerce by placing its discussion in the context of events, rather than isolate individual ideas thematically. Paragraphs rather than phrases usually constitute the units of evidence. This reading provides more dialectic at the expense of less certainty about the generality of an expression. Understood this way, political economy was a crucial part of early American political culture, but it was not a synechdoche of American "social character" and values.[6]

———

I AM DEEPLY GRATEFUL to Joyce Appleby, Jack P. Greene, Gordon S. Wood, and Michael Zuckerman for their support of this project at crucial times. Peter Onuf provided an encouragingly critical reading of the manuscript. Research grants or fellowships from the John Carter

Brown Library, the American Philosophical Society, the Massachusetts
Historical Society, the American Council of Learned Societies, and the
Social Sciences and Humanities Research Council of Canada (410-91-
1744), and a residency at the Rockefeller Foundation's Bellagio Research and Conference Center, provided financial support.

THE PRIVILEGES OF INDEPENDENCE

Matthew Darly, The *Commissioners* (1778).
Courtesy of the Print Collection, Lewis
Walpole Library, Yale University.

1 ...ld your trade, with the hope of starving ye, ...uild your Lands, went your Towns, and caus'd your captive Heroes ...ed your sons to war against their Bretheren.

2 ...nany to perish by Cold, pestilence & famine ...heart spurn'd your place of Divine worship, derided your virtue and piety, and scoff'd ...ave ravag'd your brought us thus on our knees before ye.

3 ...where Ravish'd, Scalp'd, and murder'd your People, even from Tender infamcy to Decrepid age, altho supplicating for Mercy.

4

5 For all which material services, we the Commissioners from the most pious & best of sovereigns doubt not your cordial duty & affection towards us, or willingness to submit your selves again to recieve the same, whenever we have power to bestow it on Ye.

COMMISSIONERS.

Pub.ᵈ April 1 1778 by M.ˢ Darly 39 strand.

Mercantilism in the Enlightenment

Most mid-eighteenth-century political economists had a "neo-mercantilist" optimism about the liberalization of markets, especially in foreign trade, because they also assigned critical importance to the regulation of colonial trade. Enlightened economic thought in France and Britain during the 1740s, 50s, and 60s provided only a contradictory and implicit critique of the arch instance of illiberal political economy, namely, imperial monopolies of colonial trade. It subjected foreign trade, not colonial trade, to serious rethinking. This rethinking had immediate hypothetical implications for the regulation of colonial trade, but writers did not make them explicit; on the contrary, colonial trade remained peculiarly resistant to revisionist thought.

The case of Richard Cantillon demonstrated the possibility of making original contributions to economic thought without being antimercantilist.[1] Among contemporary nonphysiocratic political economists, Cantillon stood out with his emphasis on theory rather than policy, but he remained quite conventional in his view that foreign trade, exceptionally, needed regulation in order for a country to realize its benefits, which were political, not economic: "Foreign trade is only half supported when no care is taken to increase and maintain large merchants who are natives of the country, ships, sailors, workmen and manufactures, and above all that care must always be taken to maintain the balance against the foreigner."[2] The *Essai* did not deal explicitly with colonial trade, but nothing in Cantillon's views on foreign trade implied a revision of mercantilist policy toward imperial commerce.

Soon thereafter the *Encyclopédie*'s discussion of colonies offered a similarly conventional discussion of the economic importance of colonies, though Diderot would later identify with Raynal's political anticolonialism. The *Encyclopédie* presented a succession of six types of colonies from the death of Noah to the European discovery of the Americas. Before Columbus's discoveries colonies for commercial pur-

[1]

poses had been highly exceptional. Only Tyre, Carthage, and Marseilles had depended on commerce for their power. Other premodern colonies resulted from population pressure and the spirit of conquest. Since Columbus, however, all European colonization had commerce and production as its priorities. The *Encyclopédie* did not exploit this association as an opportunity to criticize mercantilist principles or to assert the economic benefits of liberal market relations. On the contrary, the entry on colonies explicitly repudiated liberal pieties about the economic advantages of free markets. Modern colonization aimed forthrightly at economic benefits for the "metropole." Colonies ought to depend administratively and strategically on the metropole, and their trade should focus there exclusively. These political principles determined the economic advantages colonies could offer—to augment the agricultural produce of the metropole, to provide for the subsistence of a larger number of its subjects as manufacturers, and to enlarge its profits from foreign trade. Colonies provided these benefits by consuming commodities and goods produced in the metropole, supplementing its needs, and providing a surplus for export.

The rigidity of the *Encyclopédie*'s mercantilism emphasized that the economic benefits of colonies to the metropole could not be taken for granted. On the contrary, only scrupulous attention to regulation could prevent colonies from being national liabilities rather than imperial assets. Colonies posed the liability of increased commercial competition for the metropole, both internally and externally. Unless colonies remained economically underdeveloped, their agriculture and manufactures could compete with metropolitan production rather than supplement it. Unless restrained, they would engage in trade with foreign nations. Such robbery of the metropole diminished its power relatively and absolutely.[3] Thus, in allowing privileged status to the colonies in economic analysis, the *Encyclopédie* also imposed exceptional economic liabilities on them.

The *Encyclopédie* borrowed its discussion of modern colonies from Montesquieu, whose *Spirit of the Laws* provides a more elaborate demonstration of the oblique conflict between nascent economic liberalism and mercantilism with respect to colonial trade. Montesquieu's discussion of commerce implicitly repudiated mercantilist views on national commercial competition and on the need for state regulation of markets. He associated foreign trade with "agreeable manners" and international peace. Commerce established mutuality among nations: "Two nations who traffic with each other become reciprocally dependent; for if one has an interest in buying, the other has an interest in selling; and thus their union is founded on their mutual necessities." Commerce might alienate people individually by making "a traffic of all the humane, all the moral virtues," but the "economy" natural to republics enabled their citizens to trade. Republics depended "on the practice of gaining little, and even less than other nations, and of remedying this by gaining incessantly." The principle of luxury prevented such economy in monarchies. Security of property in a republic made its inhabitants willing to entertain ambitions of long-term gains: "A nation in slavery labors more to preserve than to acquire; a free nation, more to acquire than to preserve." For some kingdoms it was proper to enact laws "to humble the states that have entered into economical commerce." But to do so tacitly sanctioned an inefficient, backward, and straitened commerce. Exclusive commercial regulations irrationally prevented the "competition which sets a just value on merchandise, and establishes the relation between them."

Despite his economic liberalism on foreign commerce, Montesquieu acknowledged that monopolies of colonial trade presented special cases of law. The whole point of establishing colonies in the Americas was "to trade on more advantageous conditions than could otherwise be done with the neighboring people, with whom all advantages are reciprocal." "A fundamental law of Europe" held that the metropolis should have a monopoly of colonial trade.

In summarizing his discussion of the commercial effects of modern colonization, Montesquieu drew a mercantilist conclusion. The most important effects had been geopolitical and fiscal: "Europe has arrived at so high a degree of *power* that nothing in history can be compared with it, whether we consider the immensity of its expenses, the grandeur of its engagements, the number of its troops."[4]

The physiocrats went a step beyond Montesquieu's economic liberalism by disregarding the distinction between foreign and colonial commerce. In the 1750s and 1760s they relentlessly advocated free markets, but they chiefly concerned themselves with grain markets, whether domestic or foreign. They inverted the priorities typical of mercantilist commercial policies: foreign trade had no privileged status in their analysis, and political priorities were unimportant in their analysis of commerce. Quesnay warned against being "taken in by a seeming advantage in mutual trade with foreign countries . . . In the mutual trade of the raw produce which is purchased from abroad and the manufactured commodities which are sold abroad, the disadvantage usually lies on the side of the latter commodities, because much more profit is yielded by the sale of raw produce."[5] Imperial controls over colonial trade presented hypothetical opportunities to manipulate these relative advantages, but the physiocrats' warnings against the regulation of markets precluded them from saying much about colonial trade. Because the physiocrats applied a strictly economic analysis to the organization of markets, they largely ignored the formal distinction between domestic and foreign markets.[6]

As the author of the decade's biggest books on economic topics, Malachy Postlethwayt most fully represented the amalgam of liberal and regulatory mentalities in neomercantilism. In his pretentiously authoritative volumes, dogmatically conventional mercantilism coexisted with liberal revisions and haphazard infusions of French theory. A gifted plagiarist, he was current and catholic. Postlethwayt had mercantilist leanings in favor of the export of manufactures, the restriction of colonial economic development, and the need for governmental regulation of markets, but he allowed himself to be influenced by David Hume, Richard Cantillon, and the physiocrats.[7]

Postlethwayt clearly defined the interest of the mother country in colonial trade: "(1) a greater consumption of the productions of her lands: (2) occupation for a greater number of the manufacturers, artizans, fishermen and seamen: (3) a greater quantity of such commodities as she wants: (4) a greater superfluity, wherewith to supply other people."[8] The colonies had a "plantation business," Postlethwayt argued, to supply "materials for our capital manufactures we shall not be capable of raising amongst ourselves." The seventeenth-century acts of navigation and trade were holy writ in defining this "plantation business": only vessels belonging to British subjects could export goods from British colonies; foreign goods could enter Britain only directly from their places of origin; only British ships sailing from Britain could bring European goods to British colonies. These laws, "the bulwark of the English commerce," had "two essential objects in view; one, the encrease of the naval power (by making her own people the sole carriers of the whole British commerce); the other, the appropriating and securing to herself, and her own subjects, all the emoluments arising from the trade of her own colonies." This commercial strategy had no imperative for efficiency, fairness, or reciprocity with the colonies or foreign countries. The "dependency of our colonies upon the mother-country" was a forthright goal. The requirement of a "double voyage" for European commodities imported into British colonies, for example, deliberately made them less competitive with British manufactures, while providing British merchants additional profits from freight. The more contracted the market for French goods, the better the market for British goods.[9]

Postlethwayt presented the colonies as a special category of trade for regulation. Although integrated with the domestic economy, colonies should be kept underdeveloped by commercial regulations that deliberately imposed economic inefficiencies. Colonial trade performed the same functions as foreign trade in providing a market for surpluses and in increasing a strategically advantageous navigation, but only if their commerce remained "independent of all other states." Only if they grew correctly could the growth of colonies benefit the metropolis: "Colonies become a strength to their mother kingdom, while they are under good discipline, while they are strictly made to observe the fundamental laws of their original country, and while they are kept dependent on it; but that otherwise, they are worse than members lopped from the body politic, being like offensive arms wrested from a nation, to be turned against it, as occasion shall serve."[10] Because the colonial trade ambiguously seemed part of both domestic and foreign trade, the development of colonial manufactures posed the worrisome liabilities of replacing importations from Britain and entering into competition with British products in foreign markets. Colonies could not "in justice" consume foreign products when there was an equivalent available from the mother country, nor could they sell products to foreign buyers when the mother country had an interest in importing them: "Every infringement of those laws is a real, though too common, robbery of the mother country's labourers, workmen and seamen, in order to enrich the same classes of men belonging to rival nations, who will soon or later take advantage of it against those very colonies."[11]

Such a strategy for the regulation of colonial commerce reiterated the principles of the seventeenth-century acts of navigation and trade. But Postlethwayt qualified it with a more liberal "maxim in trading states viz. that no trading nation can maintain an intercourse of commerce with others, if they expect to sell all, and to purchase no commodities in return."[12] He expressed an appreciation of the greater potential for economic growth from liberalized foreign trade than from protectionism. Britain, Ireland, and the American colonies could be economically self-sufficient, but commercial policy should not seek sheer economic independence. For if the British domains traded only among themselves, then other countries, particularly France, could expand their foreign trade and with it their power.

Postlethwayt's confidence that "the wants of mankind are sufficient to give full employment to those that want it" implied mutual international interests in the expansion of foreign trade. The paradigm for commercial legislation was not necessarily the zero-sum game that underpinned mercantilist trade policy:

> If every nation, instead of having occasion for such restraints or prohibitions would make their produce, &c. cheap enough; which, by the means suggested, is always in their power to answer to the real benefit of every part of the community; their good and cheap commodities will force themselves by these commanding qualities, on some other nations at least; and in some degree on those too, perhaps, who shall endeavour to restrain

them. Does this not seem to be the more natural, and, therefore, the more effectual way to preserve and advance our maritime commerce? Do not these obvious reflections indicate the folly of restraining trade this way, and discover plain and easy methods to make our people happy in trade without such restraint, or indeed without ever going to war about it? for war is no less destructive of trade than it is of the peace and felicity of human nature.[13]

This positive, neomercantilist, view of foreign trade depended on a reevaluation of the potential of the domestic economy for growth. By the 1750s the domestic economy had a new analytical autonomy in British political economy. The "home trade" of the nation, where consumption and industry reinforced each other, became an analytical concern in its own right, and the populousness of the state measured the value of this home trade. This dynamic view of economic development envisaged an improvement in the standard of living, without the previous concerns with backward-sloping labor supply curves as consequences of prosperity or of increased dependency ratios arising from population growth.

Imperialism and liberal revisions of mercantilism, as their coexistence in Postlethwayt's thought demonstrates, did not have an inverse relationship in the middle of the eighteenth century, such that one displaced the other. Criticism of mercantilism developed simultaneously with the strengthening of simplistic imperialist views in conventional economic wisdom. Support for aggressive colonial expansion became a component of opposition politics in the 1740s, as "the final stage of the opposition to Walpole . . . [stimulated] the articulation of a popular mercantilist vision of empire as the sole means of national greatness."[14] By midcentury support for aggressive colonial policy came from a broad spectrum of respectable society, ranging from dissident nobles and gentry through "metropolitan and provincial merchants" to artisans and tradesmen. The "extra-parliamentary nation" took it as a given that the prosperity of Britain depended on the scale of its imperial trade. The very popularity of imperial expansion made it vulnerable to criticism as vulgar and uninformed.[15] Commercial imperialism was vulnerable to expert opinion, but the intellectual elitism of antimercantilist thought ensured that it would be a minority view.

In this context David Hume made the most self-conscious revision of the conventional wisdom that *The Wealth of Nations* would label "the mercantile system." In his essays "Of Commerce," "Of the Balance of Trade," and "Of the Jealousy of Trade," Hume directed his skepticism at the shibboleths of the privileged importance of foreign trade.[16] Whereas mercantilists had voiced a fear of consumption, Hume adopted a relativistic understanding of "luxury," in order to show that it might be a good for individuals as well as society: "It means great refinement in the gratification of the senses; and any degree of it may be innocent or blamable, according to the age, or country, or condition of the person. The bounds between the virtue and the vice cannot here be exactly fixed, more than in other moral subjects." Luxury was only a vice when "pursued at the expence of some virtue, as liberality or charity," or when indulged self-destructively. Hume explicitly repudiated the Mandevillian paradox that private vices were public virtues. He identified "vicious luxury" and subordinated his positive view of commerce to the need for public virtue. But he went on to say that "two opposite vices in a state may be more advantageous than either of them alone": "By banishing *vicious* luxury without curing sloth and an indifference to others, you only diminish industry in the state, and add nothing to men's charity or their generosity." The refinement of taste had historically contributed to the greater use of reason in commerce, in government, and in the liberal arts: "Where luxury nourishes commerce and industry, the peasants, by a proper cultivation of the land, become rich and independent; while the tradesmen and merchants acquire a share of the property, and draw authority and consideration to that middling rank of men, who are the best and firmest basis of public liberty."[17]

If luxury caused, as well as followed from, social improvement, Hume argued, then so did foreign trade. As luxuries, foreign commodities had the advantages over "home manufactures" of novelty and immediate accessibility. Foreign trade profitably exchanged domestic superfluities for foreign ones having little competition back home. But the intrinsic advantages of foreign trade were short-lived, because it stimulated domestic emulative consumption to a scale that foreign supplies alone could not meet. Hume worried little about British competitiveness overseas because foreign trade had this capacity to displace itself by stimulating domestic production: "It is true, the English feel some disadvantages in foreign trade by the high price of labour, which is in part the effect of the riches of their artisans, as well as of the plenty of money: but as foreign trade is not the most material circumstance, it is not to be put in competition with the happiness of so many millions."[18]

Hume repudiated the conventional economic wisdom of giving priority in commercial policy to a favorable balance of trade. He could grant that *some* taxes on "foreign commodities" might not be "prejudicial or useless" if they encouraged a country's manufactures or provided a national revenue, but he criticized the "numberless bars, obstructions, and imposts, which all nations of Europe, and none more than England, have put upon trade, which never will heap up beyond its level, while it circulates." Money, like water, "remains always at a level," and that level was dynamically "proportionable to the art and industry of each nation." "Jealousy of trade" among nations could not provide a rational basis for commercial policy. Most wealth in a nation derived from "the domestic industry of a people," which the prosperity of other nations only indirectly affected. The prosperity of one nation could stimulate the development of its trading partners as they sought to imitate the profitable imports in order to displace them. These developments, in turn, resulted eventually in exportable goods: "But if our neighbours have no art or cultivation, they cannot take them; because they will have nothing to give in exchange."[19] Hume's liberal arguments only bore implicitly on the colonies, but they taught that the dynamic potential of consumption patterns, whether national or international, provided the stimulus of economic development.

Contemporaneously with these physiocratic and liberal revisions of British mercantilism, Benjamin Franklin developed the most sophisticated and wide-ranging Anglo-American analysis of colonial political economy. His *Observations on the Increase of Mankind* showed how even Britain's colonies in temperate climates had harmonious economic interests with the metropole, though subject to its regulation. Whereas Postlethwayt compared poorly regulated trades with a gangrenous limb that was better amputated, Franklin compared "a Nation well regulated" with a "Polypus": "If you have Room and Subsistence enough, as you may by dividing, make ten Polypes out of one . . . or rather, increase a Nation ten fold in Numbers and Strength."

Franklin readily accepted policies that subordinated colonial commerce and judged their success in conventional mercantilist terms of sheer "Increase of Trade and Navigation" at the expense of other nations.[20] He sought to reassure British policymakers that the colonies would not develop manufactures as long as they expanded agriculturally. Although the population of the colonies increased much more rapidly than that of Great Britain, and could be projected to surpass it in the next century, this expansion would continue to provide a lucrative market for British manufactures. Here Franklin established a theme in colonial political economy that would have many echoes during the imperial crisis of the next two decades, as he sanguinely portrayed this "glorious Market" "wholly in the Power of Britain." Similarly, he accepted the need for legislation to prevent the importation of "Foreign Luxuries and needless Manufactures," because "such Laws likewise strengthen a Country, doubly, by increasing its own People and diminishing its Neighbours."

From Franklin's perspective, the colonies' economic dependence on Great Britain contributed to their prosperity and economic growth. He contentedly noted that this economic dependency arose from an emulative desire "to indulge [our]selves in finer cloaths, better furniture, and a more general use of all our manufactures," not from the needs of subsistence. When he tabulated a comparison of British exports to the northern colonies and to the West Indies, he optimistically noted that those of the northern colonies were now larger and continuing to grow. Franklin's physiocratic sympathies allowed him to be untroubled with the American lack of manufactures, but he assumed that American prosperity depended on favorable exchanges in foreign trade.[21] Although he had a great deal of pride in colonial economic expansion, he understood it from a metropolitan perspective.

Franklin elaborated these views of colonial economic relations when he adopted a British persona in order to take part in the controversy in 1760 over whether to acquire Canada or Guadaloupe. Again he warned British politicians that the colonists needed area for agricultural expansion, or else they would develop manufactures once they could no longer subsist on the land. He found it unimaginable that manufactures could develop except out of a necessity for wage labor arising from the deprivation of agricultural livelihoods. American dependence on British exporters would continue even as American settlement extended far into the continent. He drew on comparisons with European continental trade to show that "whatever charges arise on the carriage of goods, are added to the value, and all paid by the consumer," and then reassured British legislators of their control over colonial "trade, manufactures, [and] commercial connection." Thus Britain would continue to enjoy the benefits of a growing colonial export trade, and with it the strategic advantage of a large navigation. He calculated the cheapness of British goods in the colonies relative to Americans' investment in agriculture, not to the availability of goods in an open market.

None of these relations was oppressive. Franklin did not refer to denials of economic opportunity as grievances. The only context in which he referred to the potential for exploitative and tyrannical colonial subordination involved outright threats to property and to civil and religious rights.[22] Franklin identified how Britain disproportionately benefited from its privileges in American trade, but he stopped short of condemning the trade regulations themselves. It was their own taste for "British Luxuries" that made Americans liable to disadvantageous trade and taxable wants.[23]

During the imperial crisis of the 1760s and 1770s Josiah Tucker became the best known critic of conventional wisdom on the economic advantages of colonies.[24] As rector and prebendary in Bristol and later the dean of Gloucester, as well as royal tutor on economics, Tucker was a paradox of respectability. He made an intellectual career of telling people things they did not want to hear. In the 1750s he argued for the naturalization of foreign Protestants and Jews; in 1763 he criticized the prosecution of war for commercial purposes; and throughout the imperial crisis of the 1760s and 1770s he showed how the loss of the American colonies would benefit the British economy.[25] In the 1750s, when he established his authority on political economy, his writings already expressed the confident economic liberalism and the acerbic view of privileged interests that would underpin his anticolonial analysis, but he did not yet give them that direction. From the start of his career as an economic authority, Tucker presented himself as an advocate of economic freedom. As a political economist, he explained to the people at large how neither they nor the nation needed much commercial regulation for their economic benefit: "The Physician to the Body Politic may learn to imitate the Conduct of the Physician to the Body Natural, in removing those Disorders which a bad Habit, or a wrong Treatment hath brought upon the Constitution; and then to leave the rest to Nature, who best can do her own work."[26]

Tucker drew political, not economic, distinctions between foreign and domestic trade. Because of the possibility to deal comprehensively with domestic commerce, "our first Concern should be to set that Trade *free,* which circulates, or might circulate at Home, and then to extend our Attention to those Fabrics and Commodities which are, or might be exported Abroad." Tucker reversed mercantilist priorities on two counts: he located greater potential for growth in the domestic economy rather than in foreign trade; he identified problems of economic regulation as ones typically of obstruction rather than exquisite adjustment. Tucker discussed both domestic and foreign commerce with unrelenting, often sarcastic, denunciations of economic privilege. Besides their frequent association with the corrupting effects of political favoritism, such measures were economically irrational, because they impeded profitable adjustment to markets: "Every Manufacturer must, and will endeavour to suit his Fabrics to the Taste, or Pocket of his Customers, let the Standard be what it will."[27]

Tucker applied this optimism to foreign as well as domestic markets. He expressed little concern about the dangers of competition, and he did not present international trade as a zero-sum game. He dismissed bullionist arguments, and he showed little concern for the dangers of unfavorable balances of trade. He mocked the trading companies' defenses of their privileges. Without them, British goods would be exported in such quantities and the reciprocal imports would become so cheap to British consumers that the companies' rates of profits would diminish. Tucker believed that the elimination of commercial privileges in foreign trade would benefit the liberalizing country even more than its trading correspondents: "Every exclusive Grant is a reciprocal Disadvantage, and a Stop to mutual Industry." Rather than urge privileges for "Shipping and Navigation," he simply included them with other "Mechanic Trades and Manufactures." He appreciated that some people thought shipping "ought to be considered as the *primary* Object of our Attention, because we are a maritime People," but he resisted giving navigation privileged status in political economy. Shipping was an effect, not an imperative, of commerce: its "Sea-Carriage" depended on goods to be carried.[28] He had none of the "fear of goods" of earlier generations of mercantilists, and he emphasized the mutuality of interests among agricultural, commercial, and manufacturing interests.

But Tucker did not at first extend his liberal critique of economic privilege to the largest monopoly of all, namely, the colonial trade. Here only his silence was telling: he did not explicitly perpetuate mercantilist pieties. Nearly all of the principles he applied in advocacy of liberalizing domestic and foreign trade could have been brought to bear on colonial trade as well, but the structure of interests was different. The monopolies he denounced "were established with the very Intent of being detrimental to the *many,* in order to be exorbitantly profitable to the *few.* The Question therefore is no more than this, Whether the *few* or the *many* shall get the better in this Struggle; a Struggle in which the one Side are contending for their natural Rights and Liberties, and the other for the Continuance of an unjust and odious Usurpation."[29] The question was enormously more invidious when directed at imperial economic relations.

In response to the Seven Years' War, Tucker began to ask this invidious question. The war arose from a combination of "the Inveteracy of bad Habits, such [as] the bewitching, tho' empty Sounds of Conquest and Glory," and the calculated motives of particular special interests. Vulgar "military and political Folly" sought "Empire by Means of Desolation" and "national Riches by introducing universal Poverty and Want." No necessarily *economic* advantages resulted from securing political control over potential markets: "Trade will always follow Cheapness, and not Conquest." Borrowing a phrase from Hume, Tucker asked rhetorically, "Is this Spell, this Witchcraft of the Jealousy of Trade never to be dissolved? . . . of all Absurdities, that of going to War for the Sake of getting Trade is the most absurd." Tucker condemned the self-defeating policy of commercial warfare and forthrightly urged consideration of mutual interests in international trade, just as in domestic markets. The chief opposition to such principles was vulgar chauvinism: "To excite that Man (whom they ['the blood-thirsty Mob'] have long called their Enemy) to greater Industry and Sobriety, to consider him as a Customer to them, and themselves as Customers to him, so that the richer both are, the better it may be for each other; and, in short, to promote a mutual Trade to mutual Benefit: This is a Kind of Reasoning, as unintelligible to their Comprehensions, as the Antipodes themselves."[30] In 1763 Tucker criticized policies of colonial conquest. He had not yet directed his antimercantilism against the supposed advantages of colonial trading privileges—as he would after the Stamp Act crisis.[31] But when in the later 1760s he reflected on colonial resistance to imperial authority he was virtually the first public figure on either side of the ocean to recommend economic independence for Americans.

———

AS EVEN Postlethwayt demonstrated, conventional British wisdom on the privileged importance of external trade encountered profound skepticism in the 1750s and early 1760s, when colonial officials became critically concerned with inadequacies in the regulation of colonial trade. In the 1760s Postlethwayt's confused eclecticism epitomized the contradictory directions Anglo-American political economy had taken in the matter of colonial trade. On the one hand, arch-mercantilists insisted on the need for effective regulation in order to realize the peculiar benefits of colonial trade. On the other hand, some few writers touted the economic advantages of liberalized markets. The latter arguments implicitly denied the distinctiveness of colonial trade and therefore subverted the economic rationale for restrictions on colonial trade. However, the contrary tendencies in political economy agreed in denying conventional wisdom that imperial trade necessarily brought metropolitan wealth.

CHAPTER ONE

The Prosperity of
Colonial Dependence

CONVENTIONAL WISDOM in Britain held that colonial markets had provided most of the growth for British export trade in the eighteenth century. This dynamic capacity of the colonial economy impressed British commentators, whether they pessimistically worried about the potential for its manufacturing capacity to displace British suppliers, or whether they optimistically noted the continuing increase of its purchasing power. Because conventional wisdom also associated the general prosperity of Britain with its foreign trade, the state of colonial trade had important implications for the well-being of the whole country. Estimates in the 1750s of the importance of colonial trade calculated it to be worth over five million pounds per year, approximately one-third of Britain's foreign trade, and to employ over forty thousand seamen in about two thousand ships.[1]

British plenty and power depended critically on the colonial trade, and only due regulation could secure its advantages. No matter how large the colonial trade, it needed improved regulation if "the whole advantage thereof does not center in England." For example, the barter of provisions for molasses and rum between the British northern colonies and the French sugar colonies provided the French with "a new *mine* of profit," while for Britain it "not only deprived the nation of a profit to which they have a natural right, but many persons employed in our manufactures have been reduced to beggary."[2] The "dependence" of the colonies on trade with the metropole critically measured the effectiveness of their commercial regulation. As colonial writers well knew, the litmus test of such dependence was the colonists' consumption of British manufactures, and hence they so frequently played down the economic imperatives for the development of colonial manufactures.

Metropolitan Orientations during
the Imperial Crisis

During the Seven Years' War the need to regulate colonial trade appeared critical regarding trade with the enemy. A Board of Trade investigation into reports of illicit trade between the French islands and the British colonies documented decades of systematic, large-scale smuggling in peacetime as well as wartime.[3] Supplying the enemy with provisions in wartime presented an immediate strategic problem, but from a mercantilist perspective colonial trade with the French involved more important long-term liabilities for British wealth and power. In buying foreign molasses and rum the colonists reduced the earnings that West Indian planters could spend on British goods, and by smuggling foreign manufactures the colonists directly reduced the sales of British manufactures in the colonies. With information from the Board of Trade and reports from the Commissioners of Customs, the Treasury Lords in October 1763 urged the Privy Council to consider "the proper Regulation of their Trade of immediate Necessity, lest the continuance and extent of the dangerous Evils . . . may render all Attempts to remedy them hereafter infinitely more difficult, if not utterly impracticable."[4] Officials assumed that increased trade among the American colonies and foreign nations must come at the expense of British economic interests.[5]

Colonists' anticipation that the end of the Seven Years' War would bring the renewal and more stringent enforcement of the Sugar Act of 1733 called forth several detailed analyses of imperial trade and commercial regulation. Advocates of colonial interests provided such detailed analyses because they did not object in principle to parliamentary regulation of colonial trade, or to the principle of a metropolitan definition of commercial priorities. Effective criticism of commercial regulation had to show that undesirable policies harmed British as well as colonial interests.

Rather than condemn the recognizable commercial advantages of the metropolis, colonial writers employed a mercantilist analysis to emphasize the linkages of commercial prosperity throughout the empire. From a New England perspective, for example, "a prohibition or a prohibitory duty on the produce of the foreign sugar islands" would deeply "wound" the New England fisheries because it would increase the cost of provisions (specifically rum) for voyages. If the fishery declined, navigation available for the seasonal West Indian trades would decrease. The West Indian planters would soon find themselves with less income as they hired more expensive freight, and their supply of slaves from Africa would become constricted and more expensive as well. As the cost of producing sugar increased, the British islands' lack of competitiveness with the French West Indies would worsen, and a policy intended to lessen French wealth and power would before long serve to encourage French trade and navigation. The market for British manufactures in both the West Indian and the northern colonies would lessen, as the West Indian economy contracted and the northern colonists turned to domestic manufactures. As Britain's commerce and manufactures lessened, so would its "revenue and naval power."[6] The value of the colonies arose from their capacity to consume British manufactures, and that capacity depended on the mutual prosperity of the colonies and the metropole.

In this context Governor Stephen Hopkins of Rhode Island, in his *Essay on the Trade of the Northern Colonies,* came closest "to speaking for the entire colonial merchant class" in criticizing renewal of the Sugar Act.[7] Several colonial newspapers printed the essay in the spring of 1764, and it appeared in London as a pamphlet later that year. Hopkins' essay addressed a metropolitan audience in order to inform them about the "Commerce of the British Northern Colonies in America." He frankly acknowledged that he had to overcome both the indifference and the ignorance of his British readers with respect to the peculiarities of colonial commerce.

Hopkins may have felt alienated from the metropolitan understanding of the colonial political economy, but he wished to take part in it. He analyzed only export trades. He identified the economic regions of the North American colonies with their staples—from north to south: fish / "lumber, horses, pork, beef, tobacco (of a poor and unmerchantable kind)" / wheat / and in the "most Southern . . . tobacco, naval stores, rice." Having differentiated the colonies by exports, he then analyzed the trade of each colonial region regarding its final market in the metropolis. Hopkins explicitly accepted colonial commercial subordination. He calculated the commercial advantages of the regions by the relative directness of their trade with Britain, not by their terms of trade or rates of earnings.[8]

Unlike most European colonies in the Americas, the northern colonies produced little that could be sold directly in metropolitan markets. Faced with this inability "to make remittances in a direct way," the northern colonies had developed an extensive small-scale shipping that engaged in a highly circuitous commerce, unlike that of any other colonial region. Most of the products shipped had such marginal profitability that they "must be consumed in the country where first sold," and their high bulk/value ratio often meant "that no one market will take off any great quantity."[9]

Hopkins did not propose a positive alternative, even hypothetical-

ly, to imperial commercial regulation. On the contrary, he "acknowledge[d] that whatever business or commerce in any of the Northern
Colonies interferes with, or is any way detrimental to the true interest, manufactories, trade or commerce of Great Britain, we reasonably expect will be totally prohibited." He noted with embarrassment
some "illicit commerce (not before spoken of)" with "Holland and
Hamburgh," and he defended the harmlessness of the importation of
"perishable fruits" in return cargoes from the fish trade to southern
Europe.[10]

Only in reference to the British West Indies did Hopkins insist on the
rights of commercial interests in the northern colonies.[11] He disagreed
with the Sugar Act on political, not commercial, principle. The different colonies deserved a parity of interests within the empire. He resented the privileges that "the rich, proud, and overbearing planters
of the West-Indies" apparently enjoyed from political advantages at
home. The West Indian planters took for granted that they could use
"two millions of free and loyal British subjects" "for their own use,
advantage, and emolument," much as they used their slaves.[12] The
British West Indies simply could not absorb all of the exports from the
northern colonies. Northern merchants sold their goods there at half
the price obtainable in the foreign islands, and they bought products at
twice the price in the non-British islands. If the northern colonies
could not trade in the foreign islands, their exports would "dwindle
down into the diminutive size of these markets," with a corresponding
decline in imports of British manufactures.[13]

Hopkins also criticized a hypothetical policy to prohibit colonial
trade with foreign colonies. Although he predicted that such a policy
would be "absolutely ruinous" to the northern colonies, he did not
argue that it fundamentally violated their rights. He warned instead
that it would result in "a thorough alteration in their whole domestic
economy" and fundamentally damage the economic interests of both
Great Britain and the colonies. Deprived of half their export markets,
the colonies could not maintain remittances to Britain, whose exports
would inevitably decline. He calculated that twenty thousand seamen
and fishermen would be unemployed, as would half the agricultural
labor force. These displaced people, as well as those with lessened
incomes from British trade, "must be compelled, by mere necessity, to
employ themselves in such coarse and homely manufactures, as their
ability and skill will enable them."

Hopkins' only alternative model of colonial economic development
projected colonial self-sufficiency as a response to the arbitrary prohibition of colonial exports. He did not project a more optimistic development that depended on an invidious comparison of economic op-

portunity and imperial regulation. On the contrary, he cautioned colonists not to evade laws "made for limiting and restraining their commerce," or to rely on the "indulgence" of Customs: "Such methods are equally unjust and ineffectual, expensive and odious; and render the colonies in which they are practised, obnoxious to the resentment of the administration at home; and tend to justify an extraordinary exertion of power employed for carrying these laws into execution." The colonies should provide their agents in Britain with analyses of their trade, to be put before the Board of Trade for recommendation to Parliament, "where doubtless it will be farther examined, and duly considered, and every branch of our commerce that coincides with the general interest of the nation, be countenanced and established; and if we practise any, which are found to have a contrary tendency, they must be given up and forsaken." Parliament could unquestionably justify such restrictions if they ensured that the advantages of colonial commerce did not "center in any other kingdom or state, but that of the mother country."[14]

Hopkins referred the desirability of "a free commerce" to the relative priority of fiscal and commercial goals in commercial regulation. He advised his metropolitan readers of the cautionary analogy of the Spanish empire, where "the want of a free commerce has checked their navigation, hindered their increase of shipping, and kept them poor and weak in the midst of riches." Hopkins called for an enlightened imperial self-interest in British commercial policy, one recognizing that the expansion of the colonial economy brought wealth to the metropolis, but he accepted that such a policy would regulate colonial trade and give priority to metropolitan interests.

As Hopkins and other American petitioners feared, the American Duties Act of 1764, subsequently better known as the Sugar Act, comprehensively addressed imperial concerns about colonial commerce— "for improving the Revenue of this Kingdom, and for extending and securing the Navigation and Commerce between Great Britain and your Majesty's Dominions in America."[15] The act paid particular attention to the fundamental mercantilist principle that the benefits of colonial trade go to the metropole and not to foreign nations. The list of products enumerated for export only to Great Britain increased to include numerous lesser but newly popular commodities such as cacao, coffee, and whale fins. Their enumeration would provide British manufacturers with a secure and cheap supply of raw materials, while denying the colonists opportunities to obtain foreign manufactures by smuggling. To encourage further consumption of British manufactures, the act increased duties on foreign cloth imported from Britain. In the instances of detrimental colonial trades too well established to eliminate, measures would reduce the incentive to smuggle and make an administrative revenue more feasible. Thus the act lowered duties on wines imported from Great Britain and on foreign molasses.

Much of the act dealt with more elaborate procedures to prevent or to punish illegal trade, but Grenville intended it and related statutes to improve the linkages of the colonial and metropolitan economies, not just to constrain the colonists. Grenville wanted to reduce British as well as colonial smuggling, and he extended commercial privileges to colonial as well as British enterprises. Because British manufacturers and shipowners enjoyed the most privileged commercial interests on both sides of ocean, the act also encouraged the production and export of particular commodities. It increased the bounties for naval stores, added new ones to encourage the production of hemp and flax for sailcloth and rope, and reduced duties on raw materials such as furs and whalebones. As an extension of the principle that direct colonial trade with foreign markets enhanced colonists' purchasing power to buy British goods, an act now allowed the direct export of rice to foreign territories in the Americas. The Navigation Acts forbade foreign ships from any of these trades, while they continued to define colonial ships as British for the privilege of commercial navigation.[16]

Grenville's secretary, Thomas Whately, made the most important apology for the Sugar Act and the other recent measures to enforce the regulation of colonial commerce. His pamphlet, *The Regulations Lately Made Concerning the Colonies, and the Taxes Imposed upon Them, Considered,* shaped the presentation of the colonists' economic grievances during the imperial crisis because it provided a fund of commercial statistics in comparing their high levels of prosperity with low levels of taxation. Only the last dozen pages of the 112-page pamphlet discussed the fiscal and constitutional rationale for commercial regulation. Most of the pamphlet presented a flattering and benign analysis of the commerce of the mainland colonies. Whately favorably contrasted the consumption patterns of the continental colonies with those of sugar islands. In the northern colonies "the plain, the industrious and frugal Republican of America" happily absorbed the "good, rich, and solid, but not delicate" manufactures of Great Britain, while the "wealth," "luxury," and "extravagance" of the West Indian planters "induce them to prefer the finer productions of other countries." Because of the primary value of the northern colonies as consumers, their "benefit" to the metropole depended chiefly on the size of their population.[17] British subjects "in Europe and in America" were "the same people, and all equally participate in the adversity or prosperity of the whole." "The difference of their situations" warranted the differences in policy toward them. The colonies had advantages of "extent of country, fertility of soil, cheapness of land, variety of climate, and scarcity of inhabitants," which "naturally lead the Americans to cultivation." In Britain, little land "still remains improvable to any considerable degree"; the people of Britain "are more than sufficient for its cultivation, and must seek for fortunes, and even for subsistence in trade and manufactures."[18]

Because economic advantages throughout the empire depended on complex networks of exchanges, Whately argued, there had to be a single "supreme authority" to regulate them. When "local purposes" harmed general interests, as with legal tender laws for paper money, then the British government had to constrain the colonies. But many mercantilist changes in commercial regulation favored colonial trade at the expense of established British interests—here Whately elaborately discussed the changes regarding duties on furs and whalebones, bounties on hemp, and the enumeration of rice.[19] The crucial principles encouraged manufactures in Britain and agriculture in the colonies.

The Sugar Act applied exquisite adjustment such that "the degree of restraint put upon the French trade in this article [sugar products], is proportioned to the stage of manufacture, in which the commodity may be at the time of importation." For example, the act prohibited French rum in order to encourage American rum production, but it would not make American rum so cheap that it competed with British suppliers of fishing vessels. Sheer protectionism for British West Indian interests would be counterproductive, however, because the regulations also aimed to provide a revenue from the colonial importation of French molasses.[20] Despite the colonists' fears, ministerial encouragement of the British and American economy did not require prohibition of trade with the foreign islands. But the ministry could not tolerate the violation of "those wise laws to which the great increase of our trade and naval power are principally owing."[21]

The colonists could criticize the new regulations of trade without claiming authority to reject specific measures. Arguments for colonial legislative sovereignty accepted the principle that Parliament had authority to regulate trade because it dealt with the colonies generally, not just individually.[22] For example, the petition of the New York Assembly in response to the Sugar Act claimed an exemption for the colonists from any parliamentary impositions of internal taxes or duties on consumption, but the Assembly advanced the claim in the name of the protection of property.[23] There was also a "Freedom to drive all Kinds of Traffick," but the petition interpreted that as "a Subordination to, and not inconsistent with, the *British* Trade." In denying any colonial "Desire of Independency upon the supreme Power of Parliament," the petition immediately referred the point of political subordination to commercial relations: "What can be more apparent, than that the State which exercises a Sovereignty in Commerce, can draw all the Wealth of its Colonies into its own Stock? And has not the whole Trade of *North-America,* that growing Magazine of Wealth, been, from the Beginning, directed, restrained, and prohibited at the sole Pleasure of the Parliament? . . . [Yet] the Authority of the Parliament of Great Britain, to model the Trade of the whole Empire, so as to subserve the Interest of her own, we are ready to recognize in the most extensive and positive Terms."

The New York Assembly equally recognized how the colony's economic dependence resulted from imperial commercial regulation. Despite a structural subordination, such "that all we acquire is less than sufficient to purchase what we want of your Manufactures," the Assembly perceived a mutuality of commercial interest between New York and Great Britain: "The more extensive our Traffick, the Greater her Gains; we carry all to her Hive, and consume the Returns; and we are content with any constitutional Regulation that inriches her, though it impoverishes ourselves." The petition criticized several new commercial constraints imposed by the Sugar Act of 1764, such as that on colonial trade with the foreign West Indies, but it did not repudiate them even though they harmed colonial economic interests. Instead, it predicted that they would "prove equally detrimental to us and *Great-Britain.*"[24]

The Stamp Act and the Affirmation of Colonial Dependence

After the Stamp Act constitutional issues regarding taxation came to the fore in discussions of imperial government. In circumscribing the authority of Parliament in the individual colonies, however, controversy over the Stamp Act also more explicitly acknowledged parliamentary authority regarding imperial commerce.[25] Although numerous writers had challenged Whately's economic justifications of the Sugar Act, Daniel Dulany, in one of the most important pamphlets repudiating the Stamp Act, cited *The Regulations Lately Made* with approval to make the point that while "a right to impose an internal tax on the colonies without their consent *for the single purpose of revenue* is denied, a right to regulate their trade without their consent is admitted."[26] Dulany went out of his way to acknowledge "the subordination of the colonies and the authority of Parliament to preserve it." He appreciated that Britain's "welfare" and "perhaps the existence of the mother country as an independent kingdom" depended on its commerce with the colonies.

To secure the benefits of this commerce required Parliament to exercise its "unquestionable" authority to regulate colonial trade.[27]

Dulany's extravagant concession of parliamentary powers to regulate commerce did not prevent him from making a bitterly detailed analysis "of the obstructions, or regulations as they are called." In an appendix Dulany worked out in careful detail how the enumeration of tobacco, combined with the British monopoly on the sale of manufactures in the colonies, was "effectually a tax." Enumeration gave British importers a buyers' market and denied Chesapeake planters access to the final markets for their commodity; consequently, the "re-exported tobacco pays double freight, double insurance, commission, and other shipping charges." As for imports to the Chesapeake, when they originated in foreign countries they bore added costs from "double freight, insurance, shipping charges, the merchant importer's commission, the English tradesman's profit, the merchant exporter's commission, and subsidies retained." Dulany calculated that "the whole tax is upwards of 65 per cent." The colonists, "being confined in their consumption to a particular manufacture, and the commodities they export being chiefly raw materials," did not have "the means generally in the power of other people, by raising the price of labor to throw their burdens upon others." Instead, they "are for the most part obliged, both in their exports and imports, to submit to an arbitrary determination of their value." Dulany acknowledged that he did "not perceive the policy in laying difficulties and obstructions upon the gainful trade of the colonies with foreigners," if "the balance gained by the American merchant in the pursuit of that trade centers in Great Britain and is applied to the discharge of a debt contracted by the consumption of British manufactures in the colonies, and in this to the support of the national expense."[28] But Dulany directed his painstaking analysis toward making a metropolitan, not a colonial, audience aware of its real economic interests. Rather than mobilize the colonists to demand commercial reforms that would enhance their pursuit of self-interest, Dulany simultaneously advised and threatened the British that the imposition of the Stamp Act would weaken an already precariously inefficient trade.

Colonial *under*development meant increased domestic manufactures. Lacking direct foreign competition, "British manufactures come dearer and not so good in quality to America as formerly." Dulany did not expect the British monopoly to be lifted or broken, but if the colonists' lessened capacity to consume reinforced the "increase of price and falling in the goodness of quality" inevitable with monopolies then the colonists would of necessity increase their manufacturing. Dulany had no illusions that colonial production would truly replace British suppliers. He associated the development of colonial manufactures with a simplification of taste and technology. He reminded British readers of the privileged position of manufactures in mercantilist political economy in order to pose an economic threat to the political viability of the Stamp Act.

Discussions of the Stamp Act characteristically raised hypothetical *economic* objections to commercial regulation in order to reinforce *constitutional* points. Now pamphleteers put their arguments more starkly than the earlier, more piecemeal, objections anticipating the Sugar Act.[29] For example, in pursuing the argument that rights imply equality, Richard Bland asked, "Why is the Trade of the Colonies more circumscribed than the Trade of Britain?" But he did not argue that colonial commerce ought to be free. Instead he reduced to an apparent absurdity the argument for parliamentary authority to tax the colonies—by saying that such power would be rightful only if the colonists had the same freedom of commerce as subjects in Britain.[30] Similarly, when William Hicks reacted to the Declaratory Act by denying Parliament's "sovereign jurisdiction over the colonies," he argued that such power threatened the livelihoods of the colonists. He anticipated what might follow from parliamentary arbitrariness; he did not object to commercial regulation thus far. Hicks did not call for an end to Britain's commercial regulation of the colonies; he still assumed that an imperial economic interest existed. Because the colonies could no longer rely on Parliament for commercial regulation, they would need to apply "to their Prince for the establishment of such a partial policy as may be the best adapted to their particular circumstances, and, at the same time, the most conducive to the general good."[31] Colonial spokesmen recognized that commercial regulation amounted to an alternative source of imperial revenue, and they appreciated the hypothetical possibility that Parliament, with its "power to regulate the trade of the whole empire," could "draw all the money and all the wealth of the colonies into the mother country." But given the interdependence of imperial commerce, such a policy would be self-defeating beyond the short term.[32]

During the Stamp Act crisis, colonial writers usually made their most thoroughgoing condemnations of imperial commercial regulation in order to reinforce the rhetorical impact of political arguments against taxation. Arguments that restrictions on colonial trade denied the colonists opportunities for wealth did not then call for a reform of trade. For example, James Otis could question the basic justice of imperial regulation of colonial commerce, just as he could see the stark difference for the colonies between the justice and the authority of parliamentary taxation.[33] He doubted there were any good arguments "why trade, commerce, arts, sciences and manufactures, should not be as free for an American as for an European." In particular, he repudiated the authority of Montesquieu, whom "half thinking mortals" quoted "to prove, that it is a law of Europe, to confine the trade and manufactures to the mother state, 'to prohibit the colonists erecting manufactories,' and 'to *interdict* all commerce between them and other countries.' "[34] Such strong statements remained rhetorically subordinate in Otis's criticism of the Stamp Act. He asserted the entitlement of the colonists, as British subjects, "to all the rights, liberties and privileges essential to freedom," and he analyzed imperial commercial regulations to show how "indirectly and eventually the colonists are and have long been amazingly taxed by Great Britain." He located the origins of the regulatory system in Restoration legislation which borrowed from Spanish example to "restrain [the colonies] in their trade and commerce" by the enumeration of commodities to be shipped only to Britain and by the prohibition of imports from anywhere but Britain. Having shown the restraints on colonists' commercial opportunity, Otis forthrightly offered advice to British politicians to encourage Americans' collective self-deception about the commercial benefits of empire:

> A merchant who could bring matters so to bear, as to force all his neighbours to buy his goods, and sell him theirs, and both at his own price, would as soon grow rich; and all his neighbours would soon grow poor; and while obliged to trade with him, upon such unequal terms, must ever remain so. But if he could persuade those neighbours, that he was the most generous fair trader in the world, & that they were very happy that he would trade with them, he must be a mad man to try any further projects that might by any possibility undeceive them.[35]

What could have been the starting point for a radical reassessment of the political and economic rationale for mercantilist regulation of colonial trade—"with overtones of Adam Smith's famous *Wealth of Nations*"[36]—Otis instead used to demonstrate the colonists' allegiance to imperial subordination. He asserted the exploitativeness of imperial commercial regulation in order to demonstrate the lack of any colonial desire for independence. The longevity of the exploitation implied its acceptability, and Otis could happily anticipate its increase: "What better assistance can be given to madam ['Dear mother, sweet mother, honored mother-country'], than by yielding, as her American sons have, for more than a century, subsistence for half Britain? . . The time is hastening when this fair daughter will be able, if well treated, to purchase and pay for all the manufactures her mother will be able to supply." Otis identified colonial economic regulation as a burdensome tax de facto, but one he hoped would be borne indefinitely: "The

[23]

colonists pride themselves in the real riches and glory their labours procure for the best of kings: liberty is all they desire to retain for themselves and posterity."[37] Involuntary, direct, exorbitant taxation threatened this liberty in ways and degrees that commercial regulation did not. In showing that imperial commercial regulation amounted to a tax, Otis did not intend to arouse colonial militancy against such regulations; rather, he sought to undercut the ministry's justification of direct taxation on the grounds that the colonists paid no taxes toward the maintenance of the empire.[38]

John Dickinson's widely circulated *Letters from a Farmer in Pennsylvania* more closely typified colonial views on the imperial economic relationship. He compared the Navigation Acts benignly with the measures of Grenville's and Townshend's administrations.

> He who considers these provinces as states distinct from the *British Empire,* has very slender notions of *justice,* or of their *interests.* We are but parts of a *whole*; and therefore there must exist a power somewhere, to preside, and preserve the connection in due order. This power is lodged in the parliament; and we are as much dependent on *Great Britain,* as a perfectly free people can be on another.
>
> I have looked over *every statute* relating to these colonies, from their first settlement to this time; and I find every one of them founded on this principle, till the *Stamp Act* administration. *All before,* are calculated to regulate trade, and preserve or promote a mutually beneficial intercourse between the several constituent parts of the empire; and though many of them imposed duties on trade, yet those duties were always imposed *with design* to restrain the commerce of one part, that was injurious to another, and thus to promote the general welfare.

Dickinson took for granted that such mutuality required commercial regulation, and the prohibition of colonial manufactures left him untroubled precisely because "this country is a country of planters, farmers, and fishermen; not of manufacturers." The restriction of manufactures and the monopoly for British suppliers troubled him because they potentially enabled a duty on American imports to extort a revenue from necessities.

Dickinson accepted colonial underdevelopment because "the prosperity of these provinces is founded in their dependence on *Great Britain.*" He uncritically adopted a metropolitan perspective on the advantages of colonial trade to the interests of the colonists themselves. Writers such as Sir Josiah Child, Charles Davenant, and Malachy Postlethwayt, who closely identified Britain's prosperity with the proper regulation of colonial trade, provided him economic authority. Without irony, Dickinson assumed that "perfect liberty" had characterized a process of economic development shaped by regulations directing colonial production to Britain and providing it with an exclusive export market. "All history" proved "that trade and freedom are nearly related to each other."[39] This "freedom" secured property, not economic opportunity.[40] From the mercantilist perspective, trade regulations did not themselves deprive Americans of their wealth or freedom. For this reason Dickinson used the test of intent, not economic costs and benefits, to assess the threats to liberty posed by parliamentary regulations on trade: Were they to regulate trade, or to raise a revenue?[41]

It could be said, and Josiah Tucker did say so, that the colonists did not object systematically to the acts of navigation and trade because they systematically violated them. If evasion was tacit objection, however, then explicit condemnation of British regulation of colonial trade should have increased following the stricter enforcement after 1763. Colonists robustly resisted the more stringent enforcement and forthrightly detailed injuries to their self-interests, but grievances about commercial regulations rarely aroused systematic condemnation. Most calls for redress took for granted that the mutual economic interests of the colonies required commercial regulation.[42] The most apparent exception was the minority of smugglers among the merchants of Boston, New York, and other northern ports. They insinuated themselves into leadership of the resistance movement and unrelentingly remonstrated against imperial constraints on colonial commerce. However, even they stopped short of defending the smuggling of foreign manufactures, which continued to be held dishonorable. Nor did they ever develop either a viable analytical alternative to relatively orthodox mercantilism or an ideological alternative to the benefits of imperial commercial privilege.[43]

Individually and in groups, colonial merchants often bitterly contested imperial regulations of trade. In New York in particular, "local conditions from the outset led many Americans to question mercantilist premises." They frequently asserted the colonists' needs and rights for the easing of restrictions on their trade and manufactures, and "by the 1750s . . . [argued] for the expansive potential of unregulated trade." However, appeals to free trade never acquired much ideological authority because they transparently served self-interests and often contradicted the simultaneous pursuit of privilege by their proponents. From the mid-1760s to the mid-1770s such liberal economic ideas ran afoul of the restraints on consumption and trade by the nonimportation movements and the Continental Association, as the sacrifice of individual economic benefits became a test of public virtue. The opportunity to broaden the claims of colonial resistance to include specific eliminations of colonial commercial regulations—not to mention the promise of true economic sovereignty—went unseized. Be-

cause liberal ideas regarding commerce became of *less* ideological relevance during the imperial crisis, it remains debatable whether they ever
really challenged "mercantilist premises" in such ways as to amount
to sustained, systematic criticism—comparable to that beginning in
Britain—of imperial commercial regulation.[44] In the 1760s most
American and British commentators viewed freedom and the regulation of trade as compatible; for most British colonists in America,
inextricably so. After all, at that stage in their resistance to imperial
policy, the American Whigs represented themselves as defending their
British liberties.

Parliamentary Sovereignty and
Commercial Regulation

Once precipitated by the issue of repeal of the Stamp Act, parliamentary debate on the imperial crisis linked parliamentary sovereignty with
maintenance of the Navigation Acts and the regulation of colonial
trade. Grenville's ministry had already justified the Stamp Act on that
connection: "The acts of trade and navigation, and all other acts that
relate either to ourselves or to the colonies, are founded upon no other
authority; they are not obligatory if a stamp act is not."[45] In debate on
the Declaratory Act, Lord Lyttleton immediately tied the justifiability
of taxing the colonies with the regulation of their trade: "But it is said
they will not submit to the Stamp Act as it lays an internal tax: if this be
admitted, the same reasoning extends to all acts of parliament. The
Americans will find themselves crampt by the Act of Navigation and
oppose that too."[46] Opponents of the repeal of the Stamp Act insisted
that such leniency simultaneously ignored and encouraged the manifest intent on the part of colonial merchants to free themselves of
British commercial regulation. Precisely because the colonists made
constitutional objections to the Stamp Act, Parliament should reject
them, lest it concede on the inextricable issue of commercial regulation
as well: "Should they ever be encouraged to procure for themselves
that absolute Freedom of Trade which they appear to desire, our Plantations would become not only of no Benefit, but in the highest Degree
prejudicial to the Commerce and Welfare of their Mother Country."[47]
   Parliamentary defenders of the colonists' rights to taxation exclusively by their representatives also linked the preservation of parliamentary authority with colonial conformity to the acts of navigation
and trade. The opposition saw no inconsistency between the colonists'
insistence on taxation only by representatives and their acceptance of
imperial restraints on their economic interests: "The Americans have

acknowledged our right of restriction of trade and submitted to it, but they will not be deprived of their property which they acquire under this restriction."[48] Should Americans deny parliamentary authority to regulate their commerce, however, their defenders in Parliament, particularly Pitt, threatened to turn on them fiercely: "We must not tax hereafter. But if they set up manufacturers or combine not to take the manufactures of this country, he should look on it as a combination approaching to a revolt."[49] Similarly, the Rockinghams particularly insisted on the maintenance of the acts of navigation and trade. As Burke straightforwardly informed the New York Assembly, "all the true friends to the Colonies, the only *true* friends they have had, or ever can have in England have laid and will lay down the proper subordination of America, as a fundamental, incontrovertible Maxim, in the Government of this Empire."[50]

During the imperial crisis, Josiah Tucker continued to be the sharpest critic of conventional wisdom on the commercial benefits of empire. He insisted that the colonies, not Great Britain, effectively enjoyed economic privilege out of the imperial relationship. For example, bounties, such as that on hemp, applied to colonial but not metropolitan production. American raw materials, such as naval stores and indigo, entered Britain duty-free, while British consumers had to submit to prohibitive duties on foreign supplies. In the case of tobacco, American planters enjoyed the dual advantages of a captive market and privileged production, because British law prohibited the domestic growth of the plant, while American tobacco could be reexported duty-free when the British price was too low. When it came to supplying their own needs, however, Americans repudiated any regulatory constraints: The typical American "will ever complain and smuggle and smuggle and complain, 'till all restraints are removed, and 'till he can both buy and sell, whenever, and wheresoever he pleases. Any thing short of this, is still a grievance, a badge of slavery, an usurpation on the natural rights and liberties of a free people."[51] Tucker saw nothing exceptionable about Americans in such commercial self-seeking. On the contrary, the historical record of colonial administration was one of "mutual discontents, mutual animosities and reproaches," because colonists had "no other marks of attachment to their antient parent, than what arose from views of self-interest and self-love." "All Colonies, whether ancient or modern, from the Days of Thucydides down to the present time . . . aspire[d] after Independence, and to set up for themselves as soon as ever they find that they are able to subsist without being beholden to the Mother Country." The "bold free constitution which is the prerogative and boast" of all British subjects accounted for Americans' readiness and "daring" to seek independence earlier than the colonies of France and Spain. Consequently, Tucker warned against using force to bring Americans into commercial compliance with the imperatives of empire. Such "government à la prusse" would soon "contaminate" the free part of the Constitution as it required increasing numbers of troops.[52]

In 1774, as the North government adopted a policy of coercion to respond to American resistance, Tucker recommended complete separation. A decade earlier he had advised against the use of military force for imperial administration by employing an analogy that Smith would present more benignly: "A shop-keeper will never get the more custom by beating his customers: And what is true of a shop-keeper, is true of a shop-keeping nation."[53] Tucker appreciated that most people explained the "prodigious increase of trade . . . since the happy revolution" in reference to the development of the colonies, but he attributed that growth to a complicated set of internal developments—the reduction of monopolies in foreign trade, the attrition of guild privileges, the repeal of taxes on imported raw materials and on exported manufactures, better communications through turnpikes and canals, the mobilization of larger concentrations of capital for agriculture and manufactures, and "improvements in various engines, with new inventions and discoveries for the abridgment of labour." In this context the colonies, along with the East India Company, hampered Britain's economic development. The colonies cost hundreds of thousands of pounds annually in bounties and civil and military expenses, and both the colonies and India involved Britain in "frequent ruinous and expensive wars."[54]

With the American colonies peacefully independent, Tucker concluded, Britain would enjoy all the economic benefits of their commerce without the expenses of their government. There would be no loss of profitable trade, because Americans had long shown that they "will trade with any people, even with their bitterest enemies, during the hottest of a war . . . provided they shall find it their interest so to do." Britain simply provided the best market for most American products and the best supplies for colonial needs: "Were the whole trade of North America to be divided into two branches, viz. the Voluntary, resulting from a free choice of the Americans themselves, pursuing their own interest, and the involuntary, in consequence of compulsory Acts of the British Parliament; this latter would appear so very small and inconsiderable, as hardly to deserve a name in an estimate of national commerce."[55]

PARLIAMENTARIANS on both sides of most issues regarding colonial rights agreed that the regulation of commerce was the *sine qua non* of parliamentary sovereignty in the colonies.[56] Yet as colonial resistance to parliamentary authority moved toward outright denial, the colonists seldom presented such regulation as a fundamental grievance. Right through to their declaration of independence, American patriots expressed a prevailing, and explicit, desire to maintain commercial dependence on Britain.

CHAPTER TWO

Commercial Monopoly and Parliamentary Sovereignty

T HE IMPERIAL CRISIS put sovereignty at issue, and the acts of navigation and trade had become a shibboleth in British politics for parliamentary authority. Yet between the repeal of the Stamp Act in 1766 and the Coercive Acts in 1774, commercial regulation of the colonies virtually disappeared as an issue in parliamentary debate. Colonial patriots simply did not make them a constitutional grievance. They depended on authorities in Great Britain, either the royal prerogative or Parliament, to regulate colonial trade. The regulation of colonial trade reemerged as an issue in British politics when Parliament framed the Coercive Acts in response to the Boston Tea Party.[1] For the next two years nearly all colonial patriots tried to avoid seeing the crisis as one involving commercial regulation.

British Assertions and American Evasions of Commercial Sovereignty

In response to the Boston Tea Party, the king asked Parliament, on 7 March 1774, to consider "what further Regulations and permanent Provisions may be necessary" to secure "the just Dependence of the Colonies upon the Crown and Parliament." The king's immediate concern was the Bostonians' obstruction of "the Commerce of this Kingdom." Their subversion of the Constitution, as an implicit means to that end, was an integral but subsidiary concern. Parliamentary debate on the king's message started with the same emphasis on the effectiveness of commercial regulation rather than its constitutional implications. In his motion of thanks to the king, George Rice, a treasurer of the chamber, reminded the Commons that "we cannot subsist without the advantages which are derived from our commerce in America. Those advantages can never be maintained if we [do not] keep up the sovereign authority of this country."[2]

North presented the Boston Port Bill with the justification that the destruction of the East India Company's tea had shown that British trade with Boston was not safe for British merchants or for customhouse officials. He acknowledged the act's punitive nature, which he intended to caution colonists elsewhere from imitating Boston's "various insults and outrages" to "those laws and rules to which Parliament has in former time wisely subjected the trade of the colonies."[3] North dealt with a perceived repudiation of Parliament's authority, not just a grievous violation of a particular statute: "We are not entering into a dispute between internal and external taxes, not between taxes laid for the purpose of revenues and taxes laid for the regulation of trade, not between representation and taxation, or legislation and taxation. But we are now to dispute the question whether we have or have not any authority in that country."[4] Britain needed that authority in order to maintain the colonial monopoly: otherwise, "Where will it end? Will not the Americans likewise be desirous of rescinding the Act of Navigation?"[5]

During debate on the Boston Port Bill, the Navigation Acts changed from a parliamentary shibboleth to an issue of substance and principle in the imperial crisis. Burke introduced this theme by observing that if Parliament had punitive intents regarding Boston's commerce, then it ought to appreciate that colonial commerce already depended on invidious relations: "You have taken a monopoly to yourselves. You have given the inhabitants of that country only a limited and circumscribed form of acquiring wealth."[6] Thereafter Burke repeated and elaborated on the equivalency of colonial policy, the acts of navigation and trade, and commercial monopoly.[7] Burke explained that the colonists continued to accept the invidious political relationships of the colonial monopoly, partly out of habit but mostly because they owed their prosperity to it: "Their monopolist happened to be one of the richest men in the world." British capital "(primarily employed, not for their benefit, but his own)" underpinned "their fisheries, their agriculture, their ship-building (and their trade too within the limits)." As long as "England pursued trade, and forgot revenue," the imperial relationship, however unequal politically, provided reciprocal economic benefits: "This whole state of commercial servitude and civil liberty, taken together, is certainly not perfect freedom; but comparing it with the ordinary circumstances of human nature, it was a happy and liberal condition." To be sure, the colonists violated the Navigation Act, but "its authority never was disputed": like the British themselves, they systematically violated trade regulations only when "pressed hard." Burke denied any implication that Americans could negotiate the terms of the acts of navigation and trade: "They were born with that on their head." But too strict an application of those acts, too ready a disposition "to believe regulation to be commerce," would make the regulations themselves counterproductive: "It is the nature of all greatness not to be exact; and great trade will always be attended with considerable abuse." Without such tolerance and flexibility, efforts to reform commercial regulation defeated themselves. Grenville, confronted with the phenomenon of the "rich redundance" of American trade during and after the Seven Years' War, had mistakenly made the acts of navigation and trade "his idol."[8]

North's associates readily accepted Burke's characterization of imperial commercial regulation as a monopoly, and they appreciated that the colonists might resent it as such.[9] But they had taken Tucker's point that the advantages of the monopoly ran both ways: the colonists enjoyed bounties on whale products, "on naval stores, on iron, on lumber, on indigo," and they had access to inexpensive manufactures that they could buy on ready credit for their products. Wedderburn argued that the monopoly of colonial trade nearly disadvantaged Britain, and he questioned whether to maintain it in the face of colonial disregard: "I shall advise giving up a great deal more. Don't keep a lingering contest, dissatisfying to you, prejudicial to both. With regard to America give up the rest." Wedderburn was not yet "of the opinion of Mr. Tucker. I do not think the period is come when you . . . submit your authority, give it up without a struggle." But he anticipated how the commercial rationale for control of colonial commerce could mistakenly become of subsidiary importance to the psychological imperatives of political power.[10]

The regulation of trade, rather than duties on it, became an issue on the colonial side of the imperial crisis when Parliament passed the Boston Port Act in March 1774, as the first of the Coercive Acts— Intolerable Acts to the patriot colonists—intended to discipline Boston for the Tea Party. The act closed Boston's port by eliminating its custom house. No ships could enter or leave the port except to bring food and firewood from other American ports, and these exceptions required an escort from the Salem custom house. News of the Boston Port Act immediately precipitated calls throughout the colonies for what became the first Continental Congress.[11] In the light of previous conflicts arising from commercial boycotts organized in individual colonies, an intercolonial meeting provided the most popular and least controversial way to deal with the appeal of the Boston Committee of Correspondence to the other colonies to cease trade with Britain.[12]

In Virginia, the Assembly had adjourned, but the burgesses who remained in Williamsburg called for a provincial convention in August to respond to the Boston appeal. Meanwhile open meetings in the counties discussed the appeal from Boston. The Resolves from Fairfax County, largely drafted by George Mason, became the most influential expression of Virginians' view on the crisis. George Washington carried them to the provincial convention in Williamsburg, where they provided the terms for Virginia's association for commercial boycott, and they served a similar function at the Continental Congress. Having identified "the fundamental Principle of the People's being governed by no Laws, to which they have not given their Consent, by Representatives freely chosen by themselves," and having asserted that Parliament could not provide such representation, the Fairfax Resolves then immediately dealt with the apparent contradiction posed by the colonists' acceptance of commercial regulation by Parliament. The Resolves explicitly recognized that, as Britain had provided protection to the colonies, Parliament had justifiably regulated colonial trade to the advantage of "the People of Great Britain." These regulations included a monopoly for British goods in the colonies, as well as exclusive British privileges to purchase needed colonial goods. Although the Resolves manifested scrupulousness on other constitutional issues, when it came to trade they acknowledged the constitutional repugnancy of the imperial commercial monopoly and still conceded that "such a Power directed with Wisdom and Moderation, seems necessary for the general Good of that great Body-politic of which we are a Part." Virginians' submissions to such regulations for over a century had acknowledged their "Utility, and the reciprocal Benefits flowing from it produced mutual uninterrupted Harmony and Good-Will, between the Inhabitants of Great Britain and her Colonies." Even when the regulatory powers "stretched beyond the original Design and Institution," the colonists avoided "Strife and Contention with our fellow-subjects," because they were more "strongly impressed with the Experience of mutual Benefits."[13]

Thomas Jefferson became ill on his way to the August convention, but he sent on a draft of instructions for the Virginia representatives to the Continental Congress. Immediately published as *A Summary View of the Rights of British America,* Jefferson's proposals supported a program of nonimportation and nonexportation, but they went beyond the Fairfax Resolves in denying the legitimacy of any parliamentary legislation for the colonies. Jefferson used the language of natural rights, and his crucial word was "free." "Free inhabitants" had settled the colonies, in accordance with the "universal law" of "public happiness." The Navigation Acts had tyrannously prevented the "exercise of a free trade with all parts of the world, possessed by the American colonists as of natural right." Britain's commercial regulation of the colonies had repeatedly made their "rights of free commerce . . . a victim of arbitrary power."

As a consequence of so-called regulation, Americans paid inflated prices for imports available more cheaply elsewhere, and they received lower prices for exports than they could find on other markets.

But Jefferson disputed the injustice of parliamentary power in the colonies, not commercial regulation.[14] Jefferson analyzed the invidious economic effects of Parliament's commercial regulations in order to show "that bodies of men as well as individuals are susceptible of the spirit of tyranny." The Hat Act of 1732, not the Navigation Acts, provided his extreme example of Parliament's commercial tyranny—"an instance of despotism to which no parrallel [sic] can be produced in the most arbitrary ages of British history." In Jefferson's own time the colonists accepted Britain's regulation of their commerce as a "gift" to the British in exchange for the protection of their mutually valuable commerce. When Jefferson defended the rights of Americans to "free trade," he asserted their sovereignty to regulate themselves. He expressed no objection in principle to commercial privileges, and at this point he took for granted that they would exist between Great Britain and its American colonies. Jefferson expected there to be "such exclusive privileges in trade as may be advantageous to them, and at the same time not too restrictive to ourselves." His calculations for American trade policy had more political than economic precision: "Accept of every commercial preference it is in our power to give for such things as we can raise for their use, or they make for ours. But let them not think to exclude us from going to other markets, to dispose of those commodities which they cannot use, nor to supply those wants which they cannot supply."[15]

Along with Jefferson's *Summary View*, James Wilson's *Considerations on the Nature and Extent of the Legislative Authority of the British Parliament* most thoroughly denied Parliament's legislative authority in the colonies, whether internally or externally. Yet until its very end Wilson's pamphlet avoided the topic of commercial regulation.[16] Only in a footnote to the last sentence did Wilson take up the "only one objection that can be offered against" his argument "that all the different members of the British empire are distinct states, independent of each other, but connected together under the same sovereign in right of the same crown." This objection, he conceded, "will, by many, be deemed a fatal one[:] 'How, it will be urged, can the trade of the British empire be carried on, without some power, extending over the whole to regulate it?'" Wilson dealt evasively with this hypothetical objection. First he replied that the whole world carried on trade without "one superintending power," and "some politicians, of no inferiour note," thought "that all regulations of trade are useless; that the greatest part of them are hurtful; and that the stream of commerce never flows with so much beauty and advantage, as when it is not diverted from its natural channels." But Wilson would not commit himself to this liberal theory. Instead he asserted that "commerce is not so properly the object of laws, as of treaties and compacts." Because commerce was a diplomatic matter, and because the king had the prerogative to make treaties, "Where is the absurdity in supposing him vested with the same right to regulate the commerce of the distinct parts of his dominions with one another, which he has to regulate their commerce with foreign states?" Wilson did not even argue that the king should negotiate commercial relations with the individual colonies: in order to maintain his argument against Parliament's legislative authority in the colonies, he conceded "a power in the crown to regulate trade, where that power is exerted for the great end of all prerogative—the public good." His simultaneous enhancement of royal prerogative and denial of parliamentary sovereignty may well have been in bad faith, but it highlighted the colonists' difficulty in assuming commercial sovereignty with political independence.[17]

Despite the forthright repudiations by Jefferson and Wilson, the first Continental Congress itself conscientiously stopped short of denying "Parliament's authority over colonial trade," and in framing the Continental Association its members remained "clearly unhappy about contravening, even by implication, the Navigation Acts."[18] American views on their "commercial system" during the imperial crisis expressed virtually no systematic criticism of the acts of navigation and trade or of economic regulation more generally. Even writers in New England, who emphasized the costs of economic regulation more than its mutual benefits, still reiterated that British protection of American trade sufficiently justified the restrictions that benefited Britain's commerce. Conversely, the commercial advantages that Britain enjoyed from the protected market for its exports and from the privileges it had as purchaser of colonial exports constituted an "indirect tax" that made any further levy inequitable.

Colonial patriots differed on the constitutional basis of the acts of navigation and trade—did they arise from agreements between individual colonies and Great Britain, or did they manifest a more general imperial authority?—but adherents of either view accepted the economic regulations themselves and seldom exploited the regulations' debatable constitutionality to argue for the elimination of colonial commercial subordination. For example, in contrast to Jefferson's proposed instructions for Virginia's delegation, the instructions John Dickinson drafted for the Pennsylvania delegation to the first Continental Congress readily accepted Parliament's power to regulate colonial commerce, as "the only judge between her and her children in commercial interests." Dickinson proposed that if the colonies should be successful in eliminating the objectionable taxes and coercive measures then "it will be reasonable for the colonies to engage their obedience to the acts of navigation."[19]

Against this background, short-term boycotts of Anglo-American trade did not contradict affirmations of the existing dependencies in colonial commerce. Accordingly, in October 1774, Congress bound "ourselves and our constituents" to the Continental Association. The Association sought "to obtain redress" of colonial constitutional "grievances" by establishing "a non-importation, non-consumption, and non-exportation agreement" among the colonists. After 1 December 1774, colonists would cease importations of British goods, as well as goods exported from Great Britain, East Indian tea, exports from the British West Indies, and other duties goods (such as Madiera wines). From the same date importations of slaves would stop, and the inhabitants of the united colonies would cease all involvement in the slave trade. To reinforce these provisions for nonimportation, colonists would not "purchase or use" proscribed goods after 1 March 1775.[20]

Congress adopted a less forthright policy regarding nonexportation to Great Britain. The South Carolina delegation, with the exception of Christopher Gadsden, boycotted Congress in order to prevent what they saw as an unfair policy of nonexportation. Because the Association intended to abide strictly with the acts of navigation and trade, the northern colonies would continue to be able to export their products directly to Europe, while rice, as an enumerated product, would not be generally exportable.[21] Eventually the South Carolinians conceded on indigo, and Congress made an exception of rice exported to European markets through Britain. Anyway, the policy of nonexportation of goods to Great Britain, Ireland, and the West Indies would not begin until 10 September 1775, because Virginia's delegates had insisted on postponement until the 1774 tobacco crop had been cured and shipped. Congress sought to have its cake and to eat it too in the staple economy—to deny income to British exporting interests while maintaining the exporting interests of the colonists. Conversely, British merchants who dealt in colonial staples would continue to do business for a year, while colonial retail merchants would almost immediately be denied goods for sale. Both politically and economically, foreign trade remained privileged according to mercantilist priorities.[22]

At the same time as Congress drafted the Continental Association, it also prepared an "Address to the People of Great-Britain." The "Address" sought to convince them that since Lord Bute's administration began there had been "a plan for enslaving your fellow subjects in America." The "Address" also elaborated on the commercial advantages that people in Britain had long enjoyed over colonial commerce:

"You restrained our trade in every way that could conduce to your emolument. You exercised unbounded sovereignty over the sea. You named the ports and nations to which alone our merchandise should be carried, and with whom alone we should trade." Congress identified such commercial relations, not in order to insist that they be liberalized, but in order to show "our loyalty and attachment to the common interest of the whole empire." According to Congress's address, the successful resolution of the colonists' constitutional grievances would affirm and reestablish the commercial subordination of the colonial economy.[23]

As an apparent denial of British sovereignty, the Continental Association, not the Continental Congress, critically challenged North's ministry.[24] The breadth of the colonial boycott forced North's government to reconsider the character of imperial commerce. North now characterized the "restraints of the Act of Navigation" as the colonies' "Charter; and that the several relaxations of that law, were so many acts of grace and favour." The colonists had no right to trade. Parliament conferred the privilege of trade on the colonies, and therefore, if they refused to trade with Great Britain, "we should not suffer them to trade with any other nation."[25] On 30 March 1775 Parliament gave statutory form to its reaction to the proceedings of the first Continental Congress by prohibiting the New England colonies from fishing on the Newfoundland banks and by restricting the colonies that had enacted the Association from trading anywhere except with Britain, Ireland, and the British West Indies. (The act therefore initially exempted New York, Delaware, North Carolina, and Georgia.) North intended the policy to be politically coercive and strategically the equivalent of a blockade.[26]

To North's supporters, the Association challenged the acts of navigation and trade and the general regulation of colonial commerce. The Association aimed forthrightly at "the total overthrow of that great Palladium of the British commerce, the act of navigation."[27] The conflict had gone beyond the "right of taxation." Parliament had to address the question whether "commerce" would be "laid open at the will of the factious Americans, who were now struggling for a free and unlimited trade, independent of their mother country." Such free trade derogated "the honour and dignity of the imperial crown of England" and posed the dangers that the colonies "would not only be independent, but carry all their trade to a foreign State."[28] Lord Lyttelton "urged the necessity of asserting the sovereign right of Great Britain by the most speedy and resolute measures." He insisted that the advantages of colonial commerce depended entirely on the effectiveness of "the navigation act, and all other regulatory acts."[29]

While leading the opposition to the government's plan to retaliate against the Association by restraining colonial commerce, Pitt emphasized that he agreed with Lyttelton's assessment of the importance of the acts regulating colonial commerce, "so wisely framed and calculated for that reciprocity of interests, so essentially necessary to the grandeur and prosperity of the whole empire." He disparaged as "metaphysical refinements" efforts to show that their lack of parliamentary representation freed Americans of liability to "obedience and commercial restraints." Pitt reiterated that he would support attempts "to resist and crush" any effort on the part of Americans to "defeat" the Navigation Acts. He had no difficulty in understanding how a "glorious spirit of Whiggism" could animate Americans to defend their liberties and to "prefer poverty with liberty, to gilded chains and sordid affluence," and yet they could still abide by British regulation of their commerce. "Property is private, individual, absolute:—Trade is an extended and complicated consideration;—it reaches as far as ships can sail, or winds can blow; it is a great and various machine:—To regulate the numberless movements of its several parts, and combine them into effect, for the good of the whole, requires the superintending wisdom and energy of the supreme power in the empire." Pitt and other opponents of the Restraining Act denied any evidence to support the government's analysis of colonial political economy.[30] As Wilkes pointed out, the Continental Congress simply had not voiced any complaints about the commercial regulation of the colonies.[31]

Less sanguine petitioners warned Parliament about the economic consequences of the Association and elaborated on the linkages between colonial trade and Britain's domestic economy and foreign trade. The London merchants trading to North America explained how they exported the manufactures of Great Britain and Ireland to the colonies, "in particular the Staple Articles of Woollen, Iron, and Linen, also those of Cotton, Silk, Leather, Pewter, Tin, Copper, and Brass, with almost every *British* Manufacture, also large Quantities of Foreign Linens and other Articles imported into these Kingdoms . . . which are generally received from those Countries in Return for *British* Manufactures." They also sold the colonists "great Quantities of the various Species of Goods imported into this Kingdom from the *East Indies*." From North America these merchants imported "Pig and Bar Iron, Timber, Staves, Naval Stores, . . . Bees Wax, Pot and Pearl Ashes, Drugs, and Dying Woods, with some Bullion, and also Wheat Flour, *Indian* Corn, and Salted Provisions, when on Account of Scarcity in *Great Britain*, those Articles are permitted to be imported." From Ireland came more complicated circuitous returns, "(for Flax Seed, etc. exported from *North America*) by Bills of Exchange on the Merchants of this City trading to *Ireland,* for the Proceeds of Linens, etc. imported into these Kingdoms, from the West Indies, . . . for the Use and Support of the *West India* Islands, by Bills of Exchange on the *West India* Merchants, for the Proceeds of Sugar, Mellasses, Rum, Cotton, Coffee, or other Produce, imported from those Islands into these Kingdoms." Colonial trade eventually returned to Britain from all over Europe, where colonial merchants obtained bills of exchange for their direct exports of "Wheat, Flour, Rice, *Indian* Corn, Fish, and Lumber." The linkages provided £2,000,000 in trade between the colonies and London alone, as well as the employment of thousands of British ships and tens of thousands of British seamen to transport the goods. The petitioners did not specify any particular measures for Parliament to resolve the imperial crisis, except to "restore and establish the Commerce between *Great Britain* and her Colonies on a permanent Foundation" for "that System of Commercial Policy, which was formerly adopted, and uniformly maintained, to the Happiness and Advantage of both Countries."[32]

The government's supporters had no patience to hear about the immediate commercial implications of their coercive policy, for if colonial commercial pressure led Parliament to hold back on firm measures, then "whenever the Americans had any point to gain, let it be ever so unreasonable, all they had to do was to refuse to pay their debts, to threaten to stop all commercial intercourse with us, and their business would be done." It would be better immediately to give up altogether claims to parliamentary supremacy "than remain open to demands which could have no bounds, and must be irresistible, when they were brought forward in the present form."[33] Government supporters asserted that everyone expected "that whilst the disputes between Great Britain and America subsist, their trade would undergo a temporary stagnation," as a necessary cost of Britain's long-term commercial interests: "Unless the supremacy of Parliament and the rights of sovereignty were vigorously asserted by Great Britain, the American traffic could not subsist." Investors in the "funds," "landed property," and commerce should accept short-term losses "for the sake of those permanent advantages which they would undoubtedly reap when the Americans were subdued, if, per adventure, a subduction, obtained by force, should be found expedient."[34] The short-term losses of trade arose from political imperatives, but they amounted to investments in effective commercial regulation.

Faced with objections to the commercial costs of its coercive policy, the government increasingly invoked the analogy of war to rationalize the statutes restraining colonial commerce. Wedderburn acknowledged that the coercive measures might harm British merchants and manufacturers, but interests of "greater consequence" were at issue. The Continental Congress had "invaded and denied" the power of Parliament and thereby put itself "in actual and open rebellion": "An enemy in the bowels of a kingdom is surely to be resisted, opposed and conquered; notwithstanding the trade that may suffer, and the fabrics that may be ruined . . . the question is not now the importance of American colonies, but the possession of the colonies at all." The government's hardliners readily drew the implications of the Restraining Act for the eventuality of "actual rebellion": they introduced a state of war, and therefore all subjects had to bear their costs.[35] Critics of the Restraining Act charged that it, not the actions of the Continental Congress, provoked war. It "put an end to all that remains of the legislative authority of Great Britain over America" because it gave the colonists no alternative to denying parliamentary authority altogether and therefore to resist it by any means necessary.[36]

The more the opposition elaborated on the negative implications of the Restraining Act, the more frequently supporters of the government asserted a radical willingness to have no colonial trade at all rather than to have an unregulated one: "Life itself was not worth keeping in a state of uncertainty and fear."[37] Burgoyne taunted the "merchants and manufacturers . . . [to] take example from the Americans, and render it glorious by adapting it to a better cause." He asserted that the Restraining Act tested their patriotism:

> If they do not feel insult and affront in the suspicion, that while one country dares the interruption of commerce to effectuate her chimerical claims, the other will not exert equal fortitude to vindicate her fundamental rights; if this be our wretched state, I agree that the sooner a formal surrender is made the better; let Great Britain revert to her primitive insignificancy in the map of the world, and the congress of Philadelphia be the legislature to dispense the blessings of empire.[38]

The Fisheries and the West Indies: Navigation versus Trade

At the climax of the imperial crisis, the most elaborate and many-sided parliamentary discussion of colonial commerce involved the fisheries. Rather than call on Parliament to ease its coercive policies, West Country fishing interests supported the prohibitions on the New England fishery as an opportunity to reorganize the fishery to Britain's advantage. The fishery conducted directly from Britain, they predicted, could readily expand to replace that from New England. Commercial policy had long given priority to such a fishery because it reliably served as a nursery of seamen and its profits were all returned to Britain.[39] Americans in the fishery, in contrast, had no obligation to carry "green" hands for training and did not have liabilities to impressment.[40] Now Americans must be setting up their own manufactures of nets, lines, canvass, and so forth, "or such other Sources of Supply discovered, and Connections formed, as will for ever deprive them [the West Country-men] of a Return of this Trade."[41]

The initial title of the so-called Restraining Act marked a clear difference in policy regarding the fisheries: the act "restrain[ed]" the trade of New England to Britain, Ireland, and the British West Indies, but it "prohibited" the American fishery in Newfoundland. Once it became known that North intended the Restraining Act to include a prohibition of the New England fishery in Newfoundland, then the opposition raised a new set of commercial objections. The London merchants trading to the colonies presented a new petition, which claimed that a prohibition of the colonial fishery would result in deprivation and even famine in the colonies, in unemployment of fishermen and seamen who would then either become privateers or else migrate to French territories, and in the loss of remittances earned by the colonists in southern Europe and the West Indies.[42]

As a committee of the whole, Parliament called several witnesses, both merchants and captains, for information on the American fisheries. Their evidence showed that New England fishermen and merchants inevitably dominated the Newfoundland fishery. The British fishery could not fully supply foreign demand for fish. The West Country already faced a scarcity of maritime labor, with capital in its fishery already fully extended. Witnesses testified that the American fishery had inherent advantages of proximity for early fishing; it relied on the more efficient shares system for wages; and its smaller vessels put all hands to fishing. Americans simply had a monopoly of skills in the spermaceti whale fishery. Nonetheless, profits from the New England fisheries returned eventually to Britain, because British merchants extended most of the credit for fishing supplies, as well as for goods imported for personal consumption. Critics warned that the Fishery Prohibitory Act threatened to disrupt the Newfoundland fishery permanently. In the best of circumstances the New England fishery had a competitive advantage in Newfoundland, and the imminent war would handicap the British fishery further.[43] Subsequent testimony in support of the West Country petitions did not refute the explanations of New England's advantages, or explain the sources of capital and labor for an expanded British fishery, but it did describe a large and thriving fishery conducted in Newfoundland but based in Britain.[44] Henry Dundas said it "was as clear as any demonstration of Euclid" that the

English capital supporting the New England fishery would simply shift to that of England, "and thus our merchants could suffer no loss whatsoever."[45]

When pressed on whether any British alternative to the New England fishery existed, one witness sarcastically suggested the alternative of subsidy: "If government would supply men, money, and ships, they will find merchants enough to carry it on."[46] Because the Newfoundland fishery enjoyed status as a sacred cow in British politics, such sarcasm was ironically misplaced. For example, Shelburne complained that concerns about the shortcomings of the Newfoundland fishery distracted debate about the broader implications of the Prohibitory Act's constraints on the New England fisheries: "How nugatory and ridiculous it is, then, to talk of commercial regulation, which is supposed to include improvement and protection, when that regulation is immediately directed to starve and oppress one part of your subjects, to whom there is not so much as any crime or offence imputed, in order to give commercial advantages to another." But he also claimed to be readily disposed to consider reform of the Newfoundland fishery as a separate topic: "If the several laws in being, for the improvement of the Newfoundland fishery are not sufficient, or that the admiralty, in whose department it is, satisfy Parliament that those powers have been properly exerted, and are found to be inadequate, let a bill be brought in for that purpose."[47]

Officials had chronically criticized the Newfoundland fishery throughout the eighteenth century. Now, some of them seized the opportunity to urge that the prohibition of New England be more than temporary. Former governors Palliser and Shuldham rehearsed how New Englanders interfered with the benefits due from British policy toward Newfoundland. New England fishing ships' crews enjoyed exemption from impressment and carried off British seamen as well. Their illegal trade with the French harmed Britain doubly, because they sold French fishermen fishing supplies with which to compete with British fishermen and then took French manufactures in payment. Because the British crews in the Newfoundland fishery provided a reservoir of British naval recruitment, and British merchants controlled southern European markets for fish, the temporary benefits arising from prohibition of the New England fishery should be made "perpetual."[48]

While the Prohibitory Act for the New England Fisheries moved through the final stages of passage in April 1775, Parliament turned to consideration of improvements in the British fisheries.[49] The Newfoundland Act of 1775 eventually resulted. To encourage the fishery conducted from Britain to the Newfoundland banks, the act estab-

COMMERCIAL MONOPOLY AND PARLIAMENTARY SOVEREIGNTY

lished bounties for fishing ships owned, built, and crewed in Britain. Each year the first twenty-five qualified ships to make two trips to the banks and land their catches on Newfoundland would receive a bounty of £40; the next one hundred would receive £20 each; and the second one hundred would receive £10 pounds each. Ships received these bounties on return to their British home port. Similarly, the act encouraged the British whale fishery in the seas around Newfoundland. British ships taking whales in the northwest Atlantic and then returning to Britain would compete for bounties, with the ship bringing the most oil receiving £500, the second £400, and so on until the fifth most successful had received £100. Starting in 1776, this program of bounties would last for eleven years.

Parliament intended such encouragement of the Newfoundland fishery to come at the expense of the New England fishery. In presenting the proposed bill to the Commons, North forthrightly observed "that there could not be a doubt but it would be infinitely for the advantage of this country, to make Newfoundland as much as possible an English island, rather than an American colony."[50] Therefore Irish merchants could now ship provisions and fishing supplies directly to Newfoundland for the resident fishery there. Similarly, Irish ships could for the first time receive bounties in the Greenland fishery, as well as for the new ones in the waters around Newfoundland.[51] With little debate, it took only a month to enact the proposals.[52]

Besides the Newfoundland fishery, only the West Indies had representatives of its commercial sector granted the privilege to inform the Commons directly about the economic effects of the Restraining Act. Witnesses on behalf of the West Indian planters and merchants' petition categorized the islands' economies as manufacturing, not agricultural. With the partial exception of Jamaica, their production specialized in the production of staple exports, and they could not provision themselves. Most of their food came from the mainland American colonies, even though these supplies arrived irregularly and in small shipments. The West Indian colonies, they advised, received only a little fish and flour from Great Britain. Ireland provided large quantities of salted meat and butter, but otherwise North America provided the islands with grain, animals, and salted fish. Salted fish crucially provided "the meat of all the slaves in all the West Indies." The planters had no practical alternatives to supplies from North America. Even before the nonexportation provisions of the Association had gone into effect, Great Britain faced grain shortages. Ireland could not divert much produce from its established markets. Canada exported no maize, and little wheat. And New Englanders actually caught the fish shipped from Newfoundland to the West Indies.[53]

The development of alternative supplies for the West Indian colonies required long-term efforts. Meanwhile the islands faced an immediate prospect of famine: "It is inconsistent with the nature of commerce, to furnish an adequate supply to a vast, an immediate, and an unexpected demand; the demand and the supply must grow up together, mutually supporting and supported by each other." For example, new European suppliers, such as northern European lumber merchants, would commit themselves to the West Indian market only if they had assurances of long-term access, not "upon the speculative idea of a continuance of a most unnatural quarrel." If such trades developed as a consequence of the efforts of Parliament to reinforce its control over the colonial economy, they would undermine the intent of the navigation system to maximize metropolitan trade.[54] Any lessening of the islands' dependence on the northern colonies for provisions, even in Jamaica, could only come at the cost of "diminishing the growth of the staple commodities of sugar and rum." Although the expansion of provision grounds on the large island might be a marginal cost over the long run, the expense of self-sufficiency in lumber products would be prohibitively high even there.[55]

At the same time that the witnesses on behalf of West Indian interests explained the islands' dependence on the North American colonies, they elaborated as well on the islands' crucial linkages with the British domestic economy. Estimates of fixed investments in the islands by residents of England ran as high as fourteen million pounds, and at any one time an "immense" amount of commercial credit was extended toward the islands. Although physically separated from the metropole, "the sugar colonies are really no other than a British manufacture, established at the distance of three and four thousand miles for reasons of convenience. And the dependence of this manufacture is the same as if it was situated in the heart of the kingdom." The distance of the islands from England simply conferred additional economic benefits by encouraging "a commerce and a navigation, in which multitudes of your people, and millions of your money are employed . . . the support which the sugar colonies receive in one shape, they give in another. In proportion to their dependence upon North America, and upon Ireland, they enable North America and Ireland to trade with Great-Britain." The economy of the islands underpinned British trade to Africa and the Far East as well. The slave trade conducted from England underpinned Britain's trade with Africa, while the islands' planters consumed large quantities of "Asiatic commodities." If the West Indian staple economy declined, British customers would not be willing or able to "pay in money to the foreigners, the large sum for West India commodities, for which the British manufactures, and the profits of a circuitous commerce, are now given in exchange." As imports of West Indian products decreased, so would "the manufactures and commerce the West Indies supported." Fiscal resources would decline as revenues from colonial duties lessened. Even tea duties would decline, because tea consumption would lessen as sugar became scarce: "In trade, as in the human body, nothing suffers singly by itself; there is a consent of parts in the system of both, and the partial evil grows into universal mischief."[56]

The representation of West Indian planters' interests involved the most sophisticated economic discussion during parliamentary debate on the restraint of commerce in the American colonies, and it forthrightly faced up to the need for commercial privilege. On the one hand, their advocates said that the staple economy of the islands required privileges of unhampered supplies from the united colonies; on the other, they assumed that the value of colonial trade to the metropolis depended on maintenance of an imperial monopoly: "All in Europe are our rivals, all devoted to manufacture and traffic, as capital pursuits of policy: while we, struggling with such competition, have in some instances already experienced its hurtful effects, and must prepare for more; we had always one consolation left, that our colony-trade, kept to ourselves by old and salutary regulations, hath been augmenting from period to period, till at present it constitutes more than half of the whole, with a prospect of further growth, rather than diminution, unless we create our own rivals."[57]

The failure of the West Indian representation, and the success of the West Country interests, demonstrated the jeopardy of the colonial trade's privileged status in commercial policy just as the government prepared to go to war in order to establish its authority to regulate imperial commerce properly. North reportedly ostentatiously ignored "the examination of the evidences who came to prove any of the injuries that this country would suffer by the loss of her American commerce."[58]

Radical and Opposition Commitments to American Commercial Dependence

In March 1775, at the conclusion of debate on the Restraining and Fisheries Prohibition Acts, Edmund Burke made his celebrated speech on conciliation with the colonies. Burke knew that even North's more moderate supporters saw American resistance to taxation as only "a cloak" to "attack the trade laws." Because Burke's argument for a policy of accommodation on matters of taxation depended on a strict distinction between "commercial servitude and civil liberty," North could undermine it by using Tucker's analysis of imperial trade. To the consternation of Burke, North had perversely "borrowed [Tucker's] ideas, concerning the inutility of the trade laws," to rationalize a coercive policy of colonial administration in order to maintain restrictions on colonial trade. Burke charged that "you keep up revenue laws which are mischievous, in order to preserve trade laws that are useless." Burke saw this as an argument in bad faith, because almost everyone, including himself, recognized how Britain's prosperity and power depended critically on American trade, which in turned depended on imperial regulation. Because Burke knew that the compromise did not fundamentally disturb the leaders of American resistance, he could be exceptionally explicit about how laws regulating colonial commerce compromised American liberty.[59]

Burke argued that North miscalculated his program of coercion because he ignored the basic economic realities of the colonies. The colonial trade played a crucial structural role in Britain's Atlantic commerce: "It will be said, is not this American trade an unnatural protuberance, that has drawn the juices from the rest of the body? The reverse. It is the very food that has nourished every other part into its present magnitude." The colonial population was large and growing, "not a mean dependent, who may be neglected with little damage, and provoked with little danger." Even more important than the colonial potential for demographic growth, "the commerce of your colonies is out of all proportion beyond the numbers of the people." Exports to the colonies had increased twenty-five times in the eighteenth century and now made up two-fifths of all present-day export trade, nearly equaling the entire export trade at the beginning of the eighteenth century.[60]

Throughout the imperial crisis, the parliamentary opposition who sympathized with American claims to political rights had also insisted that Parliament had supreme authority to regulate trade. Because they juxtaposed political rights and economic subordination, Chatham and Burke could forthrightly acknowledge British exploitation of Anglo-American commerce by balancing it against the preservation of colonists' liberties.[61] In contrast, Adam Smith benignly assessed Britain's and America's relative economic advantages in colonial commerce in ways similar to those of Tucker. His view of the connection between economic and political issues contradicted Burke's. Smith advocated colonial representation in an imperial parliament, and he justified taxation of the colonies on grounds that the colonial relation had imposed increasing fiscal burdens on Great Britain at the same time that the metropolitan disadvantages of colonial trade had also increased.[62]

While utterly at odds on the principle of parliamentary sovereignty in the colonies, on the issue of policy regarding colonial trade, the views of the parliamentary opposition and of extraparliamentary radicals had more similarities than differences.[63] At the climax of the imperial crisis, but before war had broken out, British radicals typically urged an easing of constraints on the colonies, both economically and politically. They devoted most of their attention to the constitutional aspects of the imperial crisis, particularly the colonists' right to self-government and the implications of its denial for Britain's domestic polity. But while repudiating parliamentary authority in the colonies, they still supported the principle of privileges in imperial trade, and therefore they often found themselves haplessly becoming advocates of the prerogative in the particular matter of trade regulation—much as had James Wilson. Thus in the spring of 1774 John Cartwright, at that point the most prominent radical on the colonial issue, urged that Great Britain immediately recognize American independence by a treaty declaring that "his Majesty is, and shall be held to be the sovereign head, in like manner as he is of the legislature of Great Britain." Such a treaty would also provide a mechanism to arrange "a firm, brotherly, and perpetual league" between Great Britain and the individual states "for their mutual commercial benefit, and their joint security against all other kingdoms and states." What Cartwright's precisely titled pamphlet, *American Independence: The Interest and Glory of Great Britain*, gave away with the main title, it took back with the subtitle. In a half-hearted reaction against Tucker's *True Interest of Britain*, Cartwright advocated recognition of "the respective governments in America" as "independent nations," free of any parliamentary authority, in order that there might be "brotherly affection" to "cement a lasting union with them as between the separate branches of one great family." With Americans securely independent, Parliament and the former colonies would reciprocate "good offices," and "all will be ready to contribute their respective shares, and that due respect and deference will ever be paid to the elder house."

Cartwright disavowed the legitimacy of political empire, but he contentedly recalled that in the colonies "government's first object was, as indeed it always ought to be, to extend the commerce of this kingdom." Political accommodation with the colonies should be the means to the end of the continuation of special commercial relations between America and Britain. Cartwright, the political libertarian, optimistically anticipated how sheer economic power would allow Britain to control American commerce more effectively than formal empire ever had. "The superior advantage of our trade" would provide "the same power to awe America into a faithful observance of her treaties that we now have, to enforce a disputed and odious sovereignty, and with this manifest advantage, that treating with each state separately, we shall only have one at a time to contend with." Just as under the acts of navigation and trade, there would now be a tacit reciprocity between protection from Great Britain and "exclusive trade" from the colonies. Cartwright disavowed that the "proposed league" would be based on anything but Americans' "free consent," but just as under the acts of navigation and trade, one would be the "planting," the other the "manufacturing country." Of their own free will, Americans would recognize "what it is *their* advantage to restrict themselves to in manufactures and trade; and will be ready to take care to confine themselves to such branches, as will be most consistent with that first political maxim, of securing, at all events, *the protection of Great Britain,* and her valuable trade, from which they have benefits to expect, that no other European market can yield them."[64] Among British radicals, Cartwright typified a paradoxical anti-imperialist mercantilism. Unlike Tucker, from whom he took so many cues, he had little confidence that Anglo-American trade could be prosperous without political arrangements to shape its course.

———

ONCE the rebellion began, the Dissenting minister Richard Price came to political prominence in Britain for his denunciation of the war as a threat to both British and American liberties. By the early 1760s Price's liberal theological and moral writings had gained him the acquaintance of Benjamin Franklin, David Hume, and Joseph Priestley. His friendship with Lord Shelburne began in 1769, and at that time Price's interest in political and financial matters became apparent. The liquidation of the national debt became his special interest. Once the American resistance became armed rebellion, his writings in opposition to the war made him the most widely read, and controversial, public commentator in Britain. His *Observations on the Nature of Civil Liberty, the Principles of Government and the Justice and Policy of the War with America,* first published in February 1776, eventually appeared in over sixty thousand copies. At the climax of the imperial crisis, Price urged reconciliation through reform of earlier abuses. He concurred with Cartwright that American liberty required self-government for the individual states, but he thought that Anglo-American trade required an imperial legislature.[65] Yet when Shelburne reviewed a draft of the pamphlet and urged that Price state that Parliament already constituted such an imperial legislature, Price reluctantly went along with the editorial advice. Therefore Price presented his views on the importance of American trade by summarizing Shelburne's speech condemning the American Prohibitory Bill: "Prescribe the most explicit acknowledgment of your right of regulating commerce in its most extensive sense; if the petition and other public acts of the Colonies have not already, by their declarations and acknowledgments, left it upon a sufficiently secure foundation."[66] In that speech Shelburne had referred to the Navigation Act as "that great Palladium of our commerce, that great source of all the advantages we now happily enjoy, as the first commercial and trading nation in Europe."[67]

CHAPTER THREE

Commercial Diplomacy during the Revolution

ARGUMENTS for the lessening of British commercial regulation could not mobilize either resistance to coercive imperial administration or militancy for independence. The awareness of loyalists on this count led them to charge militants with wanting to eliminate, not just to evade, British commercial regulation. To forestall such charges while organizing the Continental Association and condemning the four "Coercive" acts against Boston and Massachusetts, the first Continental Congress had "cheerfully consent[ed] to the operation of such acts of the British parliament, as are bona fide, restrained to the regulation of our external commerce, for the purpose of securing the commercial advantages of the whole empire to the mother country, and the commercial benefits of its respective members."[1] Even Congress's later justifications for taking up arms in 1775 explicitly accepted Great Britain's "monopoly" of colonial trade in order to juxtapose that "heavy contribution" with taxes. Even the hypothetical alternative, presented as a *reductio ad absurdem*, implied a subordination to British regulations: "If we are to contribute equally with the other parts of the empire, let us *equally with them* enjoy free commerce with the entire world."[2]

War and American Perpetuation of the Navigation Acts

The war required reconsideration of the political strategy behind the Association.[3] After learning, in July 1775, that Parliament had extended to other colonies the restraining act on New England's commerce, Franklin presented Congress with resolutions from the committee "to devise ways and means to protect the trade of these colonies." The committee recommended that on 20 December 1775 the custom houses be closed and the ports opened to "the Ships of every State in Europe that will admit our Commerce and protect it;

who may . . . expose to Sale free of all Duties their respective Produce and Manufactures, and every kind of Merchandize, excepting Teas, and the Merchandize of Great Britain, Ireland, and the British West India Islands"—in other words, free trade. Congress should assure countries entering into such trade that this "Freedom of Commerce" would continue for two years, regardless of "any Reconciliation between us and Britain," or as long thereafter as "the late Acts of Parliament for Restraining the Commerce and Fisheries, and altering the Laws and Charters of any of the Colonies, shall continue unrepealed."[4] The rationale for this apparently liberal measure, however, would have been political coercion and retaliation, not free trade. Because it would not go into effect unless Parliament failed to repeal the Restraining Act within a year, the measures proposed by Franklin's committee actually sought, in part, to *restore* British control over colonial trade.[5] Nonetheless, Congress would not go even that far to disrupt imperial commerce, and instead it tabled the resolutions. American trade remained officially closed to foreign ships until 6 April 1776.[6]

While Congress considered opening the Confederation's trade, it acceded to the insistence of John Dickinson to send another, "Olive Branch," petition to the king. The petition voiced a complete identification of the American colonists with the "British Empire": "The apprehensions that now oppress our hearts with unspeakable grief being once removed, your Majesty will find your faithful subjects on this continent ready and willing at all times, as they ever have been, with their lives and fortunes to assert and maintain the rights and interests of your Majesty, and of our mother country."[7] Franklin had drafted a remarkable proposal for the Continental Congress to consider as a supplement to the Olive Branch Petition. "In order to remove her [Britain's] groundless Jealousies, *that we aim at Independence and an Abolition of the Navigation Act, . . .* and to avoid all future Disputes about the Right of making that and other Acts for regulating our Commerce," Congress would "Covenant" with Britain that it would have a "Right" for one hundred years to make such regulations, "the same being *bona fide* used for the common Benefit." Congress would have advised each state to confirm the agreement, on the understanding that it could not be repealed without royal assent. Congress reportedly found little hypothetically objectionable about the proposals, but viewed them as premature in the context of the Olive Branch Petition, which requested that administration of the colonies be restored as it had been in 1763.[8]

Congress confounded itself with devising a strategy to obtain supplies for the rebellion without violating the Continental Association's ban on exportations. The ban would come into complete effect in the fall of 1775, half a year after the outbreak of rebellion.[9] Not only had the Association failed to anticipate the commercial implications of a colonial revolt, but the British government had sought to divide the colonies on the basis of commercial privilege. New York, Delaware, North Carolina, and Georgia enjoyed exemptions from the initial acts restraining the commerce of the rebellious colonies.

Paradoxically, arguments for easing the Association in order to allow the continuation of imperial trade pointed out the imperatives of market relations. Delegates from the colonies exempted from the Restraining Act argued for a pragmatic assessment of the advantages to be had from compliance with imperial commercial regulation: "We must regulate our trade, so as that a reconciliation be obtained, or we enabled to carry on the war." If the colonies exported to Britain, they would secure specie credits they could use for the purchase of war supplies. The rebellion would have political as well as logistical liabilities if all the colonies denied themselves the opportunities of exportation: "What will disunite us more than the decay of all business? The people will feel, and will say, that Congress tax them and oppress them worse than Parliament." Delegates opposed to the closure of custom houses advised that patriotic virtue not be put to too stern a commercial test: "We can't do without trade; we must have trade . . . I would use American virtue as sparingly as possible, lest we wear it out." "Are we to do hurt," John Jay asked, "to remove unreasonable jealousies?" There should be a distinction, he urged, between invidious policies among the united colonies themselves and those imposed by the British government: "Let us lay every burden as equal on all the shoulders as we can. If Providence or Ministry inflict misfortunes on one, shall we inflict the same on all?" Commercial as well as political realities dictated against the closure of custom houses. Neither French nor Spanish merchants gave any indication of new interest in American trade: they probably appreciated that to do so would violate treaties of peace with Britain. Lastly, should the united colonies open their ports to foreign traders, it would weaken their support in Britain: "The people of England will take it we design to break off, to separate."[10] As long as other colonies boycotted British imports, commercial pressure could continue in British domestic politics.

Rather than emphasize how a successful boycott would eliminate British control over American trade and thereby widen commercial opportunities, staunch supporters of the Association expressed a mercantilist distrust of the political consequences of unregulated trade. Congress's allowance of exports could be to the advantage of Great Britain, either by providing a revenue if imported there, or by supplying provisions necessary for the economy of its West Indian colonies.

Provisions nominally exported to French and Spanish destinations would eventually find their way to the British islands, with their higher demand. Despite the price of lessened trade, the rebellion's cohesion required adherence with the Association's restraints on imports and exports rather than surrender control over American navigation: "The grower, the farmer, gets the same, let who will be the exporter, but the community does not. The shipwright, rope-maker, hemp-grower, all shipbuilders, the profits of the merchant, are all lost, if foreigners are our sole carriers, as well as seamen."[11]

Throughout the fall and winter of 1775–76, Congress could not devise an alternative commercial policy to the rejected recommendations of Franklin's committee that custom houses be closed and that commerce be conducted in disregard of British regulation. Congress's commercial policy consisted of contradictory exceptions. The Association would continue: "We shall shut up all our ports, and be all on a footing." But some members also frankly hoped that supplies of arms and ammunition would "be obtained by what is called smuggling." Others had confidence that patriot committees could issue trading licenses for the sole purpose of obtaining powder. Critics of such a licensed trade warned of its liabilities for favoritism, while others responded that an open trade would supply the British islands after all. In September 1775 Congress formed a Secret Committee of Correspondence with authority to export goods to the non-British West Indies in order to secure war supplies; early in 1776 the committee began negotiations in France for a direct trade of tobacco for arms credits. In this context debate concluded with recognitions of confusion: "We are making laws contradictory in terms. We say nobody shall export, and yet somebody shall . . . one proposition is to be made public, and the other kept secret."[12]

Congress repeatedly considered and then referred back to the committee its report on trade. Congress had already altered the Association in order to allow exportations for the purpose of securing military supplies, but it could not devise an alternative general commercial policy. During this period of indecision, Congress added further qualifications to the terms of the Continental Association—such as prohibiting altogether the export of lumber, livestock, and leather (lest they find their way to the British West Indies as provisions), or allowing the export of flax seed to Ireland in exchange for "military Stores and woolen Yarn," or allowing the tobacco colonies to secure salt by exporting produce anywhere except Great Britain and its proscribed domains—but support for an alternative policy remained insufficient to warrant simple disregard of imperial commercial regulation. Instead Congress made well-meaning recommendations to the colonies to keep their "Roads in good Repair," and for members to set an example of wearing "leathern waist coats and breeches" when the manufacture of woolens did not develop fast enough to "furnish an immediate supply of clothing."[13]

Because John Adams' diary provides the fullest record of congressional debate on commercial policy during the period of rebellion before the declaration of independence, it is difficult to separate his colleagues' confusion and uncertainty from his own. His views while a member of the second Continental Congress illustrate how economic separation from the metropole presented a conceptual problem as much as a political one. One of the most militant members of the Congress in his attitude toward resistance to Great Britain, he was troubled only slightly by the possibility of "the disagreeable necessity of assuming a total independency." In July 1775 he already complained about Congress's reluctance to exercise sovereignty: "We ought to have had in our Hands a month ago the whole Legislature, executive and judicial of the whole Continent, and have completely modeled a Constitution; to have raised a naval Power, and opened all our Ports wide."[14] Because armed rebellion had begun, Adams saw no reason for Congress to abide by British regulation of American trade, but he found himself uncharacteristically indecisive about what sort of commercial policy the American colonies should actually enact. He found it heartening that Congress urged each colony to defend its trade along the Atlantic coast, but he expressed uncertainty about any new commercial policy: "We have had in Contemplation a Resolution to invite all Nations to bring their Commodities to Market here, and like Fools have lost it for the present. This is a great Idea. What shall We do? Shall We invite all Nations to come with their Luxuries, as well as Conveniences and Necessaries? or shall We think of confining our Trade with them to our own Bottoms, which alone can lay a Foundation for great Wealth and naval Power?"[15]

Even though "a more intricate and complicated Subject never came into any Man's thoughts than the Trade of America," Adams' consideration of commercial policy remained almost entirely short-term and political. He did not anticipate that independence from Great Britain would either result in enduring commercial realignments or provide economic opportunities denied under British rule. When reflecting on the appropriate commercial policy for the Continental Congress, Adams' only economic calculations were to assume that Americans themselves could not "bear a total Cessation of Commerce" (because "such Numbers [would] be thrown out of Employment and deprived of their Bread, as to make a large discontented Party") and that "our Country furnishes a vast abundance of materials for Commerce" to foreign nations (and therefore "many private foreign Adventurers would find Ways to send Cargoes here thro all the Risques without Convoys)."[16]

Commercial policy presented Adams with diplomatic, not economic, riddles. The "Thirteen united Colonies" really only controlled their trade through an ability to cut it off in an uncertain attempt to coerce new trading privileges from countries other than Great Britain. European nations might fear that Great Britain would take a violation of its colonial monopoly as a cause of war. If so, then the colonies would need to rely on the initiatives of an illicit trade by "Smugglers, by whom I mean private Adventurers belonging to foreign Nations." Such merchants would be liable to seizure by their own government, as well as by Great Britain. If the colonies sought formal commercial treaties with foreign nations, they would confront a likely suspicion that "These People [the British American colonists] intend to make Use of us to establish an Independency, but the Moment they have done it Britain will make Peace with them, and leave us in the Lurch, and we have more to dread from an Alliance between Britain and the United Colonies as an independent state, than we have now they are under one corrupted Administration."[17]

Adams anticipated that his "one Plan" that might satisfactorily meet American wartime needs for credit and supplies would appear "wild, extravagant and romantic." The colonies would simply provide smugglers from any country with assurances that they would have protection from British capture. Conversely, American merchants would send out ships, "especially in Winter, and would run thro many Dangers, and in both these Ways together, I should hope We might be supplied with Necessaries." In order to give the "Utmost Encouragement" to trade for "the present," Adams advocated that "we must lay no Duties at present upon Exports and Imports, nor attempt to confine our Trade to our own Bottoms or our own seamen."[18] His commercial strategy proposed illegal free trade in default of successful commercial diplomacy.

In matters of commerce, as in matters of government, the expatriate Thomas Paine led American Whigs toward a radically optimistic assessment of the consequences of American independence.[19] He labeled as "ancient prejudices" and "superstition" the notions that British protection provided Americans critical security and that America's economic development depended on "her former connection with Great-Britain." British strategic involvement in America had created European enemies for the colonies: "What have we to do with setting the world at defiance? Our plan is commerce, and that, well attended to, will secure us the peace and friendship of all Europe; because it is the interest of all Europe to have America a free port." Commerce between those colonies and Europe would flourish better without the disruptions and distortions inevitable with a dependence on Britain: "The commerce by which she hath enriched herself are the necessaries of life, and will always have a market while eating is the custom of Europe."

Paine's analysis of the commercial implications of American independence went no further than these generalizations—with the exception of military resources. Only for naval armaments did Paine actually calculate the production, costs, and markets of an industry: "We ought to view the building of a fleet as an article of commerce, it being the natural manufactory of this country." America had the natural resources to be self-sufficient in naval stores; naval construction involved considerable added value; and naval vessels readily found international markets and thus improved the balance of trade. Paine had a mercantilist optimism for American commerce: "To unite the sinews of commerce and defence is sound policy; for when our strength and our riches play into each other's hand, we need fear no external enemy." When he thought of commercial policy, he thought of power, not plenty.

The other theme in Paine's discussion of the relation of liberty and commerce had a classical republican orientation. He feared that Americans would fail to realize that "the present time, likewise, is that peculiar time which never happens to a nation but once, viz. the time of forming itself into a government." The time for independence was right precisely because the American economy was in an "infant state." The population was sufficiently large to support a unified confederation, but not so large as to have begun the erosion of virtue by commerce:

> 'Tis a matter worthy of observation, that the more a country is peopled, the smaller their armies are. In military numbers, the ancients far exceeded the moderns: and the reason is evident, for trade being the consequence of population, men become too much absorbed thereby to attend to any thing else. Commerce diminishes the spirit both of patriotism and military defence. And history sufficiently informs us, that the bravest achievements were always accomplished in the non-age of a nation.[20]

Despite Paine's lessons, the Declaration of Independence did not present the imperial commercial monopoly as a grievance.[21] Parliament, not Congress, effectively declared the rebellious colonies to be free of their imperial commercial connection. On 22 December 1775, after the king had declared Americans to be rebels, Parliament prohibited trade with the thirteen colonies and declared their commodities liable to capture as war prizes. Although the Association would end on 1 March 1776, and Congress had accordingly considered new commercial regulations, not until 6 April—after news arrived of Parliament's comprehensive prohibition of colonial trade—did Congress finally allow the export of nearly all American goods and invite the trade of all countries except Great Britain.[22]

The Pursuit of New Privileges

The need for war supplies dictated the initial priorities in American commercial policy. In March 1776, a month before Congress opened its trade to foreign nations, Congress sent Silas Deane to France on a secret mission to obtain "arms and ammunition." In order to encourage the French government to supply the Confederation's wartime needs, Deane explained how American commercial independence would be to France's advantage. He put these advantages in mercantilist terms by emphasizing the potential for a new "friendship" between France and the American states, as France replaced Britain in a privileged trading relationship. In the first place, Britain would no longer have "the commercial advantages" that had "contributed greatly to her late wealth and importance." Britain's loss would be France's gain, because "it is likely great part of our commerce will naturally fall to the share of France, especially if she favors us in this application." The former colonies now needed to find new markets for their inevitable surpluses of staples, in order to have credit to import "the various manufactures they wanted." To pay for French goods, Americans expected to be able to make remittances "through Spain, Portugal, or the French Islands, as soon as our navigation can be protected by ourselves or friends."[23] American commerce itself would remain colonial in character, even though Britain no longer had a monopoly in it. On the basis of this premise of commercial recolonization, American statesmen would often repeat such mercantilist coaching over the next two decades, as they purported to show Europeans where their commercial advantages lay.[24] In doing so they demonstrated their most coherent political economy.

Political considerations had priority in commercial policy toward France, and diplomatic advantage defined the preconditions for assessing markets. French authorities made the colonies' declaration of independence a precondition for the foreign support they needed to secure that independence. France would aid the rebellion of the colonies only if they precluded reunion with Great Britain. To this end, during the summer of 1776 Congress considered Adams' draft of a

model treaty for its negotiations with France. The model treaty represented the conviction and optimism of American statesmen immediately after independence that commerce, rather than political alliances, would have priority as the means toward diplomatic ends.
Because political considerations had priority over economic ones in
American political economy, commercial privileges provided the basis
for diplomatic initiatives in the Confederation's early exercise of sovereignty. Ironically, this diplomatic strategy to rely on commercial tactics
meant that strictly economic ends had a secondary priority even in
commercial policy. The model treaty intended to secure France as a de
facto ally by encouraging it to violate the British monopoly of colonial
trade and thereby draw it into war with Britain.[25]

The strictly commercial terms of the model treaty were simple: the
subjects of each country would have the same privileges and regulatory
impositions when trading with the other country as the subjects of that
country themselves had. The model treaty intended to establish what it
termed "Liberty of Navigation and Commerce" for the American
states. In one sense this freedom involved mutual privileges in each
other's markets for French and American commercial interests.[26] The
model treaty, however, primarily intended the more important commercial liberty of preventing interference with American trade on the
high seas. The treaty gave virtually no priority to the further liberalization of market relations as means to foster economic maximization.
Adams just did not think in such terms.[27] Its economic liberalism depended on the establishment of wartime maritime rights for the new
nation. Seventeenth-century Dutch interpretations of the law of nations, not eighteenth-century analyses of political economy, provided
the guiding principles in this commercial treaty.[28] American commercial diplomacy primarily sought to establish the Confederation's claim,
as an independent nation, for its merchants to enjoy rights of neutral
trade in commerce with the colonial possessions of nations at war.

The American states hoped to secure commercial privileges in the
French empire similar to those they had lost in the British empire as a
result of their rebellion.[29] The only specifically commercial stipulations in the model treaty aimed to provide Americans unhampered
access to the French West Indies. Exports from the French islands to
the American states would be liable to no higher duties than those paid
on exports to metropolitan France, and molasses exported from the
islands to the American states would enjoy exemption from export duties. In seeking these privileges in trade with France, Congress under-
took never to "grant to [Great Britain] any exclusive trade; or any advantages, or privileges in trade, more than to his most Christian majesty
[France]." Yet in December 1776, Congress further instructed its com-

missioners to offer to share the carrying trade between the United States and the West Indies exclusively with France if France would provide military aid.[30] If American and French forces should conquer Newfoundland, Cape Breton, or Nova Scotia, then French and American fishermen would fish there "equally and in common . . . to the exclusion of all other nations." Similarly, the American states sought to replace British with French protection for their oceanic trade. The most elaborate detail in the planned treaty dealt with the mutual protection of commerce regarding coastal trades, convoys, and pirates. In the case of American liability to Barbary "plunderings," the planned treaty called on France to provide protection "as the King and Kingdom of Great Britain, before the Commencement of the present War, protected, defended, and secured the People and Inhabitants of the said United States, then called the British Colonies."[31]

American diplomatic strategy depended on French statesmen's desire for commercial privileges in the American states. Thus John Dickinson had cautioned against a declaration of independence before commercial negotiations with France had begun, lest it prematurely give away to France the economic opportunity it most sought from the former British colonies.[32] Through the Committee of Secret Correspondence, Congress directed its commissioners in Paris to convince the French ministers of the benefits of an American alliance by encouraging them to think that they would establish "the glory, strength, and commercial greatness of [France] by the ruin of her ancient rival."[33] Just as in the colonial period, politicians simultaneously held to a conviction of the crucial commercial importance of the American states and accepted their dependence on a European power: "Whatever European power possesses the pre-emption of it ['the commerce of this country'] must of consequence become the richest and most potent in Europe."[34] From the colonial era, American politicians had long practice in making such calculations of their economic importance by analyzing it from the perspective of a metropolitan power. Now, however, they hoped to redirect that importance and thereby secure their independence.[35]

At war to secure their independence, the States sought a commercial alternative to the British empire, but not necessarily commercial independence. At the same time that Congress approved the model treaty for negotiations with France, its delegates (Franklin, John Adams, and Edward Rutledge) conferred with Lord Howe's peace commission. Because neither side considered the issue of independence to be negotiable, the conference could not abate the hostilities. But each side tried to convince the other that war could not resolve any rational political interest because of their commercial interdependence.[36] Howe disavowed any British intent to obtain an American revenue as "the smallest consideration." Parliamentary politics and ideology dictated that conciliation with the rebellious colonies depend on their recognition of Parliament's sovereignty. But taxation no longer provided the substantive test of parliamentary sovereignty. Britain only stipulated that the colonies not tax the colonial trade itself; otherwise America conferred the "solid advantages" of "her commerce, her strength, her men" on Great Britain without political subordination. Routledge saw no threat in such British interest. On the contrary, he projected that Great Britain would "derive greater advantages from an *alliance* with the Colonies as independent States than she has hitherto done." Britain would still predominate in American commerce: it would exchange manufactures for raw materials, and the United States would still efficiently supply the Newfoundland fishery and the West Indian plantations. However, Routledge advised Howe that to gain such "advantages" Britain would have to enter "an alliance with America before anything is settled with other foreign powers." Franklin treated Howe's military confidence with irony, but he did not taunt the British delegates with the economic potential of the newly independent states.[37]

The Confederation's negotiators had finessed themselves in commercial diplomacy because trade with America had low priority in French strategy.[38] Vergennes had responded to the approaches of Deane by accepting his prospectus of the potential for Franco-American trade, but he demurred from extending commercial privileges. Instead he coached the newly sovereign states in their advantages for free trade. With a genuinely commercial basis for the growth of their trade, "it was therefore the interest of both to have the most free and uninterrupted intercourse, for which reason the court had ordered their ports to be kept open and equally free to America as to Britain"—which, of course, meant equal restrictions as well.[39] Furthermore, in rejecting the commercial privileges that Americans had incorporated in the model treaty, the French also disclaimed responsibility to protect American trade.

The Committee of Secret Correspondence shared the naïve optimism of Adams' earlier committee that the offer of American trade was sufficient to secure American diplomatic objectives with the French, but the committee bowed to political necessity and accepted an alliance with minimal commercial provisions. Nonetheless, France delayed until 1778 in making a commercial treaty with the American states, and then only as part of a formal alliance—precisely what the model treaty had sought to circumvent.[40]

The Franco-American treaty of 1778 used the terms "equality," "reciprocity," and "liberty" to describe itself, but it essentially involved only a reciprocal commitment to extend the terms of most-favored nation. The treaty repudiated "all those burdensome preferences which are usually sources of debate, embarrassment, and discontent" and instead sanctioned each nation to frame its commercial policy as it chose, including the liberty to admit "other nations to a participation of the same advantages." The only terms particular to Franco-American trade involved trade between the American states and the French West Indies. The American commissioners had obtained a reciprocal concession whereby France agreed not to impose export duties on molasses carried by American ships from the French islands, and Americans agreed not to apply export duties on any American merchandise that French ships carried to the French islands.[41]

Shortly after learning about the Franco-American alliance, North secured parliamentary approval to send another peace commission, this one headed by Lord Carlisle. With no authority to negotiate independence, the commission's efforts were stillborn, but the commission marked the first formal recognition by Great Britain of the American Confederation.[42] In order to secure a peace, the commission had authority to make concessions amounting to a repudiation of the coercive policy followed by the North's ministry since 1774. Parliament vested the commission with power to suspend all acts passed since 1763 relating to the colonies. The commissioners tacitly accepted the legitimacy of a general colonial assembly—namely, the Continental Congress—as long as it did not disregard royal sovereignty. Correspondingly, the commission might suggest the possibility of (a very few) colonial representatives in the House of Commons. Even governors in previously royal colonies might now be elected, and judges and civil officers be appointed, by the colonial governments. Britain would undertake not to station any standing army in the colonies during peacetime. The commissioners should try to convince the colonies to fund colonial troops by means of duties and other sources of revenue collectible before 1763, or else by long-term assembly grants. But if the colonies would not undertake to make such contributions to colonial administration and defense, then the commissioners should accept this refusal as a precondition to peace.

The terms of the Carlisle Commission clearly showed the government's priority for the restoration of Anglo-American commerce, despite Parliament's cold hostility to their apparent concessions on parliamentary sovereignty. With peace restored, the colonies would "be protected in the antient course of their trade and commerce by the power of Great Britain." On the other hand, only commercial considerations constrained the terms for negotiation.[43] Legal tender laws for debts held outside a colony would be void. The commissioners could accept "particular demands" "in behalf of particular branches of trade" regarding the "extension of the trade of America," because the Navigation Acts had already "been relaxed in favour of many articles of American production, which are allowed to be carried directly to an European market upon condition only of touching at an English port." But such relaxations would only be exceptions: "Upon the subject of commercial regulations, the prevailing principle has always been to secure a monopoly of American commerce." The ministry calculated such harmony between colonial demands for self-government and British demands for commercial monopoly that it counted on the colonists to impose the regulatory mechanisms upon themselves. In order to sustain the regulation of colonial trade by means of duties on foreign trade, Britain would give up any claim to a colonial revenue. The colonists would fund their administrations by duties that sustained the British monopoly of colonial commerce.[44] With the French alliance finally secured, however, American confidence of victory precluded even consideration of such an accommodating restoration of empire.

The Priority of the Fisheries
in Postwar Commerce

With the crucial exception of the fisheries, commercial issues disappeared from the congressional agenda during the period from the conclusion of the French alliance in the spring of 1778 to the beginnings of peace negotiations in the summer of 1782. Intense congressional partisanship emerged in the aftermath of the French alliance, as the reciprocal character assassinations of Silas Deane and Arthur Lee became the catalysts for open conflict.[45] Their allegations of each other's misperformance while acting as Congress's agents in Europe changed foreign affairs from matters of consensus to ones of controversy. The controversy centered on the archetypically mercantilist issue of fisheries policy.

Spain's proposal in early 1779 to mediate a peace accentuated Congress's divisiveness on foreign policy issues. This proposal obliged Congress to determine its terms for peace on issues having implications for supposed sectional economic interests.[46] Sectional voting patterns sharpened with more frequent roll call votes.[47] While proposing terms presumably acceptable to Britain, Congress needed to reassure Spain about the integrity of its North American possessions after American independence. When presented with its committee's draft of the terms of peace, Congress set aside its previous insistence on free navigation of the Mississippi and on access to a port south of the boundaries of the United States. Southern states with potential interests in Trans-Appalachian commerce had apparently conceded them in order to hasten the end of hostilities as the war intensified in their region.

As an issue in congressional diplomatic policy, American fishing rights provoked far more contention than navigation of the Mississippi. Congressional debate on commercial diplomacy focused on whether the fisheries should enjoy privileged status as a national economic interest. The French alliance had encouraged frequent expressions of optimism about the territorial expansion of the United States, particularly regarding the fisheries. Even before the debate in 1779 over the terms of peace, Samuel Adams had linked maritime and territorial expansion: "I hope we shall secure to the United States, Canada, Nova Scotia, and *the fishery* by our Arms or by Treaty. Florida too is a tempting object at the South."[48] John Adams expressed the same view: "The few men of the nation [Great Britain] who think seriously see clearly, in the long train of consequences of American independence, the loss of their West India islands, Nova Scotia, the Floridas, all the American fisheries, a dimunition [*sic*] of their naval power, as well as national bankruptcy and a revolution in their government in favor of arbitrary power."[49] As the quotation from John Adams indicates explicitly, however, such optimism and emphasis regarding the fisheries focused on their strategic value rather than their strictly economic potential. The fisheries would enhance national power and provide geopolitical security after the war.

Legalistic and diplomatic arguments objected to inclusion of the fisheries among the ultimata for peace. As a term for peace, the fisheries unnecessarily presented Great Britain with an issue on which to take exception. As for legal difficulties, it was uncertain that Americans had "any other right to fishing than what they *derived from their being subjects*." If so, then they did not have a clear right at the time of independence, or at the Treaty of Paris in 1763 (otherwise, according to the alliance of 1778, French support of the American claim would be warranted), or at the granting of any of the colonial charters. On the other hand, if Americans could fish on the Newfoundland banks on the basis of international rights of common access, then they did not need to claim them in any particular treaty of peace.[50]

Thomas Paine refuted this legal argument by turning it on its head. The right to the fisheries "exist[ed] in America *naturally*, and not by *grant*, and in Britain only *consequentially*." Only because of its territorial claims in America could Britain claim "her title deed to the fisheries"— "divorced therefrom, she ceases her pretentions." France had an interest to support the American claim, because France valued American commerce, but more importantly because any American loss of the fisheries would "furnish the enemy of both with a new acquisition of naval strength; the sure and natural consequence of possessing the fisheries." In the determination of American interests in the fisheries, Paine argued, the fisheries' direct enhancement of national strategic strength mattered most. The fisheries had a privileged claim as a commercial interest, for though geographically concentrated, their scale had direct implications for the commerce of the rest of the country. As a nursery of seamen, the fisheries contributed directly to the naval capacity of the Confederation, a precondition for the overseas commerce of all the States. Advocates of the fisheries did not have to be from New England to appreciate their crucial commercial importance for the country. As Thomas Paine declared, "Without the fisheries, independence would be a bubble."[51] Advocates of the fishery, such as Paine, Samuel Adams, and the Lees, also tended to view foreign trade as a mixed blessing, and therefore to be relatively untroubled if it realized less than maximum potential, especially if large merchants bore the opportunity costs.

Despite the nation's natural endowment in naval and maritime resources, economic analysts did not observe a corresponding disposition to exploit them. On the contrary, people usually took up maritime employments only when "the country gets filled, or some peculiar advantage or necessity tempts them out. A maritime life is a kind of partial emigration, produced from a portion of the same causes with emigrations in general." Because the United States had a superabundance of "new land to cultivate," it had somehow to overcome, at least partially, the usual inverse relation between agricultural and maritime potential. New England, with its ample land but infertile soil, provided an American exception proving the rule that "greatness at sea is the effect of littleness by land."[52]

Advocates of the fisheries dismissed their importance in the domestic economy and instead emphasized their crucial role in the staple commerce of the American economy. Fishermen were a resource of maritime power, but the fish, not the fishermen, provided economic benefits: "The same supply would be produced, the same commerce occasioned, and the same wealth created, were they [i.e., the fish], by a natural impulse, to throw themselves annually on the shore." Sheer employment in the fisheries lacked crucial economic importance: "Because as no man needs want employment in America, so the change from one employment to another, if that be all, is but little to him, and less to anybody else." The fisheries' commercial value depended on the foreign destinations of their products and on the linkages their commerce established with other sectors of the American economy. The products of the fisheries, like the other staples, placed wealth in circulation throughout the country. States with fisheries, having slighted agriculture, depended on the products of the other states for subsistence. Paine took this staple analysis of the national economy to an extreme and assumed that because the fisheries provided one-quarter of the staple exports of the country then the commerce of these products provided for the "*employment* [of] one fourth of the United States."[53]

The country's naval interests overrode strictly commercial ones: "The Name only of Independence is not worth the Blood of a single Citizen. We have not been so long contending for Trifles. A *Navy* must support our independence; and Britain will tell you, that the *Fishery* is a grand Nursery of Seamen."[54] The states without a fishery had even more interest in the nursery of seamen than those with one. Their commerce depended more on naval protection, and without the nursery of seamen provided by the fishery there would be no navy. America had natural endowments for the conduct of its own foreign trade, but it could do so only with a thriving fishery:

> Has nature given us timber and iron, pitch and tar, and cordage if we please, for nothing but to sell or burn? Has experience taught us the art of ship-building equal to any people on earth to become the workmen of other nations? Has she surrounded our coast with fisheries to create strength to our enemies, and make us the purchasers of our own property? Has she brought those fisheries almost to our own doors, to insult us with the prospect, and at the same time that she bar us from the enjoyment to threaten us with the constant approach of an enemy? Or has she given these things for our use, and instructed us to combine them for our own protection?[55]

Debate over the fisheries self-defeatingly protracted discussion of the terms of peace for almost eight months.[56] The congressional committee drafting the proposed terms of peace gave a high priority to an American "right of fishing and curing fish on the banks and coasts of the island of Newfoundland, equally with the subjects of France and Great Britain."[57] As Congress considered this proposal, a series of amendments watered it down, in an apparent effort to prevent an insistence on fishing rights from becoming an obstacle to peace. Pennsylvania usually sided with Massachusetts in opposing the changes, but eventually Congress decided not to press its claim, from colonial usage, of a right to fish from the coast of Newfoundland.[58] Despite this concession, in July 1779, Maryland, Virginia, North Carolina, and South Carolina still voted against the proposition that the States would view British obstruction of the American right to fish on the Newfoundland banks as a common interest of the States and a violation of the peace.[59]

The instructions eventually given to John Adams in August 1779 for his negotiation of a treaty of peace with Great Britain acknowledged this eventual reluctance to commit American commercial diplomacy to the fisheries. According to the instructions, America's interests for "peace and Commerce" required that "Canada and Nova Scotia should be ceded [from Great Britain to the Confederation], and more particularly that their equal common right to the Fisheries should be guarantied them, yet a desire of terminating the war hath induced us not to make the acquisition of these objects an ultimatum on the present occasion." Congress directed Adams "not to consent to any Treaty of *Commerce* with Great Britain without an explicit stipulation on her part not to molest or disturb the Inhabitants of the United States of America in taking fish on the Banks of Newfoundland, and other fisheries in the American Seas anywhere, excepting within the distance of three leagues of the Shores of the Territory remaining to Great Britain at the close of the war," but Congress restricted these directions to a *commercial* treaty in order to prevent the fisheries issues from being obstacles to the negotiation of a peace treaty.[60]

In the summer of 1781 Congress revoked even these instructions to Adams for the negotiation of a treaty of commerce with Great Britain.[61] Congress also took into account Adams' offensiveness to the French minister Vergennes and placed him on a new peace commission including Benjamin Franklin, John Jay, Henry Laurens, and Thomas Jefferson. The new instructions allowed the possibility of commercial concessions to Great Britain in order to obtain peace, and they specifically removed any insistence on British recognition of American fishing rights as a precondition to a peace treaty.[62]

———

AS THESE DECISIONS indicated, policy toward the fisheries generated the most controversy when Congress dealt with issues of postwar commerce. Their privileged status as a topic in political economy demonstrated how little rethinking there had been regarding the commerce of the newly independent colonies. The most coherent analysis of issues depended on mercantilist principles that gave priority to strategic considerations over commercial ones and that judged the success of commercial policy more by its encouragement of navigation than by its successful linkages of supply and demand. Even at the end of the war most American politicians made little association between independence and alternatives to the commercial structures and policies prevailing in the colonial period.

CHAPTER FOUR

The Recolonization of Anglo-American Trade

LORD NORTH resigned in March 1782, after failing to establish separate negotiations with either France, the Netherlands, or Congress's agents, when he then confronted an oppositional majority disposed toward conciliation with the American Confederation. Parliament resolved unanimously to cease using force to restore the colonies. Although King George III recognized Rockingham as nominal head of the new ministry, he looked to Lord Shelburne to deal with the critical issue, American negotiations. As secretary of state for the Southern Department, Shelburne treated these negotiations as still a colonial matter rather than a diplomatic one. He had steadfastly opposed American independence, but he had also criticized North's policy of coercion as counterproductive for Britain's true interest, colonial economic dependence. Shelburne particularly feared that an independent America would extend commercial privileges to France and thereby restrict trade with Britain. To preempt this possibility, he would happily have reestablished privileged commercial relations with the American states.[1]

In relying on Shelburne, the king slighted members of the opposition who had advocated recognition of American independence as a way to end the war. This slight bore particularly on Charles James Fox, formerly in opposition, but now secretary of state for the Northern Department, and therefore responsible for diplomacy with foreign nations. Fox sought to separate the Americans from the French by offering them prompt independence. The death of Rockingham in July fortuitously reduced the potential for conflicts in British diplomatic strategy. Soon after Shelburne became first minister, Fox resigned because the new cabinet rejected his insistence on an unconditional grant of independence to the American states. Fox had sought to use independence as a means for a favorable peace; Shelburne intended to secure a favorable peace as a precondition for independence, should it be necessary.[2]

Commerce and Independence in the Treaty of Peace

As his agent to confer with Franklin, Shelburne chose Richard Oswald, whom Adam Smith had introduced to Shelburne. After their initial informal talks, Oswald reported that there were only four terms "necessary" to Americans for peace: independence, settlement of the boundaries between the American states and the remaining British colonies, no further extension of the boundaries of Canada than those before the Quebec Act, and fishing on the Newfoundland banks. In addition, Franklin noted four "advisable" articles: compensation for the destruction of American towns, an acknowledgment of the error in British coercion, the concession of Canada, and reciprocal trading privileges for American and British ships and goods in each other's ports. However, once Franklin learned of the change of ministry and its implication of preconditions for independence, he halted further consideration of the terms of peace until Britain would acknowledge independence. By September the government made such acknowledgment—though it ambiguously directed Oswald "to treat with the Commissioners appointed by the Colonys, under the title of Thirteen United States"—and negotiations for peace commenced.[3]

Jay's draft in early October 1782 of the preliminary articles of peace included Franklin's previous "necessary" articles (while elaborating on the fishing rights to include use of accustomed places for drying) and added a new one "stipulating freedom of navigation and commerce by both parties on the Mississippi River, *and elsewhere throughout all their dominions on the terms of nationals.*"[4] The settlement of boundaries had further direct commercial implications. Jay presumed that Britain would agree to generous boundaries for the Confederation if British merchants had secure access from Quebec and Florida to Trans-Appalachian markets. He accordingly encouraged the British negotiators to anticipate "the profits of an extensive and lucrative commerce . . . by means of which the inhabitants west and north of the mountains might with more ease be supplied with foreign commodities, than from ports on the Atlantic, and that this immense and growing trade would be in a manner monopolized by Great Britain, as we should not insist that she should admit other nations to navigate the waters that belonged to her."[5] Jay held forth this prospect for diplomatic and commercial intents. On the one hand, he wanted to undercut Spain's claims to the east bank of the Mississippi; on the other, he expected that Britain would reciprocate by allowing direct American trade into all its markets.

The Confederation's commercial strategy sought to restore prerevolutionary privileges in Anglo-American trade despite the formal severing of the imperial connection. However, Shelburne's cabinet repudiated the apparent concessions in the draft treaty and sent new instructions to Oswald that he be more firm on the northern boundaries and on the Loyalists' rights and that he deny drying rights on Newfoundland. Any reciprocal trading privileges were to be left for negotiation in a separate treaty of commerce. The preliminary articles of peace signed in November 1782 established the Mississippi as the western boundary of the Confederation and provided for free navigation of the river, but made no mention of reciprocal trading privileges. For their fishery, Americans retained the "Right" to fish on the Newfoundland banks, but they could not conduct the fishery from the island's shore. Americans would also have "Liberty" to fish along the coasts of Britain's other Atlantic possessions—Nova Scotia, the Magdalen Islands, and Labrador—and there they could conduct the fishery from shore in unsettled areas. But as soon as a bay or harbor "shall be settled, it shall not be lawful for the said Fishermen to dry or cure Fish at such Settlement, without a previous Agreement for that purpose with the Inhabitants Proprietors or Possessors of the Ground." The preliminary articles contained no other directly commercial implications, but their preamble implicitly anticipated arrangement of the reciprocal commercial privileges that Shelburne fervently sought: "Whereas reciprocal Advantages, and mutual Convenience are found by Experience, to form the only permanent foundation of Peace and Friendship between States; It is agreed to form the Articles of the proposed Treaty, on such Principles of liberal Equity, and Reciprocity, as that partial Advantages, (those Seeds of Discord!) being excluded, such a beneficial and satisfactory Intercourse between the two Countries, may be establish'd, as to promise and secure to both perpetual Peace and Harmony."[6]

Even after the king addressed Parliament in December 1782, to sanction recognition of the colonies as "free and independent states," Shelburne continued to equivocate on whether the preliminary articles made independence irrevocable. Having perpetuated this diplomatic uncertainty, for the next two months Shelburne endured a welter of criticism and denunciation—for having accommodated the independence that he had previously predicted as ruinous for Britain, for thwarting the independence necessary for peace, for betraying the Loyalists and Indian allies, and for conceding too generous boundaries. In his climactic speech to the House of Lords on 18 February, Shelburne defended the preliminary articles as the best obtainable given what he portrayed to be Britain's incapacity to continue the war, and he used the need for commercial reciprocity with the Confederation as his clinching argument.

Because Shelburne forthrightly admired Smith's thought, historians have reasonably construed that *The Wealth of Nations* helped shape Shelburne's reconsideration of the British economy after the American Revolution. But Shelburne's genuine appreciation and understanding of Smith's thought did not translate into policy. Shelburne, after all, dreaded the consequences of American independence for Great Britain, opposed it well into 1782 as secretary of state, and tried to negate its diplomatic consequences. Historians have described Shelburne as "standing on free-trade ground" as he "defended his sacrifices in America," but the themes of commercial reconciliation and the expansion of American markets were flights of rhetoric as Shelburne desperately tried to end his coldly received speech. If anything, Shelburne, realizing how little good will either he or the former colonists now enjoyed in Parliament, held back from articulating his hopes for the informal reestablishment of the previous imperial commerce. Shelburne's cabinet had already rejected Jay's proposal to include commercial reciprocity in the preliminary articles because its inclusion would have violated the Navigation Acts, and now his position became untenable when the House of Commons resolved to accept the peace but voted to censure the concessions to the American states.[7]

Because the preliminary articles left commercial relations between the former colonies and the metropolis undefined, Shelburne called on John Pownall to draft a bill for the interim regulation of Anglo-American trade until the conclusion of a treaty of commerce. According to Pownall's plan, American ships would pay Alien Duties on entering British ports, but American goods would otherwise be traded as though British. With such an arrangement, American merchants would have enjoyed a major exception to the exclusion of foreign colonial products from British markets unless they arrived in British ships. As additional privileges, exports to the United States from Britain would receive the same bounties and drawbacks as goods exported to British colonies, and American ships could trade directly to the West Indies as though British.[8] Until the American Revolution, goods from the Americas had been colonial by definition. Now American independence required new categories for British commercial policy. Shelburne's strategy treated the independent states as much as possible as parts de facto of the British commercial empire. Thus Pownall's bill would have allowed ships from the confederated states to bring their country's products to Britain's remaining American colonies and to export the products of those colonies—extraordinary privileges for Britain to grant any truly independent nation.

Pownall's draft bill corresponded closely with the desires of the London lobby of American trading interests, whose advocacy of a renewal of former trade relations provided the most elaborate economic rationale for Shelburne's "liberal" commercial policy. With unconscious irony, the introduction to the merchants' "Observations" linked the title of Smith's work with a succinct statement of mercantilist priorities: "The Balance of Trade and the Wealth of Nations depend on the exportation of their Manufactures and produce, and on the Importation of Raw Materials to be used in those Manufactures, Bullion and such other Goods as may again be exported with profit to a foreign Market." The London merchants applauded how former "Commercial Regulations which the wisdom of our Ancestors established between this Country and the Colonies in North America were calculated to procure these advantages." Now that "the Restraints on the Trade and Navigation of the Americans" had ceased, Parliament crucially needed "to determine in what Instances the soundest National and Commercial Policy will furnish motives for a continuance of the same System." The merchants' "Observations" then considered Anglo-American trade, commodity by commodity, from ships, through whale oil and naval stores, to pig iron, tobacco, rice, indigo, and a dozen other American exports. Throughout the analysis, the "mutual Interest" in Anglo-American trade explicitly lay in the de facto restoration of prerevolutionary commercial patterns.

As long as Anglo-American trade conformed to these patterns, merchants from the American states ought to have nearly free trade with Britain, but only as an exclusive privilege protecting prerevolutionary British commercial interests. Some privileges, such as allowing the sale of American ships in Britain or lowering the duties on American whale products, would protect American purchasing power for British manufactures. Others, such as the admittance of furs and pig iron duty-free, would discourage the development of competitive American manufactures while undercutting French access to cheap raw materials. The London merchants uniformly advised that American goods previously bountied for export to Britain now be admitted duty-free. However, they made no "liberal" objections to restrictions on the importation of wheat and flour in accordance with the Corn Laws. Similarly, the prohibitive duties on manufactured colonial goods such as "Chocolate and Spermacoeti Candles" should continue, lest they compete with British goods. British manufactures such as silk, linen, sailcloth, and cordage, whose export to the colonies had been encouraged by bounties, ought to continue to enjoy such privileges when shipped to the American states. After all, they furnished "employment for a very considerable number of our poor," and without the bounties there was "great Danger from the Rivalship of France" or even from the United States in the case of cordage.

American trade should be privileged because Britain had particular concerns for its goods and trade, most especially that they not go to France. Tobacco was the trickiest item to regulate because its importation also provided a significant revenue, but the liability of increased sales to France at least argued for a lowering of duties on tobacco and an easing of burdens on its reexportation. Without the concession of privileges equivalent to those Americans had enjoyed as colonists, Britain would face competition from newly opened markets. These privileges may have constituted "a liberal System of Commerce" in the minds of Anglo-American merchants, but they corresponded closely with Smith's characterization of "the Mercantile System."[9]

Because Shelburne had already fallen from office, Pitt introduced the American Intercourse Bill. Former parliamentary advocates of American rights, such as Fox and Burke, spoke against the proposal because it conceded too much to the American states and compromised Britain's commercial policy toward other countries. The devastating attack came from William Eden, who warned that if Americans regained the privileges previously enjoyed as colonies, while at the same time being free of imperial restrictions, then American shipping could dominate British navigation while developing competitive manufactures. Eden depended for his arguments on a pamphlet by Lord Sheffield, *Observations on the Commerce of the American States,* written particularly for this controversy and soon the most influential analysis of Anglo-American trade. As his friend Edward Gibbon observed, Sheffield's pamphlet on Anglo-American trade crucially influenced the consolidation of parliamentary opinion against Pitt's reintroduction of Shelburne's proposals on American trade in the spring of 1783: "The sale of his *Observations on the American States* was diffusive, their effect beneficial; the Navigation Act, the palladium of Britain, was defended, and perhaps saved, by his pen; and he proves, by the weight of fact and argument, that the mother country may survive and flourish after the loss of America."[10] Fox, now jointly heading the ministry with North, had to accept Eden's lethal amendment to the bill on American trade: the King in Council would have executive authority to regulate that trade for an interim presumed necessary for the negotiation of the definitive treaty and any commercial provisions it might contain.

David Hartley, who had replaced Oswald as British negotiator, benignly viewed American proposals for commercial reciprocity and urged them on Fox: "As surely as the rights of mankind have been established by the American War, so surely will all the Acts of Navigation of the world perish and be buried amongst occult qualities . . . Throw out a loose and liberal line." "Liberal" for Hartley meant the restoration of prewar trade, not free trade. Fox sternly reprimanded him for encouraging the expectations of Americans that their ships would again be treated as British ships. Fox readily acknowledged American independence, but he insisted that it terminated the commercial privileges that Americans had enjoyed as colonists; this was just the opposite of Shelburne's thinking. Meanwhile, in May, an Order in Council had granted permission for unmanufactured products from the American states to enter British ports in either British or American ships, with the implication that American ships could not import either foreign produce or their own manufactures. The fatal blow to the American negotiators' proposals for privileges of commercial reciprocity came when word (erroneously) reached London in June that on 24 April Congress had authorized the reopening of ports to British ships.[11]

When the Fox-North coalition could not devise a coherent policy on American trade, Parliament simply delegated regulation to the King in Council. On 2 July 1783, the council issued a set of orders, drafted by William Knox, that proved to be guidelines for commercial policy toward the United States until Jay's treaty. The orders successfully ended commercial negotiations on the definitive treaty. They prohibited American vessels from entering British colonies, but most American products (except salted provisions and fish) could be imported there; either British or American vessels could import most American products into Britain (with the notable exception of whale oil, which had prohibitive duties); most West Indian products could be exported to the United States, but only British vessels could conduct trade between the islands and the United States.[12]

Through the spring of 1783 American politicians had anticipated prompt negotiations for an Anglo-American Treaty of Commerce, whether or not as part of the definitive treaty. In March, for example, the Virginia delegation reported the terms of the provisional treaty to Governor Harrison as though they included the commercial terms that the British cabinet had rejected the previous fall—that subjects of both nations would have "liberty, to cure on the *shores* subject to either power," as well as "reciprocally to enjoy in every commercial intercourse all advantages that the subjects of each respective Power enjoy within their own dominions."[13] With apparently little American reluctance to reestablish trade with Britain, "it is our business to cultivate a friendly intercourse with every trading nation." The restoration of peaceful trade presented a crucial opportunity to do so because European statesmen had "extravagant ideas . . . of the advantages that they will derive from a trade with us": "To losé so lucky a moment, and to neglect the improving such impressions to our own benefit, would surely argue a great want of discernment, and show a great deficiency in our political character."[14] During the war, securing political recognition had priority in American commercial negotiations. Now, with independence a certainty, commercial diplomacy could have commercial priorities.

Over the summer of 1783, however, the prospect of European countries competing with one another to secure American trade reversed itself. Instead, they seemed to be in collusion to derive "advantages from our commerce, without allowing us reciprocity—for if one European nation does this, the others must pursue the same policy or submit to subject themselves to great disadvantages."[15] Shortly after the peace, the Confederation's former allies reapplied previous restrictions on American trade, particularly in their colonies. France allowed American ships to trade in its islands, but restricted exports to rum and molasses and prohibited the importation of flour, fish, and various other foods. Spain removed Americans' wartime exemptions from its monopoly of colonial trade. These shifts in the commercial strategy of European nations apparently arose "from the utmost Jealousy of the commercial Prosperity of America." Now Great Britain in particular sought "to cramp and restrain" American commerce by limiting its trade with the West Indies and "to deprive us as much as possible of the carrying trade" by—Americans mistakenly expected—allowing American ships entering Britain to carry only the goods of the individual state from which a ship originated.[16]

These unexpected restrictions on postwar American commerce precipitated a renewal of diplomatic energy. Only when pessimism set in about the restoration of prerevolutionary patterns of Anglo-American commerce did American statesmen begin to give priority to the establishment of new commercial opportunities, rather than complacently rely on reintegration into British imperial trade. As a mark of this new priority, John Jay became secretary for foreign affairs, which was a post that had been vacant for over a year since Robert Livingston had left it. In the spring of 1784 Jefferson joined Franklin and John Adams in a commission to negotiate commercial treaties with European nations. The commissioners sought to secure bilateral treaties of "Amity or commerce" to provide for the reciprocal extension of most-favored-nation status by the Confederation and each treaty partner. In this respect the treaties of "amity and commerce" were less liberal economically than the model "plan of treaties" of 1776, which had proposed reciprocal treatment of merchants from treaty partners as nationals of each other's country.[17] This commercial strategy did not anticipate free trade either with the prospective treaty partner or, of course, with nontreaty nations. In fact, the objective of most-favored-nation status in treaties of "amity and commerce" almost contradicted free trade.

Such treaties had no point at all if the Confederation opened itself to free trade with any one country, because all those other nations enjoying most-favored-nation status with the United States could then claim the privilege of free trade extended to any one country. The Confederation really sought the privilege of direct trade, with American ships carrying goods to and from treaty partners.

The Confederation's commercial diplomatic strategy sought primarily to secure privileged trading stàtus from one of the major colonial powers. Treaties already existed with France, the Netherlands, and Sweden, and eventually Prussia and Morocco signed ones in this period, but they went unsigned with the major targets, Great Britain and Spain, and France reduced its privileges for American trade. Adams lamented his lack of success in even getting a hearing on commercial negotiations with the Court of Saint James. The treaty of alliance with France in 1778 had included the guarantee that French merchants trading in the American states would have most-favored-nation status. This guarantee did not prevent France from reimposing restrictions on American trade after the war, but it did entitle France to object to the Confederation's efforts to negotiate reciprocal trade with Great Britain. Jefferson secured piecemeal concessions from France on the relaxation of restrictions on American shipping and on particular imports (whale products and rice into France, lumber into its sugar colonies), but he never secured his major object of free importation of American tobacco into France. In its commercial diplomacy with the United States, Spain pursued a dual strategy of aggressive restrictions and openness to negotiations. On the one hand, it rejected the Anglo-American agreement in the Treaty of Paris to free navigation on the Mississippi, and it restricted American traffic on the river. On the other hand, Spain's emissary to the United States, Diego de Gardoqui, proposed to John Jay a treaty that would grant American merchants privileged access to Spanish metropolitan markets if the Confederation agreed to forgo claims to navigation on the Mississippi for up to thirty years.[18]

Britain's Repudiation of American Commercial Privileges

Smith's *Wealth of Nations* thoroughly influenced just those men who shaped and spoke for much of British commercial policy between the American Revolution and the French revolutionary wars—Lord Sheffield as the preeminent commentator on government economic policy in this period; Charles Jenkinson, chairman and later president of the

Privy Council Committee for Trade and Plantations (and eventually Lord Hawkesbury and first earl of Liverpool); and George Chalmers, chief clerk of the committee from 1786 to 1824. In the aftermath of the American War of Independence, they had shared a fate of political displacement because they were reminders of the colonial debacle— Jenkinson and Sheffield as steadfast supporters of North, Chalmers as a resentful Loyalist.

During the imperial crisis Jenkinson had become notorious for his role as a "secret councilor" and for his vindictiveness toward America. In pursuit of office from his mid-twenties, Jenkinson had a succession of patrons, including Lord Bute and George Grenville, who recognized his virtues of loyalty, diligence, and intelligence. He played a critical role in devising a stamp act for the colonies and voted against its repeal, but Grenville cut him off when he accepted an Admiralty office under Pitt's administration. Jenkinson supported every administration thereafter until the Fox-North coalition, but he carefully avoided personal attachment to any potential government leader. He became the archetypal "King's Friend." Deeply suspected for his supposed influence at court, initially as private secretary to Lord Bute and later when secretary at war after 1778, he also enjoyed general acknowledgment for preeminent expertise in commercial and financial matters.[19] North twice considered giving the exchequer over to Jenkinson, and in 1782 did offer him appointment as secretary of state for the American Department, which he refused.

Best known as Gibbon's close friend and literary executor, Sheffield adopted the role of country gentleman on succession to an uncle's estates in 1768. After winning a by-election in 1780, he was a member of Parliament for Coventry and a loyal supporter of North's ministry. He became an Irish peer in 1781 and voted against Shelburne's peace preliminaries in February 1783. After defeat in the 1784 election, he showed no desire for office and did not return to Parliament until 1790, this time for Bristol. During his period of absence from formal politics, he continued in the self-appointed role of public adviser to the government on commercial policy.[20]

Chalmers had left Maryland in September 1775, rather than be forced to subscribe to the Continental Association. In 1777 he anonymously wrote pamphlets attacking Burke's arguments for leniency toward American constitutional views. In the same year Lord George Germain, secretary of state for the American Department, successfully recommended him for a stipend of £100. Chalmers then became a leader among American expatriates and represented Maryland Loyalist claimants before the Commission of Enquiry. In 1780 Germain secured him access to the Old Paper Office, which he used for documentation of *An Introduction to the History of the Revolt of the Colonies,* a relentless narrative of British administrative neglect and American rebelliousness. After the printing of the first volume in 1782, the government worried that the book would make the treaty of peace more controversial, and Chalmers apparently consented to its suppression before publication. Chalmers gave testimony to the Committee for Trade's inaugural hearings on American–West Indian trade, and he sent Jenkinson information to support the committee's recommendations. Once Chalmers was chief clerk, the two men soon developed a close administrative relationship.[21]

By becoming neomercantilists who combined economic liberalism with economic nationalism, these three men played crucial roles in the early years of Pitt's government in rationalizing the loss of the thirteen colonies. Both terms, "liberal" as well as "nationalist," were relevant to the commercial policies they formulated. (Tucker also could have provided the neomercantilists with nationalistic arguments for freer trade, but his earlier disparagement of efforts to retain the thirteen colonies was a political embarrassment.)[22] They followed Smith in making the government's encouragement of navigation an exception to a policy of freer trade, but they differed from him in giving priority in economic policy to the enhancement of the power of Britain as a nation, not to the prosperity of its people. Smith had concluded his analysis of the mercantile system by asserting that "consumption is the sole end and purpose of all production." But the neomercantilists consistently considered the applicability of Smith's thought to their divergent concerns.[23] They cited Smith as authoritative on most issues and, when they took exception to his arguments, continued to work within his conceptual framework. Each regulation and privilege for nationalist purposes had to be justified against the commercial advantages of freer trade.

The new Committee for Trade, unlike the previous Board of Trade, played a crucial role in commercial policy. Pitt initially formed it to provide advice on American–West Indian trade, and it subsequently conducted lengthy hearings on the Navigation Acts, on the Newfoundland and British fisheries, on the Anglo-French commercial treaty of 1786, on the slave trade, and on the Corn Laws. Except on the slave trade, on which the committee was resolutely noncommittal, its recommendations translated closely into legislation. Only two major areas of trade policy, Ireland and India, lay largely outside its decisions and influence.[24] Pitt used the committee to deflect and to neutralize political opposition arising from economic interests threatened by his policies. But the committee had a paradoxical political success in its use of expert political economy to depoliticize economic policy. For Jenkinson at the head of the Committee for Trade, and for his formal and informal advisers, Smith's ideas could provide a rationale for studied detachment from the threatening politics of interest. By framing its recommendations in the language of the liberal political economy to which Pitt claimed allegiance, the committee could have a measure of independence from Pitt's direction. The committee's success depended on taking advantage of the nondoctrinaire approach with which Smith had formulated policy from economic analysis.

With the publication in 1782 of *An Estimate of the Comparative Strength of Great-Britain, during the Present and Four Preceding Reigns; and of the Losses of Her Trade from Every War since the Revolution*, George Chalmers became the first of the three to come to prominence on commercial issues. The book's optimistic conclusions about the economic effects of the loss of the thirteen colonies gained it a widely favorable reception, including that of King George III. Chalmers argued against Richard Price's notion that the American Revolution was a symptom and an aggravation of Britain's declining trade and population. He reviewed the effect of economic legislation on Britain's population and repudiated Price's fashionable pessimism.[25] Chalmers identified himself with the "wide steps, during the last century, in our knowledge of the science of politics," and he looked forward to its further improvement "by substituting accurate research for delusive speculation, and rejecting zeal of paradox for moderation of opinion."

Chalmers referred most approvingly to his fellow Scots David Hume and Adam Smith as models of enlightened inquiry. He valued Smith's *Theory of Moral Sentiments* as well as *The Wealth of Nations*, and he referred to Smith's meriting "the praise of having formerly strengthened our morals, and lately enlightened our intellects." Chalmers followed Smith in being explicitly antimercantilist. He borrowed Smith's term "the mercantile system" to refer to the system of economic regulation having such "vigour" in England from the fourteenth century until Smith had "so perspicuously explained and so ably exploded it." Chalmers held that competition resulted in the expansion, not just the redistribution, of production. He looked back to the sixteenth century as the period when competition had unwisely been restricted in English domestic markets in order to promote manufactures "by monopoly." The contemporaneous poor laws had been similarly unwise because they were "at once destructive of freedom, and of the true interests of a manufacturing community, that can alone be effectually promoted by competition." He shared Smith's confidence that in a liberal context wages would rise desirably as profits increased, and he cited book 1, chapter 8, of *The Wealth of Nations*, where Smith had dealt with "the Wages of Labour, and incidentally of population, with a perspicuity, an elegance, and a force, which have been seldom equalled."[26]

Attentiveness to Smith's recent work indicated a broader awareness among the British political public that the loss of the thirteen colonies called for a reappraisal of Britain's entire economy. The desirability of privileges in trade between British dominions and the United States posed the major question of commercial policy at the conclusion of the American War of Independence. Sheffield argued against the opinion in "the common conversation, or even from parliamentary debate, during almost the last twenty years . . . that we had no trade worthy of notice, except that with the revolted colonies." Because that trade was, in principle, a highly regulated trade, he argued more generally against the association of regulated trade with Britain's prosperity. His analysis of British trade policy depended on the identification of market relations, and he doubted that regulations could advantageously shape supply and demand. Britain's economy had developed through responses to the market, not by sheer appropriation of other nations' trade. Britain had, in Smith's terms, "improved" as its merchants became more worldly and wealthy, its manufacturers more skillful and industrious, and its trade freer.[27]

Both Chalmers and Sheffield followed Smith in tracing the apparent and actual benefits of the mercantile system. The Navigation Acts of the seventeenth century had increased shipping and foreign trade, and, as this trade had drawn the wealth, knowledge, and younger sons of the landed classes into commerce, the regulations had in all likelihood contributed initially to real economic gains. The growth in colonial trade also resulted from the Navigation Acts, but this advantage was more apparent than real: "Our colonial commerce has prospered, since we have fostered it by every means which interested traders could devise, or the mercantile system admitted; we have cherished it by bounties, by drawbacks, by the obstructions that have been thrown in a way of European rivals." ("Bounties," "Drawbacks," and "Restraints upon the importation from foreign countries" are chapter headings in book 4, "Of Systems of Political Economy," in *The Wealth of Nations*.) Chalmers cited Smith's ironic observation that England's colonial trade distorted commerce and made its contributions to the nation's prosperity despite, not because of, its regulation: "If part of the capital, which had been usefully employed in husbandry, is withdrawn, in order to cultivate the cane and the coffee of the West Indies, our domestic agriculture must necessarily suffer in the exact proportion to the sum taken away."[28]

Because British capital and skills were so great, the nation had prospered under the mercantile system; that system had not created those capitals and skills, it had thwarted them. Smith referred to these costs of a monopoly of colonial trade when he considered the interests of a "nation of shopkeepers." He did not write that Britain was a nation of shopkeepers, and he did not intend a slur on shopkeepers:

> To found a great empire for the sole purpose of raising up a people of customers, may at first sight appear a project fit only for a nation of shopkeepers. It is, however, a project altogether unfit for a nation of shopkeepers; but extremely fit for a nation whose government is influenced by shopkeepers. Say to a shopkeeper, Buy me a good estate, and I shall always buy my cloaths at your shop, even though I should pay somewhat dearer than what I can have them for at other shops; and you will not find him very forward to embrace your proposal.[29]

From this perspective, the decline of American trade since the American Revolution was a healthy readjustment.[30] Chalmers calculated that since the American Revolution the reorientation of British enterprise and capital from the artificially structured colonial trades to "its original business" of manufactures, agriculture, and European trade had resulted in a dramatic growth in British commerce. Sheffield shared this confidence: "The internal trade of Great Britain is much greater than its external commerce . . . The superior state of British manufactures in general does not require other means of monopoly than what their superiority and cheapness will give." Sheffield followed Smith in viewing colonial trade as commercially inefficient: "That trade is surely the most beneficial where its returns are the quickest, where there is the least credit given, where there are fewest debts contracted, and where the customers are most under the eye of the creditor."[31]

With this view of the dynamic, expansive character of British economic life, Chalmers and Sheffield criticized mercantilist preoccupations with the balance of trade, which Smith had used to define the "mercantile system." Chalmers loftily found it "amusing" how "the Sagacious Petty, the experienced Child, the profound Temple, and the Intelligent Davenant" had taken as a "postulate which could not be disputed, that a balance of trade, either favourable or disadvantageous, enriched or impoverished every commercial country." Chalmers equated this obsession with "the metaphysical mode of induction," which should be excluded "from our researches with regard to political economy, in the same manner as it had been driven from the sciences." He deliberately omitted African, Asian, and American colonial trade from his calculation of Britain's balance of trade, because their commerce artificially resulted from mercantilist privilege and regulation. Sheffield was more aggressively antimercantilist in his repudiation of "the fallacious rule of the apparent balance." For him, the identification of the balance of trade as a shibboleth called for a reconsideration of the privileges of all colonial trade. He associated the West Indian and American interests in their mutual concern to obtain commercial privilege. He recalled how West Indian planters had urged that "the finest possessions" in the West Indies be given up for the now "despised" Canada, "because an accession of sugar colonies would bring a great quantity of produce to market, and might lower the price and their profit." Chalmers calculated Britain's balance of trade with individual European nations for the purpose of determining where commercial opportunities, not liabilities, lay. He emphasized that trade brought a nation wealth and that trade required exchange, which meant imports as well as exports: "In proportion as we discourage, by our mercantile restrictions, our imports, our exports must necessarily be depressed since in all traffic barter is implied."[32]

Precisely because Sheffield viewed economic policy from a liberal perspective, he argued the illiberal policy of the Navigation Acts so strenuously. He accepted Smith's argument that the most profitable investment of capital was in the domestic economy, next in foreign trade, and least in the carrying trade. The navigation system was the only aspect of prerevolutionary trade policy to which Sheffield gave strong approval, and he distinguished the encouragement of navigation from the encouragement of trade for strictly economic purposes: "The Navigation Act can have no enemies but those who, supposing it merely commercial, do not observe its object of naval strength." He acknowledged the inconsistency of this policy with the rest of his views on the economics of trade: "This jealousy [of navigation] should not be confounded with that toward neighbouring countries as to trade and manufactures; nor is the latter jealousy in many instances reasonable or well founded. Competition is useful, forcing our manufacturers to act fairly, and to work reasonably." The advantage of the colonial trade lay in the legal monopoly of its shipping, because freight earned its real profits: "Rather than give up the carrying trade of our islands, surely it will be much better to give up the islands themselves." Sheffield had criticized Pitt's bill on American trade with this dire view, but as he pursued the logic of this position he came to interpret the loss of the American colonies as an unintended benefit for Great Britain.[33]

For the neomercantilists the Navigation Acts differed from the rest of commercial and economic policy. To explain the difference, Sheffield drew on Smith's distinction between policies for "opulence" and those for "defense": "As defense, however, is of much more importance than opulence, the act of navigation is, perhaps, the wisest of all the commercial regulations of England." The "however" in Smith's famous sentence refers to an immediately preceding, but seldom quoted, sentence: "The act of navigation is not favourable to foreign commerce, or to the growth of that opulence which can arise from it."[34] Smith's frequently quoted praise of the Navigation Acts was typically ironic. They were the wisest of a largely unwise set of regulations, and their advantages were not commercial. Sheffield accepted Smith's point that regulations favorable toward British shipping might lessen foreign trade because foreigners could afford less in British markets if they were limited in selling there, but Sheffield added that "it is at least doubtful whether our capital can carry us farther in foreign trade, or whether it is prudent to employ more of it at present in that way."[35]

In the spring of 1784 advocates of West Indian commercial and planting interests, upset by restrictions on American trade to the islands, subjected Pitt's government to vehement complaints. Pitt responded by appointing a Committee of Council to consider a petition of West Indian planters and merchants regarding American trade. With Jenkinson as chairman, the committee began hearings in order to co-opt the issue during the general election; after Pitt's electoral success, it recommended continuation of the existing regulations. Jenkinson appealed to law rather than commercial principle in justifying the restriction of navigation to the British West Indies: "By the general law of nations acknowledged by every European state, no nation has a right to have any trade with the colonies of another." Americans had no justification to retaliate with restrictions on British shipping. The United States must accept "the rules and restrictions which other countries as independent as themselves have never scrupled to acquiesce in." British commercial policy toward the United States was fair, and even indulgent. American vessels enjoyed exemption from the Alien Duties that Britain applied to foreign shipping, yet Americans had treaties with France and Holland not to give commercial privileges to British trade. Americans seemed unable to distinguish between commercial advantage and commercial privilege, or between navigation and commerce. They objected to the exclusion of American shipping from the British colonies, even though nearly all American products could be imported there. American vessels might enjoy entry to the French islands, but French regulations subjected the actual trade to a "principle more rigid and confined, than Great Britain has hitherto adopted." The United States could only export to the French islands products that French territories could not themselves produce, which included a long list of exclusions, including salt cod and grain products. British colonial trade was comparatively open and impartial.[36]

Priority for the Navigation Acts did not contradict a *lessened* importance for foreign, and especially colonial, trade. When the Committee for Trade drafted a new Navigation Act in 1786, it altered nothing in trade policy. The act encouraged British shipbuilding only through stricter definitions of British ships and more comprehensive procedures for registration. When Sheffield urged that Britain not "sacrifice solid sense to groundless terrors, nor give up the wise system of our forefathers to the idle theories of unexperienced men, or to the interested projects of American *speculators*," he did not intend any invidious reference to Smith. He had in mind Shelburne, Pitt, and the West Indian lobbyists: "A wise nation ought to protect equally every branch of trade, and encourage many markets, without favouring or overloading any, upon the same principle as the prudent merchant himself courts many correspondents, because he finds no friendship in trade."[37]

Sheffield's critics in Britain did not separate economic considerations from political ones. They faulted Sheffield for having a naïve faith that market relations would oblige Americans to engage in a commerce that they resented politically. Critics accused Sheffield of being illiberal and employing outdated ways of thinking, but the "liberal" attitudes they recommended were ones of sympathy, generosity, and friendship, not economic calculations of self-interest. His critics did not grasp the force of his distinction between navigation and commerce. They thought that, in conceding the strategic necessity of the navigation system to provide a nursery of seamen, Britain also continued the priority of the colonial trade in commercial policy. They considered the colonies as a particular sector of the British economy, like manufactures and the fisheries, rather than simply as alternative markets overseas for domestic surpluses. In contrast to the neomercantilists' appropriation of Hume's commercial metaphor of water seeking its own level, their critics portrayed trade as a watercourse to be kept within artificial banks. For all their recommendations of a policy of liberal attitudes toward reciprocal advantage, they presented British foreign trade primarily in colonial terms. They made virtually no reference to Adam Smith's and Josiah Tucker's criticisms of the former colonial regulation of trade. They viewed the British economy primarily in commercial terms that closely identified the interests of overseas merchants with those of the nation as a whole—just the opposite of Smith's views. And the sharpest difference of all was that they viewed the scale of the colonial trade as the best measure of Britain's prosperity.[38]

Sheffield's British critics had a mercantilist view of trade policy and would have given priority to the continuation of prerevolutionary patterns of commerce. This view dictated a special place for the United States in supplying the remaining British American colonies: it equated the Navigation Acts with commercial policy more generally; it took for granted that Britain's colonial markets were more important than new European ones; it assumed that the colonial trades were the most attractive ones for investment; and it treated the British economy as a self-sufficient empire. Because the critics of Sheffield did not grasp his distinction between navigation and commerce, they could not understand why he would preclude American coastal shipping from the British West Indies but readily admit American oceanic vessels into British ports.[39]

Sheffield made liberal, not mercantilist, criticisms of Shelburne's and Pitt's proposals for trade policy toward the independent American states. Their proposals would have used reciprocal advantage as the principle for Britain's trade relations with the American states. Sheffield charged that this principle would result in commercial privilege for the Confederation among foreign nations and would discount its status as a foreign country. The encouragement of American trade through privilege erred in principle, as well as in its calculation of immediate advantage. Trade advantages themselves should shape policy, not the reverse: "Nothing can be more weak than the idea of courting commerce. America will have from us what she cannot get cheaper and better elsewhere; and what we want from her, she will sell to us, as cheap as she will to others." Sheffield then applied this principle to an item-by-item analysis of Anglo-American trade to determine where the advantages lay. He concluded sanguinely that "the solid power of supplying the wants of America, of receiving her produce, and of waiting her convenience, belongs almost exclusively to our merchants."[40]

Sheffield insisted that British trade policy toward the United States required a ruthless calculation of American economic interests. He contrasted his own "calmer reflections" with those who sought to win American trade through generosity and friendship. Americans deserved no privileges as suppliers. As for the supplies themselves, they might with equal advantage come from "all the world." Americans would sell supplies for the British West Indies if it were to their commercial advantage: "It is no object to the people of America, what ships are the carriers of their produce. There is no proportion between the number of the Americans interested in the free export of their staple commodities, and the few merchants of that country who are interested in carrying them in American bottoms."[41] When the Privy Council Committee for Trade interviewed George Chalmers about American–West Indian trade, he drew on experience as a lawyer in Maryland from 1763 to 1775 to testify that the interests of the planters and the merchants diverged with respect to competition in shipping. The planters wanted as large a market and as cheap freight as possible and would readily use British shipping to the West Indies, even if American ships were excluded there. Because British vessels also brought affordable manufactured goods, Americans were doubly likely to welcome them.[42]

Smith's views on Anglo-American trade after the American Revolution corresponded more closely with neomercantilist policy than with the reciprocity identified with Shelburne and Pitt. He thought that "the goods of all different nations" should be "subject . . . to the same duties." If this were the American policy, then "they set an example of good sense which all other nations ought to imitate." As a logical consequence, however, they should expect "that we should treat them as they mean to treat us, and all other nations," which meant explicitly that American goods should be subject to the same duties as goods of other nations. Smith conceded that the policy toward trade between the United States and the remaining British colonies posed "a more difficult question," but he recommended that it "go on as before, and whatever inconveniencies may result from this freedom may be remedied as they occur." Smith did not consider restrictions on colonial navigation as glaring instances of illiberality. Like the neomercantilists, he took strong exception to American commercial discrimination against Britain, and "suspect[ed] the Americans do not mean what they say" when advocating free trade. Like Sheffield, he had "little anxiety about what becomes of the American commerce. By an equality of treatment to all nations, we might soon open a commerce with the neighbouring nations of Europe infinitely more advantageous than that of so distant a country as America." Sheffield learned from Smith to repudiate "the fallacious rule of the apparent balance" of trade, and he accordingly criticized the efforts of American and West Indian interests to secure commercial privileges.[43] As Gibbon noted, Sheffield served the public with his reassurances that British prosperity did not depend on political advantages in American trade.

———

Britain's fundamentally liberal commercial policy toward Anglo-American trade evoked an increasingly narrow mercantilist response in the former colonies. Anticipating a reopening of Anglo-American trade on prerevolutionary terms, the newly independent states initially enacted little genuinely regulatory legislation regarding foreign trade. As their first measure for peacetime commerce after the War for American Independence, the individual states simply declared an end to the wartime prohibitions on trade with Britain. The next order of commercial legislation gave priority to fiscal considerations. At least six states imposed an impost on trade, with the revenues designated for governmental obligations regarding state debts, for the quotas required by Congress, and for payments of the states' civil lists. The states typically adopted the fiscal mechanisms already proposed for the abortive congressional impost—excise duties on a short list of enumerated alcoholic and sugar-based commodities plus coffee and tea, and a flat ad valorem duty on nearly all other imported goods. Most states also adopted a tonnage duty, which, because of the fiscal priorities, initially applied to ships of the other states as well as to foreign vessels.

As the postwar recession deepened, however, politicians and economic authorities looked for structural explanations, which they found in the restrictive commercial policy adopted in Great Britain by the Privy Council on the advice of Lord Sheffield. In response to Britain's supposed protectionism for trade and navigation, most of the states adopted retaliatory measures to discriminate against British trade and navigation. Maryland took the lead in the fall of 1783 with discriminatory tonnage and import duties on British ships and goods. Massachusetts went the furthest in retaliatory discrimination. In response to the demands of Boston merchants, who had begun a boycott of British agents in April 1784, the legislature passed a navigation law prohibiting the export from Massachusetts of any American goods in British ships. In addition, the measure levied a tonnage duty on all foreign shipping and charged double duties on all goods arriving on such ships. Meanwhile the General Court faced pressure from artisanal groups who insisted on tariff protection against any foreign competition—not just British—so it raised import duties on manufactures to protective levels.

Massachusetts called on the other states to follow suit and enact Navigation Acts against Great Britain, but when only New Hampshire and Rhode Island cooperated Massachusetts repealed the discriminations against British shipping. But in November 1784, New York doubled the duties on certain excised goods when imported in ships built in England or owned by British subjects. The next year New York doubled the duty on all goods imported in British ships. Parallel measures in other states typically encouraged American shipping as well as discriminated against British navigation, because they established differential tonnage duties for American and foreign shipping. For example, in 1785 Virginia levied a tonnage duty of two shillings per ton on all American shipping including Virginians', but discriminated between foreign ships from nations in commercial treaty with the Confederation, which paid three shillings per ton, and ships (obviously British) from nations not in commercial treaty, which paid three times the domestic rate and twice that of other foreign nations.

Truly protectionist measures were relatively unimportant in the immediate postwar years, but they increased diffusely as the enumeration of goods and the differentiation of rates increased with the retaliatory measures against Great Britain. In 1783, for example, Virginia's enumerated duties only added hemp, cordage, and salt to the goods typically named for excise duties. For most of the remainder of the Confederation, Virginia's protectionist measures remained minimal, but in 1788, in a combined sumptuary and protectionist effort, Virginia also enumerated snuff and manufactured tobacco, dressed and tanned leather, saddles, bar iron, nail rod bolts, iron pots, kettles, iron castings, axes, hoes, women's silk shoes, leather shoes, boots, salted beef, pork, candles, soap, clocks, hats, and a variety of items for personal display, such as carriages and silver lace. New York had the earliest and most elaborate tariff program, but even there protectionist intents were subsidiary to fiscal ones until November 1784, when the state began its retaliatory efforts against Great Britain.

Protectionism toward manufactures followed mercantilist preoccupations with navigation. Thus in 1786 Massachusetts prohibited importation from abroad of a long list of consumer goods, a year after the state had prohibited the exportation of goods in British ships. With the increased priority of commercial protection relative to revenue, states began to allow the entry duty-free of raw materials necessary for manufactures, just as they also established bounties to encourage the export of manufactures. As the protection of domestic production gained a higher priority in commercial policies, individual states increasingly exempted other members of the Confederation from their burdens, just as they were exempted by definition from retaliatory measures against Great Britain's navigation policy. By the time the Philadelphia Convention met, fiscal, retaliatory, and protectionist priorities in the states' commercial policies had become completely entangled.[44]

The Liberalization of Markets by British Neomercantilists

The liberalism of British neomercantilists appeared in virtually every area of policy advised by the Committee for Trade *except* navigation, the one that preoccupied Americans. At the same time that the committee drafted a new Navigation Act, it also advised the government on commercial negotiations with France. The 1783 Treaty of Paris included a British commitment to enter such negotiations, and, when Britain delayed, French retaliatory restrictions prodded Pitt into serious efforts. The Committee for Trade had the crucial responsibility to forestall parliamentary objections by taking into account the views of merchants and manufacturers. It held hearings over the winter of 1785–86 to determine their reaction to a reciprocal trade agreement with France.[45] Negotiations themselves proceeded swiftly once they began in April, with the treaty signed on 26 September 1786. Most goods from each country would enter the other with moderate, reciprocal duties, and each country's ships had the advantages of the most-favored nation in the other country's ports. Hawkesbury saw the chief regulatory question to be the calculation of the appropriate uniform duties for particular goods, regardless of their source. He advised that policy should be determined commercially, not politically: sound commercial diplomacy called for precise calculations of markets, prices, and commercial advantages. It was, for instance, pointless to hope that the tobacco trade could be restored by treaty. Its prewar scale resulted from a colonial monopoly that no longer existed: "The Share we now have or may hereafter have in that Trade must depend not on the stipulations of any commercial treaty but on circumstances which may enable us to furnish France with them more conveniently, or at an easier rate than they can be procured from the Countries where they are produced." He wanted to arrange duties so that British goods were not drastically undersold in their own market, but he would subject them to competition: "Our superiority in these Manufactures [cottons and 'mixed goods and hardware'] is so great, that we never can expect France will admit them to her markets unless in return for some advantage to be granted to her."[46]

Hawkesbury dissociated himself from the politics of particular economic interests.[47] During hearings on the treaty, Hawkesbury posed a typically leading question to George and Charles Bowles, manufacturers of glass, to show the balance of advantage he sought: "Do you conceive it would be for the Interest of the Manufacturers of Crown Glass and Plate Glass in this Country, to open a Trade with France in that manufacture, always supposing that Articles of the like nature from France must be allowed to be imported into this Country upon an equal footing."[48] Sheffield also had sanguine expectations about freer trade, and he dismissed the protectionist concerns of individual manufacturers: "I like the idea of supplying twenty-four millions of people and through them in a certain degree a greater part of the world, although many of the manufactures of all the world will find their way to this country through France, and the laying us open in that way, will be thought hazardous by some."[49]

The liberal political economy of the committee appeared again when it conducted hearings in 1789 and 1790 on the Corn Laws and then made recommendations that largely shaped the Corn Bill of 1791.[50] The Corn Laws had the capacity to encourage as well as to prohibit both the import and the export of grain. As protection to consumers in response to rising prices and increasing dependence on foreign grain, the Corn Law of 1773 had prohibited exports when the price of wheat exceeded forty-four shillings per quarter, and it lowered the import duty to a nominal level when the price reached forty-eight shillings or higher. The prohibition on export when prices were high was new, but the provision continued (from the law of 1688) for a bounty on exports. A sliding scale of duties further protected producers' interests by moving toward virtual prohibition of imports during low domestic prices. The Committee for Trade had responsibility to determine the revisions necessary for the law of 1773 because the trends toward higher prices and increased imports continued to indicate an apparent inadequacy of domestic production.[51] Hawkesbury's committee worried that Britain had gone from being a grain exporter in the period 1746–65 to being a net grain importer since 1770. Here the *Wealth of Nations* was factually out of date. Smith had calculated Britain to be a net grain exporter, and he objected to the way the Corn Bounty contributed to this pattern by increasing the real cost of living and thereby impeding agricultural improvement. Although he attributed the bounty to mercantilist fixations with exports, Smith argued for the encouragement of exports and calculated that the price to prohibit exportation was too low.[52]

The neomercantilists did not call for abolition of the Corn Laws, but they discussed them in explicitly Smithian terms. They thought that a free domestic grain market would best apportion supplies to the year-long needs of subsistence. Hawkesbury advocated that, while the long-term goal in grain policy should be to encourage domestic production, the most important measure to achieve this goal would be to raise the price allowing the export of grain.[53] He saw himself as trying to get the landowners to act with enlightened self-interest by altering the regulation of exports to permit the export of grain at a higher price, but without a bounty. He thought that the landowners saw such a change solely as an entering wedge to separate them from the export bounty. He hoped to convince them to produce more for the domestic market while becoming less reliant on the export bounty to absorb their surpluses. Correspondingly, Hawkesbury tried to convince the manufacturers that cheaper subsistence, and therefore labor, would follow from a freer domestic market in grain. He regretted the "sort of contest which had so long subsisted" over the terms of the Corn Laws. Like Smith, he identified a fundamental mutuality of interests between consumers and producers with respect to the market in subsistence commodities: "The manufacturers of this country will prosper most if the kingdom is filled with rich Inhabitants of every description but particularly with rich country gentlemen and a rich yeomanry and that it is for the interest of the manufacturer that he should purchase his subsistence at a moderate price, and not at a price unusually low and that he should always be certain of finding enough of it that is produced in his country."[54]

The Committee for Trade largely ignored the export bounty as a means to encourage production. It devoted most of its recommendations to the improvement of pricing efficiency in the domestic market. Hawkesbury's committee recommended that there be a nationwide price for the application of the Corn Laws, rather than have the prices determined port by port, in order to encourage the domestic movement of grain from areas of excess to those of shortage.[55] The committee advised against the regulation of domestic speculation in grain and urged the encouragement of large-scale grain dealing: "As, after a deficient crop, they [dealers] are thereby enabled to divide the inconvenience arising from it as equally as possible through every part of the year, and by checking improvident consumption in the beginning of scarcity, prevent a famine, which might otherwise happen before the next harvest."[56] The committee recommended repeal of the remaining provision of 15 Charles II, chap. 7, which Smith had singled out to criticize for its prohibition against buying wheat when the price exceeded forty-eight shillings the quarter and then selling it in the same market after less than three months' warehousing.[57]

Sheffield forcefully advanced the Smithian irony that the freer export of grain would increase domestic supplies. He also played down the importance of export bounties as encouragements to agricultural production and argued that the most beneficial changes would be to raise the duties on imports and to increase the price allowing exports. He wholeheartedly favored a free domestic grain market. He criticized the committee's recommendations for the warehousing of emergency grain supplies, though he suspected that this proposal contradicted the committee's independent preferences. He approved the committee's pricing mechanisms, and he agreed that "it is a steady price that is to be wished for, not a low price; and that regular price can only be obtained by our growing more corn than we can consume, and by encouraging the export of the surplus." He had virtually complete confidence in the ability of a less regulated domestic market to provide supplies that met demand in times of dearth. He criticized the proposed Corn Bill for its counterproductive preoccupations with consumers' immediate interests, and he anonymously paraphrased Smith to warn against the dangers of such miscalculations: "One of our best writers on political economy says, that bad seasons may produce a dearth, but a famine can only be produced by bad laws." Sheffield attributed the inadequacy of domestic grain supplies to the combination of laws favoring investment in pasture and discouraging it in tillage. He cited Smith as his authority to show how controls on the export of wool subsidized pasture to the disadvantage of corn production.[58]

The privileges and regulations of agricultural production and marketing appeared to have made Britain dependent on foreign countries and to have diverted its agricultural investment from tillage to pasture. Out of wariness of foreign control of British subsistence, Sheffield frankly advocated a "monopoly of the home market to our farmers." In making his case against a free market in foreign grain, he showed clear understanding of, and a basic respect for, Smith's views: "One of the objections to monopolies, bounties, and duties, is, that they turn toward particular articles a greater share of labour and capital than would otherwise have gone to them, and that they often divert men from a more advantageous employment to one that is less so." He took Smith's arguments for a freer international grain trade in only one direction. Sheffield anticipated charges of inconsistency as an advocate of free markets, and he reiterated Smith's point that "there can be no combination among the growers of corn in England. The article is in too many hands."[59] However, foreign wholesalers could act monopolistically, in ways that constituted threats to British security.

Confronted in the mid-1790s with the conjunction of harvest failures and militant antigovernment politics, and burdened with the irreconcilable responsibilities of agricultural regulation, Hawkesbury hesitated between policies of intervention and laissez-faire: "Shall we trust to the speculation of the merchant, in the regular course of commerce, to supply this deficiency, or is it the duty of government to make some provision of foreign wheat, in the manner they did early last spring; by which the inhabitants of this great city have in effect been preserved from the utmost distress, if not from famine, & the peace it secured."[60] Smith would readily have sympathized: he equated popular prejudices toward the Corn Laws with those toward laws on religion. In both instances governments had to sacrifice "reasonable system" for "public tranquility." Smith concluded his thoroughgoing critique of the Corn Laws with a sanguineness quite appropriate for his reformist followers: "With all its [the law of 1773] imperfections, however, we may perhaps say of it what was said of the laws of Solon, that, though not the best in itself, it is the best which the interests, prejudices, and temper of the times would admit of. It may perhaps in due time prepare the way for a better."[61]

———

IN 1794, after the onset of another war, Chalmers revised his *Estimate* for republication and gave a liberal, not a mercantilist, accounting of commercial policy in the decade between the revolutionary wars. He reviewed the recent encouragements for British trade, and he identified measures liberalizing trade with other nations and encouraging internal development: the Anglo-French commercial treaty of 1786 had opened new markets for British traders; the conventions with Spain had given more "certainty" to trade in the Americas; treaties with Prussia and Holland had "communicated energy to our traffic"; and renewal of the commercial treaty with Russia had "added stability to our commerce." In Britain itself agriculture had been encouraged by the return of forfeited Scottish estates, by the better use of crown lands, and by more systematic price information for the Corn Laws. Between 1783 and 1794 Parliament had passed over one thousand acts to improve domestic production and transportation.[62]

The neomercantilists presented themselves as intellectually progressive by associating their views with those of Smith. Affirmation of Smith's political economy distanced them from policies that had led to the American War of Independence. They established an Anglo-American commercial policy mutually advantageous in its openness rather than vindictive in its exclusiveness. They recommended a commercial treaty with France that aided domestic manufacturers by opening international markets rather than by protection. And in the grain trade they sought to reduce the competing privileges of producers and consumers. They interpreted their application of liberal political economy as enlightened and moderate, and they contrasted it with views that were narrow in their interests and speculative in their principles.

The neomercantilists' apparent attentiveness to the lessons of *The Wealth of Nations* has implications for the interpretation of Smith's thought, as well as of contemporary British commercial policy. Smith intended book 4, "On Systems of Political Economy," to persuade British statesmen to reform the empire politically as well as commercially in order to deal with the contradiction between mercantilism and the continuation of profit from colonial trade.[63] Despite his thoroughgoing condemnation of the mercantile system, in 1776 he advised only a "moderate and gradual relaxation of the laws which give to Great Britain the exclusive trade to the colonies, till it is rendered in a great measure free":

> Such are the unfortunate effects of all the regulations of the mercantile system! They not only introduce very dangerous disorders into the state of the body politick, but disorders which it is often difficult to remedy, without occasioning, for a time at least, still greater disorders. In what manner, therefore, the colony trade ought gradually to be opened; what

are the restraints which ought last to be taken away; or in what manner the natural system of perfect liberty and justice ought gradually to be restored, we must leave to the wisdom of future statesmen and legislators to determine.[64]

The neomercantilists apparently read book 4 so attentively because of its orientation to policy, rather than theory. The policy sought the wealth of nations; the theory urged the prosperity of their peoples. And policy, unlike theory, depended on politics and therefore was liable to compromise. Smith recognized the inevitable political tension between the principle of free trade and the exercise of state authority (even when deregulating), and he gave it episodic consideration in his political economy.[65] The neomercantilists' application of Smith's humane, antistate, liberalism for their own nationalist purposes demonstrated how Smith had allowed for half-measures. His ironic temper allowed him to be consistent in his principles without being doctrinaire. He viewed free trade as a direction, not as a condition, in which "statesmen and legislators," not "politicians," could lead their countries, and he recognized that the political process itself made arrival impossible.[66]

CHAPTER FIVE

The Madisonian Definition of National Economic Interests

D ISCUSSION of national authority to regulate the Confederation's commerce went through several phases before the Constitutional Convention of 1787. In the early years of independence such authority had little support. The Articles of Confederation, sent out for ratification in November 1777, had conscientiously denied Congress power to regulate commerce, even though it had authority to negotiate commercial treaties. Later in the war, as the Articles neared ratification, Congress only inconclusively discussed the advisability of asking the States to concede Congress a power to regulate foreign trade. The topic usually arose in conjunction with debate on the impost, because it bore directly on trade. After the Orders in Council of 2 July 1783, the perceived need to retaliate against British restrictions on the revival of preindependence trade patterns catalyzed serious discussion, as well as support, for national powers of commercial regulation.

In the name of seeking power to regulate commerce, Congress really only sought authority for retaliatory Navigation Acts. In April 1784, as part of a renewed campaign to secure commercial treaties, Congress asked the States to give it powers, again largely prohibitory, for the regulation of foreign commerce for a period of fifteen years. This appeal resulted in an unworkable combination of concessions by the States, and early in 1785 James Monroe, as chair of the congressional committee on commercial amendments, proposed a new strategy of amending the Articles themselves. The proposed amendment would have given Congress genuine authority to regulate commerce, both internally and externally, including the power to levy duties on imports and exports. The proposal had only cautious circulation for discussion, and neither Congress nor the States acted decisively on it. The next year, when Congress discussed a series of amendments for the consideration of the States, the vesting of Congress with exclusive power to regulate commerce headed the list. However, the nationalists' consensus on this power still depended on the political need to negotiate effectively with Great Britain, not from some broader and more specifically economic understanding of the purposes and needs for commercial regulation.

Besides retaliation against Great Britain, American postrevolutionary political economy had little *national* focus. State particularism carried over from the colonial period, when Americans had counted on access to metropolitan commercial privileges to harmonize the differences among their various staple economies. Economic sectionalism did not undercut a new, coherent American political economy; it expressed the prevailing desire to restore prerevolutionary commercial patterns. As long as "commercial regulation" aimed at the *short-term* goal of loosening British restrictions on American shipping in the British empire, it had strong support from nationalists, including those in the South. Sectionalist anxieties arose with the possibility that policies of commercial regulation might become more general and enduring.

Madison's Mercantilist Political Economy
for Virginia

In juxtaposition to Sheffield, James Madison played a crucial role in the 1780s—arguably *the* crucial role—in the definition of American commercial policy at both the congressional and state levels. He frequently drafted the resolutions and directives that Congress sent its agents in commercial diplomacy, and he maintained a communications network linking Virginia with the Confederation government. His senior colleagues or patrons from his father's generation in Virginia politics, such as Joseph Jones, Edmund Pendleton, and George Washington, before long looked to him for expertise in commercial policy. Just recently selected for Congress in 1780, Madison took over from a Virginia colleague and conveyed through Congress the committee report on American claims to lands on the Mississippi; then he drafted instructions to John Jay on the matter. Early in the next year, when military jeopardy in the southern states dictated a more accommodating attitude toward the Bourbon powers on the issues of fishing rights in Newfoundland and navigation of the Mississippi, Madison drafted the resolution that revoked John Adams' previous instructions to negotiate treaties of both peace and commerce with Great Britain and directed him to consult the French minister Vergennes for approval of any negotiations. Later in the debate, he successfully moved to revoke Adams' commission to negotiate a commercial treaty. After returning to Virginia in 1783 at the end of his term of eligibility for Congress, Madison maintained contact with congressional affairs through his replacement, James Monroe.

Not surprisingly, therefore, Madison gave Sheffield's argument one of its earliest and most acutely realistic American readings:

> A Pamphlet has lately come over from G. Britain which appears to be well adapted to retard if not prevent a commercial Treaty, and which is said to be much attended to. It urges an adherence to the principle of the Navigation Act by which American Vessels will be excluded from the trade between the separate parts of the Empire, and from all intercourse with the dependent territories. It undertakes to shew from an enumeration of the produce of the U. S. and the manufactures consumed by them that those of G. B. recommended by the superior credit which her Merchants can give, will be sufficiently sure of a preference in the American Market. And lastly it maintains that the interests of the States are so opposite in matters of Commerce, and the authority of Congress so feeble that no defensive precautions need be feared on the part of the U. S. and threatens that in case they should refuse to let British Vessels exclusively carry on a Commerce between the U. S. and the W. Indies as far as the interest of the Islands may require, the vessels of one State shall not be permitted to carry the product of another to any British Port. The Whole tenor of the reasoning supposes that France will not permit Vessels of the U. S. to trade with their Islands in which there is *good reason* to believe they are not mistaken. The object of the French Administration is said to be to allow a direct trade between the U. S. and their W. India possessions, but to confine it to French Bottoms.[1]

Only in response to British restrictions did Madison become an advocate of a firm national commercial policy. He interpreted the restrictions of 2 July on American trade to be a deliberate British test of "the wisdom, firmness and union of the States, before they will enter into a Treaty in derogation of her Navigation Act. Congress will probably recommend some defensive plan to the states . . . If it fails at all it will prove such an inefficacy in the Union as will extinguish all respect for it and reliance on it." Madison characteristically attributed political motives to Britain's apparent commercial policy toward the United States: "The policy of G. B. results as much from the hope of effecting a breach in our confederacy as of monopolizing our trade."[2]

Before learning of the restrictive British Orders in Council, Madison had been wary that a commercial treaty with Great Britain would become a shibboleth. The congressional committee dealing with the matter in the spring of 1783 gave priority to the reestablishment of direct trade with the British West Indies and of further rights to carry trade between the British islands and other British colonies. Madison questioned whether these were national, rather than regional, interests. He anticipated passage of Pitt's bill allowing direct American trade to the islands, and he thought that the export trade from the islands almost exclusively interested the "eastern states." Madison did not begrudge them these opportunities, but he worried that the British would insist on reciprocity—namely, "that we shall admit British subjects to equal privileges with our own citizens." Such a privilege would affect the southern states "chiefly if not alone." He wanted the southern states to be able to give "any encouragement to their own merchants ships or mariners which may be necessary to prevent relapse under Scotch monopoly or to acquire a maritime importance. The Eastern States need no such precaution."[3] In other words, Madison feared free trade because it would reduce the competition among purchasers of the South's staples. Madison wanted to manage competition in order to prevent the reestablishment of Virginians' dependency on British merchants for credit.

When Britain unexpectedly adopted what Madison took to be a discriminatory policy toward American trade, a policy of retaliatory discrimination became the crux of Madison's commercial policy. He justified such discrimination as a means to secure reciprocity in Anglo-American trade, but the good faith of that justification can be questioned in the light of his earlier reluctance to allow reciprocity when it seemed possible.

Madison was not a nationalist with respect to commercial policy at the end of the Revolutionary War. While he insisted that Congress's *fiscal* undertakings be permanent, he urged flexibility, caution, and limited duration for commercial engagements. For example, as the diplomatic negotiations on American independence reached their conclusion in the spring of 1783, he used a series of correspondence with Edmund Randolph to advise the Virginia legislature on the need to maintain control over the state's commercial regulation. Precisely because he thought of national commercial regulation primarily in reference to commercial diplomacy, he urged Virginia to maintain its autonomy: "The monopoly which formerly tyrannized over it [Virginia's trade], has left wounds which are not yet healed, and the numerous debts due from the people, and which by the provisional articles they are immediately liable for, may possibly be made instruments for reestablishing their dependence."[4] "Regulations" and "thorough emancipation" of commerce were compatible and, in the case of Virginia, necessary. He saw the advantages of free trade to lie in reference to the sale of staples: he sought competition among their buyers. Virginians should have the cake of protectionism and eat the cake of free trade.

Although he usually presented mercantilist analyses with a note of regret, Madison forthrightly expressed an expectation that over time there would be more, not less, regulation of the American economy. He disclaimed any bias toward "restrictions or preferences in matters of commerce," but he argued against surrendering such options when leaders had responsibility to later generations to maintain the protectionist option. The present predominance of agriculture in the American economy warranted "extensive privileges of all competitors in our Commerce," in order that "we shall be able to buy at cheap and sell at profitable rates," but "as our lands become settled, and spare hands for manufactures and navigation multiply, it may become our policy to favor those objects by peculiar privileges, bestowed on our own Citizens; or at least to introduce regulations inconsistent with foreign engagements suited to the present state of things." Madison anticipated that as the economy of Virginia became less colonial in its structure, as it became less dependent on imports and foreign shipping, its citizens would protect new domestic industries. As the economy of the republic came to resemble that of the Old World, so would its political economy: "Nor ought the example of old and intelligent nations be too far or too hastily condemned by an infant and inexperienced one. That of G. B. is in the science of commerce particularly worthy of our attention . . . and does she not still make a preference of her own Vessels and her own mariners the basis of her maritime power?"[5]

With these mercantilist expectations, Madison cautioned Virginia politicians against too readily conceding powers of commercial diplomacy to Congress. He assumed that any such negotiations would involve an exchange of privileges of access, so that one foreign country might be given privileged access to the American states, in exchange for Americans having access to a foreign power's otherwise restricted markets. The most likely development would be for British merchants to have advantages over other foreign merchants in access to American markets, as such a privilege might well be the price for American merchants having direct access to British home and colonial markets. Madison expected that American priorities in a commercial treaty with Great Britain would be " 1. a direct commerce with the W. Indies. 2. the carrying trade between the different parts of her dominions. 3. a like trade between these and other parts of the world. In return for these objects we have nothing to offer of which we could well deprive her, but to secure to her subjects an entire equality of privileges with our own Citizens"—an equality Madison viewed warily.

Madison assumed that Britain would readily admit Americans to its West Indian colonies because it needed cheap supplies in order to compete with the more efficient production of the French islands. But the value of the other two privileges in British trade would require compensating privileges from Americans, with invidious implications. Privileges in British trade advantaged only "those States which abound in maritime resources," while American concessions "will affect chiefly, if not solely, those States which will share least in the advantages purchased by it." Congress would have negotiated the staple-producing states back into a de facto colonial relationship with Great Britain. With these liabilities in mind, Madison had welcomed Virginia's directions that commercial treaties be conditional on congressional approval.[6]

When American independence gained recognition by treaty, Madison viewed national policy toward foreign trade primarily in fiscal, not commercial, terms. He believed that the fiscal probity of Americans tested their commitment to "unadulterated forms of Republican Government." When he recommended the impost as the best means to provide for the debts of the Confederation, he noted the intrinsic fiscal advantages of such a resource: "Taxes on consumption are always least burdensome, because they are least felt, and are borne too by those who are both willing and able to pay them." Among taxes on consumption, those on "foreign commerce are most compatible with the genius and policy of free states," presumably because they did not infringe on the *internal* commerce of the States. Lastly, he argued with unconscious irony that the impost aptly paid "the debts of a Revolution, from which an unbounded freedom has accrued to commerce."[7]

As soon as he entered the Virginia Assembly in 1784, where he continued to sit until 1787, Madison took the initiative in shaping the state's commercial policy. As chairman of the Assembly's Committee on Commerce, he sought legislation to restrict Virginia's export and import trade to an entrepôt. He acted as a commissioner to resolve the issues between Virginia and Maryland on navigation of the Potomac, and he coordinated the two states' support of Washington's plans for canals to provide transportation for Trans-Appalachian commerce. He led the self-proclaimed "federalists" in Virginia in their political maneuvering to secure Assembly support for congressional power to regulate commerce—a project they counterposed to the alternatives of regulation by state legislation or by interstate convention.[8]

The confident and ambitious participation of Madison in commercial policy has apparently encouraged historians to accept his federalism at face value and to share his willingness to blur the distinction between fiscal and commercial issues. Thus Madison's calculation that a Port Bill restricting Virginia's trade to a single port would foster a domestic shipping industry and thereby lower the costs of importations while raising the price of tobacco is accurately characterized as "a solution that was soundly grounded in mercantilist thought, if not in common sense." Although Madison thought the measure crucially important for Virginia's economy, the same historian mildly described this strategy as "ill-conceived" without finding it to be basically indicative of Madison's political economy. But the later efforts of Madison's "creditor parties" to provide Congress with power to regulate commerce is attributed to "their concern for the *free flow* of trade and credit. Just as they opposed artificial burdens on commerce as imposed by debtor-relief measures, they favored uniform regulations imposed by national authority."[9] If Madison were instead seen as a provincial mercantilist who sought to overcome the dependency of a staple economy by legislating the structure of the market, then the apparent inconsistencies disappear and the shortcomings become anachronistic. Madison did not test Virginians' commercial independence against the measure of the free operation of supply and demand. On the contrary, time after time, he devised commercial policy either to counteract market behavior or to provide commercial opportunities in lieu of market incentives.

Although he long and prominently advocated a commercial policy based on retaliatory discrimination against Britain, Madison appreciated that Virginia had a less direct concern than the northern states in a retaliatory policy toward British restrictions. In the case of the northern states, the lifting of British restrictions on the carrying trade would satisfy most of the hopes of both producers and merchants from any commercial policy. But in Virginia the conflicts of interest between merchants and planters with respect to British trade arose largely from market relations unhampered by British restrictions. Virginians' "commercial discontents" resulted from a buyer's market. Virginia's trade "was never more compleatly monopolized by G. B. when it was under the direction of the British Parliament than it is at this moment." Merchants accustomed to being agents for buyers overseas seemed oblivious or antagonistic to alternatives. Virginia planters knew that tobacco commanded prices one-third higher in Philadelphia than in Virginia, while imported goods invariably cost more in Virginia than in northern states. Although "dissatisfied," "they enter little into the science of commerce, and rarely of themselves combine in defence of their interests."[10] Madison attributed Virginians' economic dependency to British dominance in their carrying trade, but he did not yet directly attribute that domination to British navigation policy. Virginians accommodatingly continued trade relations previously dictated by imperial commercial monopoly, but now deregulated. The policy of commercial discrimination toward Britain did not cure Virginia's commercial ills, but Madison remained its paladin.

Throughout the 1780s, Madison continued to be particularist toward Virginia regarding commercial regulation. He remained convinced of the necessity to force the "rivalship" of other nations with Great Britain in order for Virginia's commerce to yield its potential benefits. Madison never came to terms with the change from a legal to a commercial monopoly of Britain's trade with Virginia. As a panacea for Virginia's commercial shortcomings, he used his chairmanship of the Virginia Assembly's Committee on Commerce to promote a Port Bill restricting Virginia's foreign trade to one or two entrepôts, thereby eliminating the commercial advantages of British merchants in buying and selling directly with planters. Madison intended the Port Bill to restructure Virginia's "internal trade" so that cargoes laden on ocean-going ships would have to be refreighted in Virginia, thereby providing an opportunity for smaller craft in Virginia to take part in distribution to the interior. He hoped that the Port Bill would restructure Virginia's "internal trade" so that "native adventurers" engaged in "the importing and retail departments," as well as individual planters, would not directly depend on overseas creditors.

The bill actually enacted deeply disappointed Madison because it applied exclusively to non-Virginian ships, be they American or foreign. He predicated his support for the Port Bill on commercial paternalism and regretted that planters did not see more clearly "the utility of establishing a Philadelphia or a Baltimore among ourselves": "It is the more to be wished for as it is the only radical cure for credit to the consumer which continues to be given to a degree which if not checked will turn the diffusive retail of merchandize into a nuisance. When the Shopkeeper buys his goods of the wholesale merchant, he must buy at so short a credit, that he can venture to give none at all."[11]

Madison viewed British merchants with economic paranoia and attributed to them a commercially irrational impulse to extend Virginians excessive credit in order to control them. According to Madison, agents for British merchants taught their American customers self-serving lessons in liberal political economy in order to arouse opposition to his Port Act panacea. Merchants who hoped for "a renewal of the old plan of British Monopoly and diffusive credit," and Virginians "whose local situations give them, or are thought to give them an advantage in large vessels coming up the rivers to their usual stations, are busy in decoying the people into a belief that trade ought in all cases to be left to regulate itself, that to confine it to particular ports is to renounce the boon with which Nature has favored our country." In opposition to Madison's plan, these merchants and planters warned that "if one sett of men are to be importers and exporters, another set to be carryers between the mouths and heads of the rivers and a third retailers, trade, as it must pass through so many hands all taking a profit, must in the end come dearer to the people than if the simple plan should be continued which unites these several branches in the same heads."[12]

Madison had a clear grasp of the liberal alternative to his efforts to shape the market, and he self-consciously rejected it. George Mason, leader of the effort to repeal the Port Act, showed the alternative's force. In a broadside submitted to the Assembly with other petitions for repeal, he mocked the mentality behind the Port Act and urged that people accept the market forces at work on Virginia's economy. Mason argued that the act perversely choked use of Virginia's great riverine endowment for transportation. Would anyone, he asked sarcastically, think it a "proper means of promoting and increasing our trade and commerce" "to stretch a chain or lay a rock, at a certain place, across the channel of each of our large rivers, leaving only a sufficient depth of water over it for small craft"? Such a measure, with its imposition of "double charges of commissions, freight, ensurance, and warehouse rent," must make imported goods more expensive to Virginia consumers, as well as lower the price for its exported commodities. Mason reminded his readers that such double charges had been a grievance against Great Britain when Virginia's trade had been subject to an earlier legal monopoly. Commercial prosperity could not be legislated: "The trade and population of Philadelphia, and some other great cities in the United States," resulted from "natural causes," not "Port Bills, and compulsive laws." The extent to which foreigners declined to trade with Virginia depended on Virginians' political malfeasance in economic matters: "In our breach of public faith—In our refusal to pay our debts—In the ex-post facto interference of our laws with private property and contracts—In our iniquitous tender laws, and other regulations calculated to defraud creditors."[13]

Despite such early liberal rebukes, Madison maintained for decades that Virginians' economic burdens of chronic indebtedness and constrained access to credit were the effects, rather than the causes, of their vulnerability to the British monopolization of Virginia's carrying trade. The Port Bill represented his most elaborate and authentic response to these shortcomings. When it failed to materialize as intended, he turned his hopes for effective commercial regulation toward Congress and adopted the much simpler device of commercial discrimination to eliminate the British monopoly on Virginia's trade. When cautioning against too forthright assertions of Virginia's interests in Confederation politics, he counted on the Confederation to maintain competition for Virginia's trade, not to elevate some presumed national economic interest over the particularist ones of Virginians. For example, at the end of the war he worried that "the easetern [*sic*] states particularly Massachusetts conceive that compared with the Southern they are greatly in advance in the general account." Fiscal resentment might motivate some northern states to form another confederacy. For Madison this potential "dissolution of the union" immediately presented the liability that the southern states, "which at sea will be opulent and weak," would become "an easey [*sic*] prey to the eastern [*sic*] which will be powerful and rapacious." This interstate vulnerability had the further implication that "alliances would be sought first by the weaker and then by the stronger party and this country be made subservient to the wars and politics of Europe."[14] From his perspective in a staple-producing state, Virginia's economic interests had little commercial autonomy because of the force of external fiscal and diplomatic imperatives. Virginia's economic autonomy depended on the union of the States.

Political Imperatives in
the Confederation's Commercial Policy

Most American statesmen besides Madison read Sheffield, but they were no more aware of the place of his writings in the broader context of British political economy. Preoccupied with a narrow feature of British commercial policy—namely, its encouragement of navigation by the exclusion of American ships from British colonies and from the carrying trade of non-American goods—they overlooked the British reorientation toward the liberalization of domestic and foreign markets. Americans accurately identified Sheffield's book with the stringent navigation policy recommended by the Privy Council's Committee for Trade, but they usually understood its argument entirely in political terms. They could not take its economic analysis seriously and instead characterized its thinking as "illiberal & senseless principles of commerce," or "silly, malignant principles." Thus, when Monroe surveyed the possibility that Britain's remaining North American colonies might replace its former colonies as suppliers of flour and timber to the West Indies, he judged the strategy commercially irrational. Britain's true motivation lay in conspiratorial political resentment toward the newly independent states.[15]

American commentators on Sheffield used a personalistic and noneconomic language to characterize and to explain British policy toward postwar trade. The governor of Virginia called on Congress to frame a policy that would "bring down the British pride." Richard Henry Lee explained that, though Pitt "does appear willing to be liberal in Commercial regulations . . . the avaricious spirit of Commerce that is so great every where, but which in England has ever been excessive, opposes his views." He considered Britain "a Nation whose appetite for Commerce has ever been ravenous, and its wishes always for Monopoly." Britain's policy seemed to be a deliberate insult to American patriotism. "The touchstone of our virtue" would be to disprove British miscalculation and to show that "we have still enough [virtue] left to induce us to forego everything that may interfere with the general good of America." A successful commercial policy would require "mutual confidence and concertion," which depended on "virtue, wisdom and temper which we know pervade the Continent and which have heretofore rendered us superiour to force, machination or intrigue."[16]

If political means had hampered American commerce, then improvement depended on political means as well. From the start, Madison's strategy sought to coerce a widening of American shipping access to British markets by excluding the British from the American carrying trade. Alternatively, British merchants would "eventually become the sole carriers even of our own produce." Madison assumed that political measures, rather than strictly economic developments, critically enhanced foreign trade and that the growth of one country's trade came at the cost of another's.[17] His commercial analysis depended on a mercantilist privileging of navigation.

Throughout the postwar decade, the explicit purpose to "strengthen" Congress's power to regulate trade more precisely sought the capability to threaten to prohibit British shipping from the American states: "Great Britain knows its [trade's] intrinsic value and if we prohibit the use of their manufactures or west india commodities except when brought by our own vessels or by those of other nations and thereby oblige them to make their purchases in cash they will very soon come to a compromise." For several years after the war even economic nationalists on fiscal questions showed little interest in conferring Congress with general powers to regulate commerce. Calls for greater congressional power to regulate trade reacted primarily to the unexpected British restrictions on American trade. Because that reaction would deny British access to American trade in order to coerce an easing of those restrictions, the initial authorizations by the States for Congress to "regulate" trade actually provided for only a narrow range of powers to *prohibit* trade. For example, South Carolina responded to the call for the States to authorize national commercial regulation by passing an act empowering Congress to regulate trade with the West Indies, but it withheld "the Power of regulating Trade generally with all foreign Nations."[18]

With its priority to secure commercial reciprocity with Great Britain, Congress forwent powers to regulate commerce. It seemed no con-

tradiction that the U.S. government should seek powers to discriminate against British trade, in order to coerce Britain to privilege
American commerce as though it were British. It also seemed no contradiction to seek such reciprocity despite the treaty guaranteeing
France most-favored-nation status—even though the terms of French
trade with the United States would, in effect, be set by Britain should
there be an Anglo-American commercial treaty. For example, when
Thomas Jefferson came to London in 1786, he and John Adams, his
fellow commissioner to negotiate treaties of amity and commerce,
again proposed to Britain a commercial treaty based on thorough reciprocity. American citizens and British subjects would be able to trade
any goods anywhere in the dominions of the other country and to
"enjoy all the rights, privileges, and exemptions, in trade, navigation,
and commerce" of the nationals of the other country. (With the exception that Americans would agree not to interfere with the rights of the
"chartered companies trading to the East Indies and to Hudson Bay.")
Ships from each country would be able to enter any of the other's
dominions and to export any goods that nationals could trade. This
proposed treaty represented an effort to regain the privileges of the
navigation system. Although Jefferson considered trade with Britain
to be ruinous for the United States, he would "tolerate" it in order to
have "free commerce with their W. Indies."[19]

Despite wariness about the implications for Virginia of a commercial
treaty with Great Britain, Madison readily supported the state's effort
to mobilize a national retaliatory policy toward British trade restrictions. Virginia acceded promptly to Congress's proposal that the States
grant it powers to regulate trade in order to coerce Britain into a
commercial treaty. The powers granted were really prohibitory, not
regulatory. They would enable Congress—for a period of fifteen
years—to prohibit imports and exports in the vessels of any country
not in commercial treaty with the Confederation, and Congress would
also be able to prohibit the subjects of such countries "from importing
into the United States, any goods, wares or merchandize which are not
the produce or manufacture of the dominions of the sovereign whose
subjects they are."[20]

Such a coercive policy toward Great Britain implicitly coerced Americans as well. After all, most restraints on British trade really bore on
Americans' disposition to buy British manufactures and to sell American commodities to British merchants. Critics charged that after the
war Americans had too readily sought to reestablish the economic
relations of the colonial period. For example, Governor Benjamin Harrison of Virginia "wished in some measure to curb the violent inclina-
tion there seemed to be for opening every avenue to them [the British]

before a treaty of commerce was entered into. I looked on the locusts that are crouding here as so many emissaries sent to sound our inclinations and to poison the minds of our people and if possible bring them back to their old and destructive paths; and I am sorry to say that I fear they will succeed unless Congress interfere." Americans' economic behavior had apparently been crucial for Britain's successful adoption of a policy of commercial jealousy toward the United States. Whether through reciprocity or through restrictions on the carrying trade, Britain "knew that by commanding our trade she would ever hold us in some kind of subservience, and would continue to reap the profits of our labour." In the spring of 1783, and coincidental with the fall of Shelburne's ministry, American merchants, consumers, and producers had shown the irrelevance of British "anxiety and fear" regarding American trade: "Our ports were opened to every thing that was called British, and our vessels, regardless of treaties and despising seizures or forfeitures crowded into the British ports in a manner that was astonishing to all Europe." It then became hopeless to make "any Commercial stipulations with Great Britain . . . because the Merchants without System or caution rushed into the British Ports and courted an intercourse with that Country."[21]

This self-criticism of consumption patterns inevitably drew on jeremiad traditions for calls of frugality in the name of moral reform. Jefferson compared Massachusetts' commercial discrimination against Great Britain with "turning a strumpet out of doors. It is saying 'we have sinned, but we repent and amend': we begin by banishing the tempter." But now such calls had additional considerations in political economy. To call on people to be "rigorously frugal" and to "despise European modes" asked "hacknied questions." People really needed to renounce the blandishments of easy British credit. *American* merchants needed to be discouraged from trading "without capital"; otherwise they would not "go to the market where commodities are to be had cheapest, but where they are to be had on the longest credit": "No man can have a natural right to enter on a calling by which it is at least ten to one he will ruin many better men than himself. Yet these are the actual links which hold us whether we will or no to Great Britain."[22] Jefferson called for "a great reformation necessary in our manners and our commerce," without juxtaposing liberty with commerce in ways characteristic of classical republicanism. He juxtaposed American liberty with *British* commerce.

Resolution, rather than legislative provisions, critically defined commercial policy. If the American states could only "convince Her [Britain] that America is too wise to be sported with, and can act in such Union as to defeat entirely her injurious attempts," then it would secure the concessions it sought. Congress needed no more "powers for the regulation of trade" than "to counteract the attempt of Great Britain to engross the carrying trade," which required little discussion of the technical application of these powers. Limitations on British trade with the American states would serve "to convince foreign Nations, that America can act in concert in guarding her Trade, as well as in defending her liberties, and to prevent our trade from being sported with and sacrificed to European policy."[23]

With exceptional forthrightness, Madison's replacement in Congress, Monroe, advocated a comprehensive national power to regulate commerce. In March 1785, Monroe presented his committee's report on amendments to the Articles. It recommended direct congressional power to regulate commerce. According to the report, Congress should recommend to the States that they alter the Articles of Confederation so that Congress had "sole and exclusive" power "of regulating the trade of the States, as well with foreign nations, as with each other, and of laying such imposts and duties upon imports and exports, as may be necessary for the purpose." The only limitations on the power of Congress would be the existing restriction that it not impose higher duties on American citizens than on foreign subjects and that the States retain a power of "prohibiting the importation or exportation of any species of goods or commodities whatsoever"—presumably slaves. Congress needed powers to bring the commercial legislation of the States into accord with the present and anticipated commercial treaties that Congress should negotiate. Successful commercial diplomacy depended on the confidence of other nations in implementing the agreed upon provisions. Correspondingly, when "necessary to counteract the policy of those powers, with whom they shall not be able to form commercial treaties," Congress must act with more than "imbecility and indecision." The report assumed that upon failure to negotiate "reciprocal advantage," "it becomes the duty of the losing party to make such further regulations, consistently with the faith of treaties, as will remedy the evil, and secure its interests."[24] For an effective strategy to meet commercial restrictions with countervailing regulations, the States needed to act in union, because there would always be an incentive for states acting individually to enhance their trade by allowing entry to trade excluded elsewhere.

The report assumed that *nations* competed for commerce. The principle of "reciprocal advantage" in commercial diplomacy served the Confederation's need to coordinate the inchoate protectionism of the states, not to facilitate the efficient linkage of supply and demand. Every nation acting alone rationally adopted economic privileges, as the states, acting individually, had demonstrated. These economic privileges bore particularly on the carrying trade, which the report virtually equated with a monopoly in the trade of goods themselves: "The policy of each nation in its commercial intercourse with other powers is to obtain, if possible, the principal share of the carriage of the materials of either party, and this can only be effected, by laying higher duties upon imports and exports in foreign vessels, navigated by the subjects of foreign powers, than in those which belong to, and are navigated by those of its own dominions." Such policies were economically rational and politically expectable: "This principle prevails in a greater or less degree in the regulations of the oldest and wisest commercial nations with respect to each other, and will of course be extended to these States."[25] The assumption of a world of commercially competitive nations made it possible to present political union as having intrinsic economic advantages.

Adoption of the recommendations of Monroe's committee would make a "deep and radical change" in the Confederation and provide its "most permanent and powerful principle." Under the present arrangement, "the political economy of each State is entirely within its own direction," and any dealing with foreign states required working through the individual states of the Confederation as well. The changes recommended by the committee would "put the commercial economy of every state entirely under the hands of the Union, the measure necessary to obtain the carrying trade, to encourage domestic by a tax on foreign industry, or any other ends which in the changes of things become necessary, will depend entirely on the Union." Monroe, the future opponent of ratification of the Constitution, happily anticipated how such changes "will give the union an authority upon the States respectively which will last with it & hold it together in its present form longer than any principle it now contains." He employed a ready appreciation of commercial realities in order to present a highly political analysis of American economic interests:

> Unless therefore they [the United States] possess a reciprocal power, its operation must produce the most mischievous effects. Unable to counteract the restrictions of these powers by similar restrictions here, or to support the interests of their citizens by discriminations in their favor, their system will prevail. Possessing no advantages in the ports of his own country, and subjected to much higher duties and restrictions in those of other powers, it will necessarily become the interest of the American merchant to ship his produce in foreign bottoms; of course their prospects of national consequence must decline, their merchants become only the agents and retailers of those of foreign powers, their extensive forests be hewn down and laid waste to add to their strength and national resources, and the American flag be rarely seen upon the face of the seas.[26]

Much more so than Madison, Monroe calculated the specifically commercial benefits of strengthening national regulatory powers.

Monroe was more genuinely an *economic* nationalist than Madison. Madison apparently drafted the November 1785 resolutions of the Virginia Assembly giving Congress power to regulate trade directly. The powers did not allow much regulation. Congress could only prohibit foreign vessels from entering American ports if they sailed from countries lacking treaties of commerce with the United States. The purpose was less regulatory than diplomatic and governmental: "The relative situation of the United States has been found on trial, to require uniformity in their commercial regulations, as the only effectual policy for obtaining in the ports of foreign nations, a stipulation of privileges, reciprocal to those enjoyed by the subjects of such nations in the ports of the United States; for preventing animosities, which cannot fail to arise among the several States from the interference of partial and separate regulations." Madison emphasized permanency in Congress's fiscal powers, in order that the United States might have creditability abroad; Monroe advocated permanency for its powers to regulate commerce for similar creditability on different questions. Whereas Madison analyzed the fiscal advantages of foreign trade, Monroe compared the fiscal burdens of the United States and other countries in order to calculate the relative advantages of reciprocal free trade.[27]

Among the Confederation's nationalists, Monroe almost uniquely conceded a hypothetical alternative to mercantilism. He agreed that the carrying trade critically required a federal power to regulate commerce, and he asked rhetorically whether its privileges "will not in effect increase the value of land, the number of inhabitants, the proportion of circulating medium, and be the foundation upon which all those regulations which are necessary to turn what is called 'the balance of trade' in our favor." But Monroe also acknowledged that "an opinion seems to be entertained by the late commercial writers and particularly a Mr. Smith on the wealth of nations that the doctrine of the balance of trade is a chimera in pursuit of which G. B. hath exposed herself to great injury." Monroe appreciated that if Smith were right, then the advantages of encouraging the carrying trade were ones of "national strength," not commerce. If the encouragement of the carrying trade did not intrinsically improve a nation's commerce, then to support it in the name of economic nationalism would actually be to give some states "advantages that will be almost exclusive & operate essentially to our prejudice: so as to lessen the price of our produce, discourage its cultivation and throw the monopoly in the purchase principally in their favor." Having taken up this hypothetical liability, however, Monroe then reassured himself by noting that the interests of the States were more similar than different because of their fundamentally commercial character: "Being all exporting & importing States—that it was of little consequence whether they exported the same or different materials, since the restrictions which tended to restrain exportation, would injure the whole, & they were all equally interested in getting their admission upon the best terms into the ports of foreign powers. That they imported nearly the same materials & of course had the same interest in that line."[28] From Monroe's perspective, the specter of economic sectionalism called for truly national powers to regulate commerce.

Madison also minimized sectional commercial conflicts, but by disparaging their economic content and by emphasizing their purely political dynamics. From his perspective, granting Congress power to regulate commerce antagonized narrow-minded state politicians more than it aggravated conflicting economic diversity among the States: "Put the West India trade alone, in which the interest of every State is involved, into the scale against all the inequalities which may result from any probable regulation by nine States, and who will say that the latter ought to preponderate?" State politicians had little reason to take effective action to serve mutual commercial interests. In addition to their reluctance to give up power, members of the state legislatures typically could not understand arguments referring to considerations beyond the state, such as those of "interests of the State as they are interwoven with those of the Confederacy much less as they may be affected by foreign politics, whilst those which plead against it are not only specious, but in their nature popular." Ironically, the most likely argument to win support for congressional power to regulate power was itself "popular": "This power is likely to annoy G. B. against whom the animosities of our Citizens are still strong."[29]

Madison assumed that if any country "imposes on our Vessels seamen etc. in their ports, clogs from which they exempt their own, we must either retort the distinction, or renounce not merely a just profit, but our only defence against the danger which may most easily beset us." He based this assumption on a fiscal, not a commercial, calculation. Such restrictions would put the United States in another country's debt: "A perfect freedom is the System which would be my choice. But before such a System will be eligible perhaps for the U. S. they must be out of debt." In this context, Madison phrased his support for congressional power in rather qualified terms, with a double negative: "Viewing in the abstract the question whether the power of regulating trade, to a certain degree at least, ought to be vested in Congress, it appears to me not to admit of a doubt, but that it should be decided in the affirmative." Experience had shown that the States acting individually "can no more exercise this power separately than they could separately carry on war, or separately form treaties of alliance and commerce."[30]

Foreign Trade and Trans-Appalachia

Rights of navigation of the Mississippi aroused intense diplomatic interest in the 1780s because commercial opportunities in the West depended critically on foreign trade. In 1780 Congress instructed John Jay, its minister plenipotentiary at the Court of Madrid, "to insist on the navigation of the Mississippi for the Citizens of the United States in common with the subjects of his Catholic Majesty, as also on a free port or ports below the Northern limit of W. Florida and accessible to Merchant ships, for the use of the former." When Madison drafted Congress's explanation for this policy, he reminded Jay of the conventional justifications that the law of nations provided for American rights regarding the Mississippi, but he emphasized the specifically commercial concerns motivating these diplomatic claims. American society would expand rapidly into Trans-Appalachia, "it being so finely watered added to the singular fertility of its soil and the other advantages presented by a new country." The people emigrating to the region, "as in all other new settlements," would engage in agriculture, not manufactures. In doing so, however, they would be responding to international markets for staples, not reverting to a simpler, subsistence-oriented way of life: "They will raise wheat corn Beef Pork tobacco hemp flax and in the Southern parts perhaps rice and indigo in great quantities. On the other hand their consumption of foreign manufactures will be in proportion, if they can be exchanged for the produce of their soil."[31]

Such an efficient regional specialization of labor depended critically on navigation of the Mississippi: "If no obstructions should be thrown in its course down the Mississippi, the exports from this immense tract of Country will not only supply an abundance of all necessaries for the W. Indies Islands, but serve for a valuable basis of general trade, of which the rising spirit of commerce in France and Spain will no doubt particularly avail itself." With opening of the Mississippi, "the imports will be proportionally extensive and from the climate as well as other causes will consist in a great degree of the manufactures of the same countries." The regional division of labor for staple trades determined the distinction in American diplomatic aims between navigation of the Mississippi and access to an oceanic port. The alternative to the Mississippi required shipping goods eastward up the rivers until they could be portaged to the lakes and rivers leading to the Saint Lawrence:

"Should obstruction of the Mississippi force this trade into a contrary direction through Canada, France and Spain and the other maritime powers will not only lose the immediate benefit of it to themselves, but they will also suffer by the advantage it will give to G. Britain."[32] One way or the other, development of the West was unthinkable without linkages to overseas trade.

Foreign commerce had priority in political economy and policymaking on westward expansion and commerce. Serious discussions of political economy in the 1780s did not blur domestic and foreign markets, or manufactures and staple trades; instead, they presented implicit and explicit expectations that the West would grow economically in direct proportion to its involvement in foreign trade and that involvement in foreign trade would shape the structure of the regional economy. In providing a justification from "nature" for American claims on western resources, the fertility of the western regions mattered less than the potential of the Mississippi to carry trade to world markets.[33]

Navigation of the Mississippi was only one-half of the West's role in the growth of American overseas commerce. The Mississippi carried staples for export. These exports provided a demand for foreign manufactures along an improved transportation system of rivers and canals. Thus "nature" had also "declared in favour of the Patowmac, and through that channel offers to pour into our lap the whole commerce of the Western world." The validation of American claims to the West would come from this augmentation of international commerce, whereas Spain contradicted its claims by perpetuating "a System, which everybody but herself has long seen to be as destructive to her interest as it is dishonourable to her character." Spain had a "system" of monopoly, which gave priority to keeping resources away from other nations, even at the cost of its own prosperity. Spain's unwillingness to allow navigation of the Mississippi arose not from a desire to exploit its opportunities, but simply because "she is afraid of the growth and neighbourhood of the U. States, because it may endanger the tranquility of her American possessions."[34]

Land policy arguably mattered less than navigation of the Mississippi as an issue bearing on the economic development of the West. In 1784, when Congress considered policy toward western lands, Madison and Jefferson exchanged letters illustrating the crucial orientation toward foreign trade in discussions of political economy. In advising Jefferson how to demonstrate to Spain its advantages from American use of the Mississippi and development of the West, Madison used the mercantilist calculus of imperial nations to remind Spanish diplomats of their own national interests in trade. The diplomatic priority of securing navigation of the Mississippi arose specifically from the potential of the

West to displace the East in the production of staples.[35] Anticipation of Jefferson's commercial negotiations in Europe encouraged Madison to formulate his famous projections of the economic development of the West and its relation to the rest of the American economy. He suggested to Jefferson arguments he could use to persuade Spanish diplomats that American territorial expansion and economic growth did not threaten European prosperity, but instead served Spain's own economic interests.

In this diplomatic brief for Jefferson, Madison projected the economic development of the West as a proliferation of expanding staple trades. He assumed that the structural relations of production and consumption would continue to be colonial in character, and he gave little priority to the goal of self-sufficiency for the American economy: "By a free expansion of our people the establishment of internal manufactures will not only be long delayed but the consumption of foreign manufactures long continue increasing; and at the same time, all the productions of the American soil required by Europe in return for her manufactures, will proportionably increase." In making this economic forecast, Madison was at least as interested in reassuring European diplomats of their captive market in the United States as he was in preserving the republic from the social ills associated with manufactures. How else to explain his equanimity with what would otherwise be a pessimistic analysis of progressively worsening terms for American trade, except as a tendentious exercise to reassure Spanish negotiators that American economic development posed no commercial competition?

> If no check be given to emigrations from the latter [the East] to the former [the West], they will probably keep pace at least with the increase of our people, till the population of both becomes nearly equal. For twenty or twenty-five years we shall consequently have as few internal manufactures in proportion to our numbers as at present and at the end of that period our imported manufactures will be doubled. It may be observed too, that as the market for these manufactures will first increase, and the provision for supplying it will follow, the price of supplies will naturally rise in favor of those who manufacture them. On the other hand as the demand for tobacco indigo rice corn etc. produced by America for exportation will neither precede nor keep pace with their increase the price must naturally sink in favor also of those who consume them.[36]

By facilitating the staple trades of Trans-Appalachia, Madison advised, European powers simultaneously encouraged a market for their manufactures and delayed the development of the United States as a competitor even in its own markets. Not a shred of republican ideology appeared in Madison's political economy here; he provided a self-servingly pessimistic economic projection to be used in negotiations. In the 1790s he would put this same economic analysis to explicitly republican purposes, but Madison first formulated it to deal with diplomatic strategy in a European context.

The priority of exports in calculations of the opportunities in Trans-Appalachia appeared again when the Jay-Gardoqui negotiations became an issue in Congress. The Virginia delegation had instructions to insist on American rights of navigation on the Mississippi. However, when it became apparent that Jay had bargained to forego navigation of the Mississippi in exchange for nearly free access to Spanish markets (except for tobacco), his opponents proposed a compromise indicating their own commercial priorities: "that exports be admitted thro' the Mississippi paying at New Orleans, as a duty, two and a half per cent. ad valorem to Spain, to be carried thence in Spanish, American or French bottoms—that imports be prohibited in that line."[37] Considerations of natural imperatives as well as priorities in political economy dictated that the orientation of the desired "navigation" of the Mississippi be toward foreign, not domestic, commerce.

The possible denial of American navigation of the Mississippi highlighted expectations of a West oriented to foreign trade. After talking with Washington about proposals for a Potomac-based transportation system, Lafayette apparently left the United States with the impression that "many people think that the navigation of the Mississippi is not an advantage but it may be the excess of a very good thing, viz the opening of your rivers." When Madison wrote Lafayette to convince him of the mutual advantages for France and the United States in a favorable outcome of negotiations with Spain over navigation of the Mississippi, he based his case on the continuation of America's staple economy.

European nations favoring American independence had calculated that "the chief advantages expected in Europe from that event center in the revolution it was to produce in the commerce between the new and the old world." However, the "revolution" in American commerce was the elimination of the British monopoly, not the structure of the American economy: "The commerce of the U. S. is advantageous to Europe in two respects, first by the unmanufactured produce which they export; secondly by the manufactured imports which they consume." However, these advantages could be maintained only if navigation of the Mississippi provided economic opportunities to make settlement in the West worthwhile. Without such opportunities, migration westward would take place more slowly than the growth of population in the East. As crowding increased there, agricultural resources would be diverted from "the culture of tobacco indigo and other articles for exportation" to the provision of subsistence.[38] European prices for

American goods would increase. Meanwhile, this decline of staple production would result in a lessening of American imports from Europe,
because they would have smaller earnings from trade to buy goods.
Quite apart from this change in the terms of trade, Americans would
increasingly be obliged to take up livelihoods in manufacturing as
those in agriculture became insufficient.

Madison associated the settlement and economic development of the
West with a retardation, rather than an acceleration, of the development of American self-sufficiency. If Spain successfully slowed settlement of the West, she "would only double the power of the U. States
to disturb her . . . she would only drive to the Sea most of those
swarms which would otherwise direct their course to the Western Wil-
derness." In those circumstances the United States would prematurely
develop a navy and thereby threaten Spain's colonial commercial monopoly much more directly.[39] Once again, Madison's most republican-
sounding mercantilism came when he framed an economic analysis to
show *Europeans* their true economic interest. In the context of political
partisanship in the new federal government, he would add an explicit
gloss of republicanism to his political economy. When first formulated,
it relied primarily on mercantilist political economy.

Other prominently federalist Virginians, such as James Monroe and
Edmund Pendleton, grew more uncertain in their advocacy of national
commercial regulations, as the turmoil over the Jay-Gardoqui negotiations encouraged them to envisage a polarity of irreconcilable economic interests between shipping and staples, as well as between manufactures and agriculture. Virginia politicians became the most prominent
self-appointed defenders of "the southern states" against the supposed
conspiratorial commercial intentions of "the Eastern men" regarding
the Jay-Gardoqui treaty. Eastern politicians and merchants were apparently so intent on expanding their trade that they would either
bargain away the commercial future of the West, or else have their
states secede from the Confederation. Out of anxiety over the likelihood that the easterners would either get what they wanted or form a
new Confederation, Monroe became convinced that the Annapolis
convention was critical for the continuation of the Confederation as
well as for a viable commercial policy. Suspicion of eastern good will
toward the commerce of the West made the enhancement of federal
power to regulate commerce something less of a shibboleth and more
of a practical issue.[40]

IN CONTRAST to Monroe's sense of urgency, Madison expressed
mixed views toward the Annapolis Convention. To George Washing-

ton, he wrote: "I think it better to trust to further experience and even distress, for an adequate remedy, than to try a temporary measure which may stand in the way of a permanent one, and confirm that transatlantic policy [i.e., Great Britain's] which is founded on our supposed distrust of Congress and of one another." To Monroe, he wrote that "the expedient is no doubt liable to objections and will probably miscarry. I think however it is better than nothing, and as a recommendation of additional powers to congress is within the purview of the Commission it may possibly lead to better consequences than at first occur." When Madison calculated the liabilities of either ineffective congressional or contradictory state regulation of commerce, however, commerce was only the initial term. The final term was fiscal: "Another unhappy effect of a continuance of the present anarchy of our commerce will be a continuance of the unfavorable balance on it, which by draining us of our metals furnishes pretexts for the pernicious substitution of paper money, for indulgences to debtors, for postponements of taxes."[41] Only as long as the primary purpose to enhance the union of the States was fiscal, rather than commercial, could Madison support the effort without his residual Virginia particularism. He was the prime example that political nationalism did not require economic nationalism, except on the particular topic of navigation, where the clinching arguments were political.

CHAPTER SIX

Commerce and
the Philadelphia Constitution

O N THE EVE of the Philadelphia convention in 1787, the "regulation of commerce," which was understood as the capacity to retaliate against British commercial discrimination, was one of the two
most important powers sought by the nationalists who intended to
govern an American republic.[1] The Articles of Confederation had left
the regulation of foreign commerce to the States, and most commentators attributed the postwar recession of the 1780s to a lack of coordinated policy for foreign trade. From the convention came a proposed
Constitution promoting free trade relations in the domestic economy.
It took away the individual states' powers to regulate commerce with
foreign nations and to impair the "obligation of contracts," and it gave
Congress exclusive power to issue money. But it also gave Congress
power "to regulate commerce with foreign nations, and among the
several States, and with the Indian tribes," powers that could contra-
vene the free workings of markets. Apparently the convention proposed a national republic with a liberal domestic market in order to
meet mercantilist ends.

The Shibboleth of Commercial Regulation
at the Convention

In opening the discussion of constitutional reform at the Philadelphia convention, Edmund Randolph of Virginia asserted that a national government could provide advantages regarding commerce
that the Confederation could not, "such as a productive impost—
counteraction of the commercial regulations of other nations—
pushing of commerce ad libitum." This need for a national power to
regulate commerce then disappeared as an issue while debate focused
on questions of representation. But even advocates of representation
based solely on state governments readily conceded that among the few

unquestionable "objects of the Union" were "regulating foreign commerce & drawing revenue from it."[2] The need for a national capability to regulate commerce was a shibboleth at the Philadelphia convention. Because of simplistic associations with retaliatory policies toward Great Britain, the principles or need for such regulation received no sustained discussion.

Instead, such questions arose infrequently, and obliquely, in debate on other topics. For example, during discussion of the length of term for senators, James Wilson explained how effective commercial diplomacy depended on long terms because the Senate had crucial powers in the ratification of treaties and therefore needed "to be made respectable in the eyes of foreign nations." Great Britain had not yet negotiated a commercial treaty with the States because "she had no confidence in the stability or efficacy of our Government." A related instance of oblique discussion of political economy arose when Charles Cotesworth Pinckney of South Carolina advised against too protectionist a commercial policy. America was a new, not an old, country, yet his fellow politicians wanted to adopt "the maxims of a State full of people & manufactures & established in credit." Pinckney's remarks may have been contentious, but they caused no debate. He made them tangentially while arguing at length that American historical and social circumstances made an aristocracy unlikely and that therefore a Senate was not a liability. He criticized protectionism in order to caution that the only likely source of an aristocracy in America would be its merchants. Although the regulatory implications of other constitutional powers often arose, the power per se to regulate commerce received almost no debate until the last weeks of the convention.[3]

The power of Congress to levy import duties related closely to its power to regulate commerce, but the convention debates maintained a sharp distinction between the fiscal and commercial intents of such duties. When gathering notes for a preliminary draft of the Constitution, the Committee of Detail listed the power to levy import duties among other powers to raise a revenue, such as a stamp tax and postage. As a separate type of power Congress would "pass Acts for the Regulation of Trade and Commerce as well with foreign Nations as with each other." Correspondingly, when Madison advocated congressional power to levy export as well as import duties, he sought to placate his fellow representatives from "staple" states by demonstrating that such duties could be neutral with respect to commerce. However, most representatives insisted that the Constitution should preclude export duties by either the States or the national government because the distinction between fiscal and commercial policy was too difficult to maintain in levying them. Import duties for purposes of revenue usually applied to a wide variety of goods consumed in all the states, but export duties on American commerce typically bore on staples and therefore varied greatly from state to state in the effects of their itemization. Sectional concerns that duties levied with apparent fiscal intent might amount to commercial regulation underlined the distinction itself.[4]

Ironically, for a document identified at the time and since with the feasibility of a national commercial policy, the most elaborate *economic* discussions at the Philadelphia convention bore on the denial to Congress of a power—namely, to levy export duties—because of its intrinsically commercial implications. Only on this issue were commercial costs and benefits discussed quantitatively. Charles Cotesworth Pinckney stated that the annual value of South Carolina exports was too great, £600,000, to allow it to be a temptation for an export duty. Hugh Williamson cited the number of hogsheads of North Carolina tobacco, twelve thousand, that Virginia dutied on export. George Clymer compared the terms of trade of wheat, flour, and other provisions, with those of tobacco and rice.[5] Gouverneur Morris explained how states would retain their relative commercial advantages in handling one another's goods, whether there was an export duty. As an advocate of congressional powers to impose duty on exports—not in reference to the general power to regulate commerce—Morris provided the convention's most detailed outline of a strategy of commercial regulation for the prospective national government:

> If no tax can be laid on exports, an embargo cannot be laid, though in time of war such a measure may be of critical importance—Tobacco, lumber, and live-stock are three objects belonging to different States, of which great advantage might be made by a power to tax exports—To these may be added Ginseng and Masts for ships by which a tax might be thrown on other nations. The idea of supplying the West Indies with lumber from Nova Scotia, is one of the many follies of lord Sheffield's pamphlets. The State of the Country also, will change, and render duties on exports, as skins, beaver & other peculiar raw materials, politic in the view of encouraging American Manufactures.[6]

His fellow representatives at the convention knew what they were doing in denying this power. The only issues with sustained discussion of their commercial implications were export duties and the slave trade. These discussions arose because the representatives from South Carolina insisted that the proposed Constitution explicitly guarantee that the new national government be *precluded* from such commercial regulations.[7]

The most forthright assertion of economic interests came in opposition to potential commercial regulation—namely, the insistence by South Carolina's representatives that the slave trade not be impeded by Congress. Rutledge asserted that "Interest alone is the governing principle with Nations." With that principle in mind, the southern states would decide whether to be "parties to the Union." Correspondingly, they advised, representatives of the northern states should realize that their interests lay with "the increase of Slaves which will increase the commodities of which they will become the carriers." The South Carolinians' steadfast defense of the slave trade provoked the convention's most sustained discussion of the commercial policy desirable from the new national government. George Mason, the Virginia antifederalist, warned about this critical decision for the economic development of the country. To deny the national government the power "to prevent the increase of slavery" tacitly accepted an economic policy of underdevelopment: "Slavery discourages arts and manufactures. The poor despise labor when performed by slaves."[8]

Replies to Mason's condemnation of slavery appealed to recognition of the market relations and economic developments bearing on slavery. Slavery would disappear where it was unprofitable. Where slavery thrived, it would be the hinge of national prosperity: "The more slaves, the more produce to employ the carrying trade; The more consumption also, and the more of this, the more of revenue for the common treasury." South Carolina's representatives also sought positive protection of the slave trade through a constitutional exemption of slaves from import duties. But when confronted with the liberal argument that such an exemption was a commercial privilege that amounted to "a bounty on that article," these representatives readily conceded the liability of the slave trade to import duties.[9]

Only in the aftermath of the debate on the slave trade, and in explicit connection with it, did the convention address the provisions for commercial regulation. At issue was the exceptional requirement that commercial regulations have two-thirds, rather than simple, majorities for their legislation. Nearly everyone appreciated that the relevant legislation would bear on Navigation Acts to encourage American shipping and to protect it from foreign competition. Advocates of such legislation argued that it would increase American shipping and that therefore southern goods would eventually be carried more cheaply. It would also sustain a navy, whose protection was also particularly necessary for southern trade. Valuable as these benefits might be, they were unattainable without a Navigation Act because commercial imperatives alone were not sufficient to produce them: "Shipping . . . was the worst & most precarious kind of property, and stood in need of public patronage."[10]

Self-appointed spokesmen for the southern states noted widespread suspicion in their section that Navigation Acts could result in a northern monopoly of the southern carrying trade. Madison sought to reassure such southern colleagues that any increased freights as a result of Navigation Acts would only be temporary, while the long-term advantages would include an increase of both southern and northern shipping, as well as an elimination of the counterproductive competition among the states in the extension of commercial privileges. Madison's arguments failed to convince most of the representatives of the southern states, but South Carolina's delegates abandoned their own amendment calling for a two-thirds majority on commercial regulations—out of appreciation of the eastern states' "liberal conduct towards the views of South Carolina" on the slave trade.[11]

Liberal principles provided the means to resolve the Philadelphia convention's crucial issues regarding commercial freedom and privilege, but fiscal policy and the encouragement of navigation remained the priorities in the regulation of commerce. The crux of commercial competition was among foreign states, not merchants. Regulatory powers remained an unquestioned good when applied to overseas trade. And overseas trade was the archetypal commercial activity.

Neomercantilism in the Federalist Papers

The *Federalist Papers*, the foremost apology for the new Constitution during the ratification controversy, explicitly asserted the mercantilist implications of the Philadelphia Constitution. The *Federalist Papers* first took up the topic of commerce when John Jay considered America's liability to war, and thereafter their discussion of commerce continued to assume the national rather than entrepreneurial basis of commercial competition. Jay expressed a classically mercantilist sense of the fixed quantity of oceanic trade: "We are rivals [of other nations] in navigation and the carrying trade; and we shall deceive ourselves if we suppose that any of them will rejoice to see it flourish; for, as our carrying trade cannot increase without in some degree diminishing theirs, it is more their interest, and will be more their policy, to restrain it than to promote it."[12] He shared the view presumed of other nations' statesmen that America's commercial prosperity could only come at their expense: the cheapness of American fish would displace the French and the British from their markets, and American trade to the East Indies would violate their monopolies. He expressed little sense that America's efficiency in shipping could contribute to an overall increase in trade.

Alexander Hamilton spoke in much more general, psychological terms than Jay about the connection between commerce and war.[13] He scorned the "visionary or designing men" who could "advocate the paradox of perpetual peace between the States, though dismembered and alienated from each other." He sarcastically reiterated their naïve assumptions:

> The genius of republics (say they) is pacific; the spirit of commerce has the tendency to soften the manners of men, and to extinguish those inflammable humors which have so often kindled into wars. Commercial republics, like ours, will never be disposed to waste themselves in ruinous contentions with each other. They will be governed by mutual interest, and will cultivate a spirit of mutual amity and concord.

But if these "projectors in politics" were right about the "true interest of all nations to cultivate the same benevolent and philosophic spirit," why had nations not pursued them accordingly? Was it not the case "that momentary passions, and immediate interests, have a more active and imperious control over human conduct than general or remote considerations of policy, utility, or justice"? The explanation was not constitutional: republics had been no "less addicted to war than monarchies."[14]

Hamilton equated the commercial imperatives of republics with political passions: "Is not the love of wealth as domineering and enterprising a passion as that of power and glory? Have there not been as many wars founded upon commercial motives since that has become the prevailing system of nations, as were before occasioned by the cupidity of territory or dominion?" Historical experience had shown him no difference between commercial and noncommercial republics in their bellicosity. Carthage was "the aggressor in the very war that ended in her destruction." The preeminent early modern commercial republics, Venice and Holland, had been no less aggressive in asserting their commercial interests—nor had Britain, where the representative branch of the government frequently took the initiative in such matters. On this count no difference marked republics from monarchies. The eighteenth-century wars between France and England arose largely from "commercial considerations—the desire of supplanting and the fear of being supplanted, either in particular branches of traffic or in the general advantages of trade and navigation."[15]

Hamilton put little emphasis on the strictly commercial, as opposed to the political, basis of the economic advantages of national union. He did not cite these historical examples in order to analyze conflicts in foreign trade. He extrapolated from such conflicts to predict how the individual American states would behave toward one another if they remained disunited: "Is it not time to awake from the deceitful dream of a golden age and to adopt as a practical maxim for the direction of our political conduct that we, as well as the other inhabitants of the globe, are yet remote from the happy empire of perfect wisdom and perfect virtue?"[16] Given the "spirit of enterprise, which characterizes the commercial part of America, [which] has left no occasion of displaying itself unimproved," citizens of one state would inevitably find themselves violating the commercial privileges of citizens of other states, which "would naturally lead to outrages, and these to reprisals and wars."

Americans should base their political economy on the system they enjoyed before the Revolution. And if there were any other nation's commercial policy that the United States should imitate, it was Great Britain's neomercantilism. Because the American states had, as colonies, enjoyed "habits of intercourse, on the basis of equal privileges," they were all the more likely "to denominate injuries those things which were in reality the justifiable acts of independent sovereignties consulting a distinct interest."[17] Rather than complain about Britain's supposed commercial illiberalism, the United States should learn from the successes of its policy.

Thus the *Federalist Papers* made navigation the privileged sector in American commercial policy, as the precondition for economic autonomy and security in a world where the political hostility of nations shaped their economic competition. Such hostility and competition bore particularly on Americans because of their potential as interlopers in European colonies: "[Europe's statesmen] seem to be apprehensive of our too great interference in that carrying trade, which is the support of their navigation and the foundation of their naval strength." Conversely, the naval strength of America would be the means and the measure of its successful commercial policy. If the States remained disunited, they would be vulnerable to "the power of the maritime nations," which would insist on carrying America's trade. Hamilton thought that an "unequaled spirit of enterprise . . . signalizes the genius of the American merchants and navigators," but it would languish without a powerful national government to assert their interests internationally. Economic opportunities in the fisheries, on the Great Lakes, and on the Mississippi all required assertion of the "rights of the Union" in the face of foreign obstruction. Americans needed a powerful government, because their economic competency so strongly aroused the commercial jealousy of other nations.[18]

The *Federalist Papers'* apparent preoccupation with considerations of political power denied economic life much conceptual or practical autonomy. An "efficient and well administered" national government was ipso facto good for commerce. It commanded the respect of other nations, which "will be much more disposed to cultivate our friendship than provoke our resentment." British experience had demonstrated the need for a national government to regulate "the navigation of Britain as to make it a nursery for seamen." Such a result would have been impossible if England, Ireland, Scotland, and Wales each had a separate navigation policy. With an effectively regulated navigation, America could establish a modestly effective navy, which if used with diplomatic judiciousness could "enable us to bargain with great advantage for commercial privileges." Conversely, if the States remained disunited, their strategic vulnerability would make "our commerce . . . prey to the wanton intermeddlings of all nations at war with each other."[19]

Hamilton urged that the States enter forthrightly into political competition for commerce. They should use "prohibitory regulations" to "oblige foreign countries to bid against each other for the privileges of our markets." To be sure, America had specifically commercial opportunities to offer other nations—a large, and growing, domestic market, "for the most part exclusively addicted to agriculture"—but the best way to capitalize on them was to manage access to them. There would be great advantages for those nations allowed to ship directly to America rather than rely on the shipping of other nations. In advocating a policy of commercial privilege, Hamilton really emphasized the reestablishment of prerevolutionary trading patterns with Great Britain. Such a strategy had priority over increasing the genuinely international competition for American trade or increasing American access to international markets.[20] The reason to have the power to *exclude* British trade from American markets was to gain privileged access to its.

Hamilton also identified ways in which a national union would enhance the domestic economy of the States, but he subordinated this discussion to questions of foreign trade. Thus, when dealing with the need for a navy, he elaborated on the advantageous contributions that different regions could make—naval stores from the South, iron from the Middle Atlantic states, and seamen from the Northeast. Similarly, though there were advantages "for the supply of reciprocal wants at home" from "an unrestrained intercourse between the States," the main advantages of domestic free trade would come from its contribution to the efficiency of foreign trade.[21]

When Hamilton discussed the "commercial prosperity of the States," he referred primarily to "the interests of revenue." "Enlightened statesmen" devoted their "political cares" to commerce because it was "the most useful as well as the most productive source of national wealth." Thus, his most elaborate treatment of economic relations introduced a discussion of the advantages of commerce as a fiscal resource. By demonstrating the mutually beneficial linkages of "the assiduous merchant, the laborious husbandman, the active mechanic, and the industrious manufacturer" in the domestic economy, Hamilton showed the equity of imposing duties on foreign trade as the chief source of revenue: everyone's economic well-being varied directly with the prosperity of overseas trade. The states individually could not take adequate advantage of this fiscal resource. If a state set duties at a level appropriate for fiscal needs, then neighboring states would lower duties in order to encourage smuggling; thereby it lost the duties as well as the trade.[22]

The federalist vanguard intended to apply only half of the art of political economy, as defined by Adam Smith. Its final terms for "national wealth" were fiscal, not the citizens' economic well-being. That Hamilton should have been more interested in power than plenty comes as no surprise. That he entirely dominated the *Federalist Papers'* discussion of commerce, however, says something generally about the character of federalism at the stage when Hamilton and Madison were political allies. In *Federalist* 42, where Madison discussed the new government's powers in dealing with foreign nations, he assumed that the topic of the regulation of commerce needed no discussion by him because it had been dealt with adequately by his coauthors.[23]

Madison's few contributions to the *Federalist Papers* on specifically commercial topics dealt primarily with fiscal considerations regarding the federal power to duty imports. Along with Hamilton, Madison argued against an exclusive reliance on duties for revenue because such a restriction would eventually be inappropriate to the American economy:

> The extent of revenue drawn from foreign commerce must vary with the variations, both in the extent and the kind of imports; and that these variations do not correspond with the progress of population, which must be the general measure of the public wants. As long as agriculture continues the sole field of labor, the importation of manufactures must increase as the consumers multiply. As soon as domestic manufactures are begun by the hands not called for by agriculture, the imported manufactures will decrease as the numbers of people increase. In a more remote stage, the imports may consist in a considerable part of raw materials, which will be wrought into articles for exportation, and will, therefore, require rather the encouragement of bounties than to be loaded with discouraging duties.[24]

Drew McCoy has shown the importance for Madison's political economy of this anticipation that the United States would eventually adopt a full-fledged mercantilist commercial policy, with manufactures becoming the privileged sector for protection and encouragement. But Madison had already shown his mercantilist reluctance to allow markets alone to determine economic relations. Madison and Hamilton shared a mercantilist political economy, but within that context Hamilton showed more interest in the economic implications of political questions, whereas Madison dwelt on the political implications of economic questions. Thus *Federalist* 10 discusses economic differences in the distribution of property but leaves aside the question of how people *acquire* property commercially:

> The most common and durable source of factions has been the various and unequal distribution of property. Those who hold and those who are without property have ever formed distinct interests in society. Those who are creditors, and those who are debtors, fall under a like discrimination. A landed interest, a manufacturing interest, a mercantile interest, a moneyed interest, with many lesser interests, grow up of necessity in civilized nations, and divide them into different classes, actuated by different sentiments and views. The regulation of these various and interfering interests forms the principal task of modern legislation and involves the spirit of party and faction in the necessary and ordinary operations of the government.[25]

Madison's "factions" and "mutual animosities" had no implications of *commercial* competition. He expected that different economic sectors would try to obtain legislative privileges for themselves, yet he did not propose liberalized market relations as means to abate such political factions. "Regulation" for Madison was less commercial than fiscal and pseudo-diplomatic, and his categories of economic analysis were mercantilist, not liberal. He disregarded the commercial consequences of factions, just as he forwent the opportunity to explain how a national economic interest could be determined for the purpose of commercial regulation. That Madison apparently gave so little thought to the pressing issues of political economy in his own time should make it less surprising that Hamilton's economic strategy prevailed among federalists.

The Cosmopolitan Antifederalists

In the past three decades, historians have shown renewed respect for the politics and constitutional views of the antifederalists, the opponents to ratification of the Philadelphia Constitution. Despite being historical losers, they are no longer marginalized from American history as "men of little faith," or "old" men of the Revolution.[26] However, the prevailing stereotype of their social and economic thought still emphasizes its traditionalist and even reactionary qualities. The combined legacy of both Charles Beard's interpretation, which identified a particular "mercantile" interest with the federalists, and of neo-Whig revisionism, which sought to repudiate Beard by eliminating the relevance of economic interests to constitutional thinking, has continued to deny a role for sophisticated political economy in antifederalism.

As one of the most sympathetic and respectful recent treatments of the antifederalists notes,

> in many ways Antifederalism was much more than simple opposition to the United States Constitution or a demand for amendments. It was a way of viewing the world. It was the political and constitutional expression of tradition-oriented people who distrusted change and who desired to live in a society and under a government that was as simple and immediately under their control as was possible. It was a world view that was also in many ways decidedly anticommercial and precapitalist.[27]

Historians reiterate the terms "agrarian" and "localist" (with its variants "provincial" and "parochial") to characterize antifederalists, whether they be juxtaposed to the "court" ideology of federalists in classical republican interpretations, or to federalists' "cosmopolitan . . . world views" according to neo-Progressive interpretations. Both terms, "agrarian" and "localist," imply that antifederalists were relatively uninvolved and unconcerned with market activity and happy to stay that way. Labeled "agrarian-localist," antifederalists were by definition distinct in their economic thinking from federalists, whose views were "commercial-cosmopolitan."[28]

From studying the controversies over paper money in the 1780s, however, Gordon S. Wood and Janet A. Riesman have proposed the alternative interpretation that antifederalists were less traditional and reactionary in their views on market society than federalists were. Wood has identified the demand for paper money, anathema to federalists, with "people who [during the war] had enjoyed buying, selling, and consuming and desired to do more of it." Federalism reacted against "this promotion of entrepreneurial interests by ordinary people." By reversing the usual association, Wood has shown how the localism of the antifederalists indicated their accommodation to commercial society. Riesman implicitly dealt with the second element in the invidious localist/cosmopolitan distinction. She found that antifederalist defenses of paper money were up-to-date in their theory and showed an awareness of "a highly complex market relationship [of the value of specie] with goods in markets all over the world . . . it was the Antifederalists even more than the Federalists who saw wealth as based primarily on the internal productivity of the country."[29]

This alternative interpretation is applicable as well to antifederalist views on foreign trade. After all, can antifederalists logically be contrasted with the "commercial-cosmopolitan" federalists on the basis of relative sophistication in political economy if it turns out that on commercial policy, and the national powers to enforce it, antifederalists strongly concurred with federalists? And what if antifederalists were at least as sophisticated regarding the regulation of trade as federalists were? Indeed, if they had more to say than the federalists about market relations in a staple economy, would it not be arguable that they had *more* commercial sophistication than advocates of the Philadelphia Constitution?

Most antifederalist writers[30] conceded the need for regulation of foreign commerce by a national government. Such regulatory power was intrinsically "of a general nature," and there were immediate imperatives for its exercise.[31] In his book *Political Parties before the Constitution*, Jackson Turner Main showed plenty of divisiveness between his "localists" and "cosmopolitans" on fiscal, monetary, and debt issues, but commercial issues aroused much less division, though they should have lent themselves readily to conflicts between localists and cosmopolitans.[32] Most antifederalist writers urged the separate states to "empower Congress to frame a *navigation act,* to operate uniformly throughout the States; reserving to Congress all necessary powers to *regulate our commerce with foreign nations, and among the several States, and with the Indian tribes.*"[33] Antifederalists could accept such an enhancement of the national government because most of them assumed that commercial regulations would not bear invidiously on the individual states, for the primary object of the regulations would be to coerce European states to open their trade to American goods and shipping.

Antifederalists typically shared with federalists the view attributing most of the underdevelopment of the American economy to the commercial policies of other nations. National capabilities to regulate trade enhanced the diplomatic clout of the States against foreign protectionist policies. With its powers to regulate commerce, Congress would have "proper controul" over the Senate and president in their treaty-making powers as they bore on commercial relations. Antifederalists recognized the diplomatic insufficiency of the Confederation, which "could make treaties of commerce, but could not enforce the observance of them and it was felt, that we were suffering from the restrictions of foreign nations, who seeing the want of energy in our Federal Constitution, and the unlikelihood of cooperation in thirteen separate Legislatures, had shackled our commerce, without any dread of recrimination on our part." Antifederalists urged that to remedy these conditions Congress should be granted powers "sufficient to command reciprocal advantages in trade"—and little more. If the Confederation Congress were only to have the power to regulate commerce and collect duties, "trade would immediately assume a new face, money and people would flow in upon us, and the vast tracts of ungranted land would be a mine of wealth for many years to come."[34]

Antifederalists readily recognized that the regulation of commerce involved restraints on some self-interests, particularly those of importing merchants and the majority of the population who consumed the goods they sold. After all, British export merchants and their agents in America were not forcing Americans to buy their wares. Americans simply had an appetite for "foreign merchandise and luxuries," which led to "excessive importations . . . and consequent drain of specie." Nor was the West Indies market the only one for American provisions, but Americans wanted to export their goods there, even in British ships, because they could obtain credits for further purchases from Britain.[35] Although antifederalists had a long list of specific concerns about how the proposed Constitution threatened liberty, there were virtually no antifederalist expressions of the idea that federal restraints on these market decisions would constitute violations of liberty. Commercial regulations per se were not infringements of liberty.

Antifederalists usually applied a mercantilist analysis to the American economy, but they prescribed a shakeout by market imperatives as the remedy for most of the commercial ills in the American states: "As long as this country imports more goods than she exports—the overplus must be paid for in money or not paid at all." With their recognition of market imperatives, antifederalists could present themselves as more realistic than federalists, whom they charged with a naïve tendency to attribute national commercial "misfortunes to the want of *energy* in our government." From such an antifederalist perspective, the proposed federal Constitution was overkill, when enhancement of the regulatory authority of the existing Confederation Congress was a more appropriately modest response. Let Congress have such powers as necessary to encourage more national sufficiency in the carrying trade, or to enact retaliatory discrimination against British protectionism. The creation of a federal republic was not a prerequisite for such powers, and it was delusive to think that a constitutional change would of itself beneficially affect the commercial policies of European states to American advantage.[36] In this vein, some antifederalists, while not disputing the need for greater federal powers of commercial regulation, could play down their necessity by taking a more sanguine view of the state of the American economy as it adjusted to the inevitable disruptions of postwar and postcolonial circumstances:

Let any man look round his own neighbourhood, and see if the people are not, with a very few exceptions, peaceable and attached to the government; if the country had ever within their knowledge more appearance of industry, improvement and tranquillity; if there was ever more of the produce of all kinds together for the market; if their stock does not rapidly increase; if there was ever a more ready vent for their surplus; and if the average of prices is not about as high as was usual in a plentiful year before the war. These circumstances all denote a general prosperity.[37]

The antifederalists' concession on the need for federal powers of commercial regulation actually allowed them to *oppose* the Philadelphia Constitution, because they believed that almost all of the Confederation's ills could be remedied simply by enhancing Congress's powers in commercial regulation, without overhauling the entire constitutional apparatus.

Antifederalist writers could be as cosmopolitan in their views of commerce as were advocates of the Philadelphia Constitution. The attribution of localism to their political economy is misplaced: for the antifederalists, commerce was foreign trade. They employed various distinctions to define the "commercial" states in the Confederation, but they all depended on the criterion of overseas trade. Antifederalist writers readily employed market analyses to explain their fiscal objections to the proposed federal Constitution. For example, an objection to the potential federal power to tax imports traced a series of commercial linkages in order to show how such measures hampered commercial life in ways that defeated their fiscal purposes as well: "If heavy duties are laid on merchandize, as must be the case, if government intend to make this the prime medium to lighten the people of taxes, that the price of the commodities, useful as well as luxurious, must be increased; the consumers will be fewer; the merchants must import less; trade will languish, and this source of revenue in a great measure be dried up." Without any criticism of market relations themselves, this writer spoke sympathetically about the ways in which people's different economic relationships made each other pay the price of increased fiscal costs:

> The merchant no more than advances the money for you to the public, and will not, nor cannot pay any part of it himself, and if he pays more duties, he will sell his commodities at a price portionably [*sic*] raised—thus the laborer, mechanic, and farmer, must feel it in the purchase of their utensils and clothing—wages, etc. must rise with the price of things, or they must be ruined. And that must be the case with the farmer, whose produce will not increase, in the ratio, with labour, utensils, and clothing; for that he must sell at the usual price or lower, perhaps caused by the

decrease of trade; the consequence will be, that he must mortgage his farm, and then comes inevitable bankruptcy.[38]

Few antifederalists voiced significant objections to congressional power to regulate commerce in order to secure "reciprocal advantages in trade." Their constitutional objections to the enhancement of federal powers to regulate trade usually focused on the association of such regulations with the congressional power to raise a revenue through duties on imports. In this respect, and only in this respect, congressional power to regulate commerce was objectionable, because it could be a stalking horse for the more general consolidation of government: "Trade seems to have been reserved, as a pretense to get Congress invested, first with an independent revenue, and since with legislative and judicial powers." Antifederalists charged that federalists held out "vain and delusive hopes" for the economic benefits of the proposed Constitution. Some of these federalist speculations were simply naïve, but others cynically calculated to divert people's minds "from contemplating its true nature, or considering whether it will endanger their liberties, and work oppression." Many antifederalist writers warned that duties on commerce would be self-defeating, but some of them went on to argue that this insufficiency would lead inevitably to an abuse of liberties in the name of fiscal necessity. For example, it might become necessary for the federal government to resort to intrinsically objectionable measures such as capitation and window taxes, which invited "a long train of impositions," as people were "numbered like the slaves of an arbitrary despot" and subjected to "the taxmaster thunder[ing] at your door for the duty on that light which is the bounty of heaven."[39] The most worrisome threat of despotism from such regulations bore not on the conduct of commerce itself, but on the property that its practitioners possessed.

In the minds of some especially suspicious antifederalists, the proposed Constitution posed direct threats to commercial opportunity as well. Commerce was no more secure from the excesses of power than was property: "Commerce is the hand-maid of liberty, a plant of free growth that withers under the hand of despotism, that every concern of individuals will be sacrificed to the gratification of the men in power, who will institute injurious monopolies and shackle commerce with every device of avarice; and that property of every species will be held at the will and pleasure of rulers."[40] If the States became a large empire, there would inevitably be commercial privileges for the capital, at the expense of the provinces. That had been the European experience: "In most countries of Europe, trade has been confined by exclusive charters. Exclusive companies are, in trade, pretty much like an aristocracy in government, and produce nearly as bad effects . . . When commerce is left to take its own course, the advantages of every class will be nearly equal." Similarly, when antifederalists expressed a seemingly classical republican concern that the Constitution would create "offices of honor and profit," which "may please the *ambition* of some, and relieve the *embarrassments* of others," they were careful to say that commerce discouraged such corruption rather than promote it.[41]

It would be stretching a point to suggest that antifederalists were *more* liberal in their views of commerce than federalists typically were, but the prominent antifederalist writer James Winthrop, in his *Letters of Agrippa*, suggests the possibility. Winthrop was exceedingly idiosyncratic both intellectually and ideologically. His persona of Agrippa referred to an antiaristocratic henchman of Gaius Octavian (later the first emperor). Agrippa's speciality was the suppression of revolts; Winthrop himself had been an anti-Shays volunteer. He was an early member of the American Academy of Arts and Sciences and a founder of the Massachusetts Historical Society, whose main scholarly efforts were interpretations of biblical prophecies. He failed to succeed his distinguished father as Hollis Professor of Mathematics and Natural Philosophy and instead became librarian of the college, a job that he eventually lost. The two consistencies of his life were polymathic intellectual range and political militancy, whether during the Revolution or later as a republican. It is not surprising to find him expressing exceptionally liberal views on political economy during the controversy about ratification of the Philadelphia Constitution.

Gordon Wood quotes Winthrop as typical of the authentically antifederalist challenge to "the whole social order the Federalists stood for": "'It is only by protecting local concerns, that the interest of the whole is preserved. No man when he enters into society, does it from a view to promote the good of others, but he does it for his own good.'"[42] Winthrop distanced himself from classical republicanism by *disparaging* the Greek and Roman republics for their citizens' *aversion* to commerce: "War was the employment which they considered as most becoming freemen. Agriculture, arts, and most domestick employment were committed chiefly to slaves. But Carthage, the great commercial republick of antiquity, though resembling Rome in the form of its government, and her rival for power, retained her freedom longer than Rome, and was never disturbed by sedition during the long period of her duration." Winthrop deflected the federalist argument that the instability of the classical republics was owing to their small size, and he argued instead that the "form of their government" was not their chief fault. Their weakness lay in their lack of priority for commercial values: "The spirit of commerce is the great bond of union among citizens.

This furnishes employment for their activity, supplies their mutual wants, defends the rights of property, and producing reciprocal dependencies, renders the whole system harmonious and energetick . . . most of the business is done in the freest states, and that industry decreases in proportion to the rigour of government."[43]

Winthrop extrapolated from the interpersonal basis of advantages in the market to sketch a mutually beneficial interstate division of commercial specialization. Commerce, not empire, most effectively united the States. Winthrop was exceptional among either antifederalists or federalists in his according the domestic market equal analytical importance with foreign trade, and he was relatively untroubled by British exclusions of American trade. Over the short term such a policy beneficially encouraged American manufactures, while over the long term the restrictions themselves could not last effectively because there was too much need for American supplies in the British West Indies and too tempting a market in America not to compel concessions eventually.[44] Winthrop's remarkable essays demonstrate that it is not anachronistic to look for examples of liberal political economy in the ratification controversy and that therefore their scarcity is of historical significance. Arguments against commercial regulation and privileges in the name of the economic advantages of freer markets were hypothetically possible, but rare.

———

IN FEDERALIST 51 Madison asked rhetorically, "What is government itself but the greatest of all reflections on human nature?" If so, then antifederalists were more likely than federalists to see a liberal "propensity to truck, barter, and exchange" as essential to human nature.[45] In the debates on the framing and ratification of the Philadelphia Constitution, federalists presented the commercial advantages of the new Constitution in thoroughly mercantilist terms: they were political rather than economic—to retaliate against other nations, to build a navy, to subsidize a merchant marine, to take oceanic trade away from other nations. The chief economic advantage of the power of the new federal government to regulate commerce was fiscal: foreign trade was a good source of governmental revenue. The antifederalists were more likely to bring strictly economic analysis to the debate and to refer their analysis to the workings of supply and demand in the market. Their political economy was less political and more economic.

CHAPTER SEVEN

Commercial Privilege in
the New Republic

T HE FIRST CONGRESS under the new federal Constitution initially concerned itself with procedural definitions—the administration of oaths, the duties of the Speaker, decorum and debate, and
arrangements for bills and committees. Its first substantive legislation,
which occupied the House from early April to the middle of May, dealt
with commercial regulation. Immediately after the administration of
constitutional oaths to the members of the House of Representatives,
debate by the Committee of the Whole began on Madison's proposals
for duties on imports. Madison urged an impost to provide the government with a revenue to meet its obligations without being "oppressive
to our constituents." He conceded that an impost bore on the "general
regulation of commerce," but he intended to restrict his discussion to
questions of revenue. He affirmed that commerce "ought to be as free
as the policy of nations will admit," but, as usual, Madison used this
economically liberal assertion not to lessen regulation but rather to
recommend its imposition.

The Priority of Commercial Discrimination

In order "to embrace the spring importations," Madison proposed that
Congress legislate the impost its predecessor had recommended to the
States in 1783; it "consisted of specific duties on spirits, wines, teas,
pepper, sugars, cocoa, and coffee and an *ad valorem* duty on all other
articles." The imposts proposed by the Confederation Congress in
1781 and 1783 had the exclusively fiscal purpose to pay off the federal
debt. Now Madison proposed an additional duty on tonnage, which
immediately contradicted his aversion from commercial regulation
and compromised his priority for considerations of revenue. Madison's
tonnage duties would protect American shipping by imposing a higher
duty on foreign than on domestic shipping, but with a less heavy rate

for ships from countries in commercial treaty with the United States.[1]

As Thomas Tudor Tucker of South Carolina pointed out the next day, such a proposal compromised the priority of revenue and the possibility of national impartiality toward competing interests. Madison's proposed tonnage duties would increase the costs of trade in some states more than in others because of their differential reliance on foreign shipping. Tucker recommended that tonnage duties either be postponed or be determined from revenue considerations alone. As long as the impost depended on discriminatory tonnage duties, Tucker warned, there would have to be political compromises in commercial policy, and these would inevitably be framed with a view toward "the various and adverse interests of the Union."[2]

In using the impost of 1783 as a model, Madison proposed a combination of enumerated duties and duties ad valorem. John Laurence of New York presciently demurred that Congress could more promptly secure a revenue from "a duty at a certain rate per cent. on the value of all articles, without attempting an enumeration of any": "If we attempt to specify every article, it will expose us to a question which must require more time than can be spared, to obtain the object that appears to be in the view of the committee. A question . . . will arise, whether the enumeration embraces every article that will bear a duty, and whether the duty to be affixed is the proper sum the article is to bear." Laurence's appeal for simplicity in the name of efficiency and administrative modesty represented Congress's lost opportunity to combine fiscal priorities with liberal trade regulation. Thomas Fitzsimons of Pennsylvania immediately countered this view by urging that Congress consider the impost in relation to "our agriculture, our manufactures, and our commerce," and then he moved an amendment to add a long list of enumerated goods to those proposed by Madison—over four dozen items from agricultural products such as beer and butter, through simple manufactures like cordage and cloth, to four varieties of luxurious carriages. Fitzsimons suggested that such enumeration of duties allowed Congress to call on its members' expertise on the economic interests and resources within their respective states. He called forthrightly for the politicization of economic interests and urged that Congress amalgamate the thinking on political economy found in the respective states.[3]

From the start, debate on import duties involved an incompatibility between strict adherence to the priority of revenue and a plethora of recommendations to frame a commercial policy on "as broad a bottom as is at this time practicable . . . to protect and promote our domestic manufactures." Madison took no exception in principle to the promotion of domestic manufactures, but he warned that "if the committee delay levying and collecting an impost until a system of protecting duties shall be perfected, there will be no importations of any consequence on which the law is to operate, because, by that time, all the spring vessels will have arrived." Madison assured Congress that once it seized this temporary advantage, it could then begin to frame a protectionist system amalgamating the programs already established in the separate states.[4]

In this protectionist context, Madison made some of the remarks cited most frequently to substantiate his "liberal" political economy:

> I own myself the friend to a very free system of commerce, and hold it as a truth, that commercial shackles are generally unjust, oppressive, and impolitic; it is also a truth, that if industry and labor are left to take their own course, they will generally be directed to those objects which are the most productive, and this in a more certain and direct manner than the wisdom of the most enlightened legislature could point out. Nor do I think that the national interest is more promoted by such restrictions, than that the interest of individuals would be promoted by legislative interference directing the particular application of its industry. For example, we should find no advantage in saying, that every man should be obliged to furnish himself, by his own labor, with those accommodations which depend on the mechanic arts, instead of employing his neighbor, who could do it for him on better terms. It would be of no advantage to the shoemaker to make his own clothes, to save the expense of the tailor's bill, nor of the tailor to make his own shoes, to save the expense of procuring them from the shoemaker. It would be better policy to suffer each of them to employ his talents in his own way. The case is the same between the exercise of the arts and agriculture—between the city and the country—and between city and town; each capable of making particular articles in abundance to supply the other; thus all are benefited by exchange, and the less this exchange is cramped by government, the greater are the proportions of benefit to each. The same argument holds good between nation and nation and between parts of the same nation.

In making this encomium to the efficiency possible with the division of labor and the allocation of resources by the market, Madison tried to keep the protection of manufactures from becoming so strong a priority in the scheme of duties on imports that it compromised their fiscal purposes. He put forward liberal truisms in order to maintain the possibility of later implementation of his scheme of commercial privileges through discriminatory duties on tonnage.

The remainder of this speech dealt with "the means of encouraging the great staple of America, I mean agriculture," and with "the exceptions that do not come within the rule I have laid down ['that commerce ought to be free, and labor and industry left at large to find its proper object']." Madison recommended that Congress encourage American agriculture because it had "unrivalled" market advantages from its low land costs. With similar contradiction, he recommended retaliatory discriminatory tonnage duties because otherwise American ships would be excluded "altogether from foreign ports," and because "by encouraging the means of transporting our productions with facility, we encourage the raising them." As additional reasons for commercial privileges, besides the immediate issue of revenue, he mentioned "sumptuary prohibition," "embargoes in time of war," self-sufficiency in military resources, and the protection of infant and established industries.

By finding common ground with Fitzsimons that the particular manufactured goods listed could bear "higher duties than those left in the common mass to be taxed *ad valorem*," Madison sidestepped the question of whether they individually deserved protection.[5] This effort to speed agreement on duties for revenue backfired because it opened up debate on the dutiability of each item. Consensus developed that the duties were no longer "a temporary expedient" and that instead "a permanent system is to be substituted in its place." Once permanency became a likelihood, then representatives began to add goods to the list of dutiables—some of them as worthy of protection, such as anchors, wool cards, wrought tin; others because they had no domestic competition, such as lemons and limes. Subsequent debate, particularly on the relative dutiability of imported rum and molasses, considered the trade-offs between opportunities for revenue, the use of differential duties to encourage the substitution of domestic products for imports, the relative desirability of duties on necessities and on luxuries, and the likelihood that smuggling would diminish returns should rates be set too high. These debates typically dealt item-by-item with questions of price, consumption and importation patterns, and the potential for increased production. Duties on some items, such as candles, compatibly provided revenue and encouraged domestic protection, but on other items, such as steel, opinion divided between advocates of a protective duty for infant industries and self-appointed spokesmen for a nominal agricultural interest.

Madison, for example, argued that there should be a bounty on *imports* of steel in order to encourage agricultural production, and he simultaneously urged that not only should cordage enjoy a protective tariff in order to encourage navigation but also that hemp should be dutied in order to encourage domestic production of a raw material for the protected industry. Disagreement arose regarding the details of virtually every duty, but consensus prevailed to distribute the fiscal burden in accordance with people's ability to pay, while having the net effect of duties encourage American manufactures, commerce, and agriculture by improving their price competitiveness with foreign goods. Virtually no one in Congress any longer argued for the compatibility between a liberal commercial policy and a priority for revenue in the regulation of foreign trade. Because the new government's commercial policy merged protectionism with fiscal measures, objections to individual duties could attack them as excessive taxation rather than as denials of economic opportunity.[6]

Just as with duties on imports, congressional debate on tonnage duties initially had the alternatives to consider them either as duties for revenue or as measures to assist American business. Virtually from the start, however, debate over a tonnage duty took for granted that it would discriminate between domestic and foreign shipping in order to encourage American navigation. The questions in debate largely dealt with the degree of discrimination and its impact on export trades. If revenue had priority, the important calculation was the rate of duties in relation to freight. If discrimination in favor of American shipping had priority, then Congress needed to know specifically how American ships were "subjected to charges in foreign ports over and above what the natives pay."[7]

Advocates of discriminatory tonnage duties took for granted that commercial regulations were retaliatory: "In these regulations, the policy is for each to obtain for its own vessels an advantage over those belonging to foreign nations." However, if foreign ships provided one-third of American freight, then any policy of encouragement had to anticipate the redirection of American commercial capital from goods to shipping. Opponents of a policy of severe discrimination objected that, however well-intentioned, it had a counterproductive potential. Because merchants would simply pass on the cost of tonnage duties as additional freight charges, the discriminatory duties on foreign ships would actually hamper the export trade of the United States by increasing the price, but not the profits, of its commodities abroad. Because of its scale, American shipping could not fully substitute for foreign shipping.[8]

Faced with these economic arguments, Madison redirected the debate on tonnage duties by arguing that discriminatory duties linked economic means with political ends. They discriminated "between nations in commercial alliance with the United States, and those with whom no treaties exist," in order to shift trade to the former from the latter. If the United States did not discriminate between British and French shipping, then it would jeopardize its policy to seek privileges in French commercial regulation. Without irony, Madison argued the need for a policy of discrimination in order to place commerce between Britain and the United States within its "natural boundary." Between the United States and its allies, "there is less of direct intercourse than there would naturally be if those extraneous and adventitious causes did not prevent it; such as the long possession of our trade, their [British] commercial regulations calculated to retain it, their similarity of language and manners, their conformity of laws and other circumstances."[9] "Natural" trade was bilateral. Madison justified commercial discrimination in the name of "reciprocity," but the advantages of reciprocity did not depend on the play of supply and demand in the market. He would replace the Navigation Acts with another form of managed trade. A successful policy of commercial discrimination toward Great Britain would result in U.S. ships carrying exactly half of Anglo-American trade.[10]

Those who opposed Madison's political argument for discrimination insisted that economic realities had to be foremost in considerations of commercial policy. If nations in commercial treaty with the United States could provide tangible commercial benefits, then they should have preferences accordingly. But expectations of gratitude could not determine a commercial policy: "We are left to act from what we may consider our best interest; for nations, as well as individuals, are guided by the principle of interest." For example, export of southern agricultural commodities depended on the extension of credit on a scale available only from British merchants. The U.S. government should not pretend to determine whether "the commerce of Britain with this country was too great in proportion to that of other nations . . . the merchants of America were well able to understand and pursue their own interests, and the advantages which they obtain tend to the wealth and prosperity of the Union." A policy of discrimination could backfire if it led to British retaliation. The profitability of goods from America benefited from competition among its foreign shippers, a competition that a discriminatory tonnage duty would lessen.[11]

Madison readily understood that arguments against discrimination showed "that G. B. made no discrimination agst. the U.S. compared with other nations" and "that if G. B. possessed almost the whole of our trade, it proceeded from causes which proved that she could carry it on for us on better terms than the other Nations of Europe." But he insisted that the primary purpose of the new federal government was to unite "the States in the vindication of their commercial interests agst her [Britain's] monopolizing regulations." Contrary to revolutionary expectations, "no new channels [had] opened with other European Nations, and the British channels [were] being narrowed by a refusal of the most natural and valuable one to the U. S." Only by aiding Britain's competitors "till they could contend on equal terms," would the United States be able to break the British monopoly.[12]

Still faced with economic counterarguments, Madison took the mercantilist high ground of advocating the strategic importance of navigation: "If it is expedient for America to have vessels employed in commerce at all, it will be proper that she have enough to answer all the purposes intended; to form a school for seamen, to lay the foundation of a navy, and to be able to supply itself against the interference of foreigners." Compared with the British neomercantilists, Madison gave even higher priority in commercial policy to navigation. He reminded Congress that debate on import duties had demonstrated a commitment to encourage manufactures through "protecting duties" because that had been the policy of the States when the Confederation allowed them to frame their commercial policies individually. The national government's responsibility to maintain the States' commercial policies applied particularly to the inherently national economic interest in "the support of navigation." The discriminatory policy of the States during the Confederation now legitimized the new national government's use of regulatory powers for an anti-British commercial policy. If this navigation policy imposed opportunity costs on American commerce, they unavoidably arose from strategic necessity. To justify this imposition of strategic priorities on a commercial debate, Madison construed British commercial policy as bellicose and anti-American: "Have we not seen her taking one legislative step after another to destroy our commerce? Has not her legislature given discretionary powers to the executive, that so she might be ever on the watch, and ready to seize every advantage the weakness of our situation might expose?"

Madison more readily analyzed Anglo-American trade relations as "commercial warfare" than as advantageous exchange. Britain depended commercially far more on the United States than vice versa, and therefore the United States could more readily "resort to a commercial contest." The United States depended on Great Britain for no item of "subsistance," and the "articles of convenience we must have from her" could be had domestically as Americans "made rapid advances in manufacturing ourselves." Because Britain depended critically on American supplies for the West Indies in time of famine and war, the United States could threaten to withhold supplies or to use the rights of neutral trade in order to gain privileges in British commerce. Great Britain "dreaded" even more a "suspension" of direct Anglo-American trade, for then Britain would lose the American carrying trade, access to American raw materials, and loss of its major export market.[13]

Madison's policy of commercial discrimination reached its political highpoint during the first session of the First Congress. The House approved tonnage duties and tariffs discriminating between countries with and without commercial treaties, but the Senate would only approve a differential between domestic and foreign shipping. Foreign vessels bore tonnage duties nearly ten times those for American vessels, and they could not engage in interstate trade. Discounts of 10 percent applied to the duty on goods imported in American ships, and explicitly protectionist duties bore on a number of goods. The commercial policy actually legislated was protectionist for American commerce, manufactures, and navigation, but not discriminatory *among* foreign nations' trade with the United States.[14]

In May 1790, in the name of reestablishing reciprocity in Anglo-American trade, Madison revived his strategy to discriminate against British commerce. Once again he called for discriminatory tonnage duties on the vessels of nations not in commercial treaty with the United States. When that proposal met strong opposition, he proposed a policy of reciprocal discrimination, whereby ships and goods from a foreign nation would be prohibited trade with the United States on the same terms that trade from the United States was prohibited in that nation's dominions. Now Madison found himself confronted by forthright arguments from liberal economy and even citations of Adam Smith. Madison replied that such arguments "went not only against the present bill, but against the passing of any bill whatever to regulate trade. It would seem as if gentlemen wished to leave our commerce, as they say, to regulate itself, but in fact to be regulated by other nations . . . As a maritime nation, the navigation act of great Britain was considered by the very author quoted by the gentleman from Georgia (Mr. Jackson) one of the wisest measures in her whole political economy."[15] This time, however, the initial proposal failed in the House as well. Defeated there, Madison arranged to have the issue of the encouragement of navigation included in Washington's address to open the next session of Congress.[16] The House referred the matter to the secretary of state, and the eventual result was Jefferson's 1793 Report on Commerce.

Commercial Policy and Political Partisanship

National political partisanship took shape in the debate over commercial policy during Washington's first administration. The federalists used liberal political economy to criticize the republicans' policy of commercial discrimination against Great Britain. In response, the republicans forthrightly acknowledged the political nature of that policy in order to make it immune to liberal criticisms and to question the patriotism of the federalists. Republican policy toward commerce inextricably linked it with political questions—such as the debt of diplomatic gratitude owed France from the alliance of 1778, the malfeasance of Great Britain regarding the 1783 Treaty of Paris, and the war over revolutionary republicanism beginning in Europe.[17]

Ironically, the precipitating issue for partisan alignment along lines of commercial policy began with Jefferson's *denial* of French claims to commercial privileges. In official protest to the renewal of the Tonnage Act in 1790, Louis Guillaume Otto, the French chargé d'affaires, had told Jefferson that the measure violated the 1778 Franco-American Treaty of Amity and Commerce because it failed to reciprocate for the exemption from tonnage duties enjoyed by American ships in French ports. Jefferson responded that the treaty's applicable principle was "most favored nation," not reciprocity. American ships enjoyed exemption in French ports along with the ships of other nations having that privilege by treaty, just as the treaty of 1778 assured that French ships bore no heavier duties in American ports than vessels from other nations. Having made this legal point, however, Jefferson recommended that Congress legislate just the exemption that Otto wanted, as reciprocation for the privileges granted (by the prerevolutionary government) in the *arrêts* of 1787 and 1788: "It is essential to cook up some favour which may ensure the continuance of the good dispositions they have towards us."[18]

This proposal to bargain commercial privileges with France led to the first major conflict between Jefferson and Hamilton. Hamilton construed a lack of reciprocity if, in American ports, French ships enjoyed the rights of American ships, while in French ports American ships had no better privileges than those of "the mass of foreign vessels" with privileges pertaining to "'most favored nation.'"[19] Rather than rely on "*ex parte* concessions," there should be "a new Treaty of Commerce with France to extend reciprocal advantages and fix them on a permanent basis." Otherwise, "apparently gratuitous and voluntary exemptions" in France's favor could be "regarded by those who do not partake in them as proofs of an unfriendly temper towards them" and "lead to commercial warfare." "My commercial system," Hamilton wrote Jefferson, "turns very much on giving a free Course to Trade and cultivating good humour with all the world."[20] Hamilton's arguments apparently prevailed in the Senate, which did not enact Jefferson's proposal.

Shortly thereafter, on 1 February 1791, as Hamilton began to draft the Report on Manufactures, Jefferson presented his Report on the American Fisheries to the House of Representatives. This report brought into the open the incipient political cleavage between republicans and federalists over commercial policy. The House had referred Jefferson petitions from the General Court of Massachusetts, and he used the opportunity to reiterate and elaborate for the American public views he had presented the French government in 1788 when successfully seeking the reinstatement of commercial privileges for the American whale fishery. The report addressed the fisheries' feeble revival after being "annihilated during the war." Since then the fisheries had "laboured under many and heavy embarrassments," particularly "heavy duties on their produce abroad, and bounties on that of their competitors: and duties at home on several articles particularly used in the fisheries."[21]

Jefferson calculated that the fisheries' economic viability depended on public support. Even without the commercial disadvantages imposed by other countries, the fishery was "too poor a business to be left to itself, even with the nation[s] the most advantageously situated" (namely, the United Provinces and the United States). On political, not economic, grounds Jefferson recommended public support for the American fisheries, to the degree necessary to compete with the subsidized fisheries of other nations, particularly Great Britain's: "The Cod and Whale Fisheries, carried on by different persons, from different Ports, in different vessels, in different Seas, and seeking different vessels, in different Seas, and seeking different markets, agree in one circumstance, in being as unprofitable to the adventurer, as important to the public." Jefferson used a history of the European fisheries to show that they had increased and declined to the degree that each nation accorded them commercial privileges. In the seventeenth century, the English, faced with new competition from New England, had revived their Newfoundland fishery by a combination of "prohibiting the importation of foreign fish," the remission of duties on fishing supplies, and the elimination of French settlement on Newfoundland. France, "sensible of the necessity of balancing the power of England on the water," "and seeing that her fishermen could not maintain their competition without some public patronage," began a protectionist policy of bounties on French-caught fish and heavy duties on imported foreign fish. Since the War of American Independence, Britain had compensated for the loss of the New England fishery by prohibiting "all foreign fish in their markets," and by a system of heavy bounties subsidizing the growth of the domestic fishery (particularly that for whales).[22]

In these circumstances, Jefferson argued, the profits "were too small to afford a living to the [American] fisherman." Jefferson calculated that the American fisheries had numerous advantages over their European competitors—a proximity to fishing grounds that enabled the use of household labor in processing the fish; the possibility of fishing in winter, "which like household manufactures, employ portions of time which would otherwise be useless"; low costs for vessels, provisions, and supplies. But he insisted that survival of the fisheries depended on supplementing these economic advantages with commercial privileges. Because of their marginal viability, they should be relieved of the fiscal burdens imposed by "Tonnage and Naval duties," as well as "impost duties on Salt[,] on Tea, Rum, Sugar, Molasses[,] hooks, Lines and Leads[,] Duck, Cordage and Cables[,] Iron, Hemp and Twine." The federal government should protect them from competition arising from "the importation of foreign fish." By defining the exchangeability of goods as something other than the relation of supply and demand, Jefferson confronted head-on the liberal counterargument that "the foreign fish received is in exchange for the produce of agriculture": the provisions from American agriculture were more "merchantable" than the foreign fish "received in exchange," and "agriculture has too many markets to be allowed to take away those of the fisheries." Jefferson even asked Congress to consider reshaping the American diet in order to maintain the American fisheries: "The loss of markets abroad may . . . in some degree be compensated by creating markets at home, to which might contribute the constituting fish a part of the military ration in stations not too distant from navigation, a part of the necessary sea-stores of vessels, and the encouraging private individuals to let the fisherman share with the cultivator in furnishing the supplies of the Table."[23]

Jefferson's informants in New England expected "that, without some public aid, those still remaining will continue to withdraw, and this whole commerce be engrossed by a single nation." This prospect of Britain's monopoly of the fishery, and with it an increased predominance in navigation—not the place of the fishery in the American economy—provided the priorities for Jefferson's recommendations. Both Jefferson and Madison appreciated how the priority of navigation in the political economy of the new republic outweighed considerations of what Madison termed the "Republican Distribution of Citizens." Far more so than manufacturers, sailors and fishermen posed categorical problems as republican citizens. Sailors might be crucial "in the intercourse, by which nations are enlightened and refined," but their lives were "distinguished by the hardest condition of humanity." On every count that favored agricultural occupations in "health, virtue, intelligence and competency," as well as "liberty and safety," workers in maritime occupations were disadvantaged. Yet the United States had to impose "counter-regulations" to deal with Britain's commercial policy to increase its navigation "on the ruins of ours." If the fisheries lost their markets, then the United States would lose one of its "three nurs-eries for forming seamen"—the others being the coasting trade, "al-ready on a safe footing," and the "carrying trade[,] the only resource of indemnification for what we lose in the other."[24]

If anything, Jefferson, like Madison, gave a higher priority to naviga-tion in American commercial policy than the British neomercantilists gave to theirs. He measured the success of American policy by the extent that American shipping displaced British, and he advocated a more discriminatory and more exclusive navigation law than that of Great Britain. It would favor France at Britain's expense, and it would apply to all British shipping, not just that to the West Indies. British neomercantilists gave priority to navigation for strategic reasons; they appreciated that such a policy had negative implications for commerce. However, Jefferson maintained a prerevolutionary identification of navigation with commercial policy. He wanted the "resumption" of the American carrying trade to "take effect so gradually as not to endanger the loss of produce for the want of transportation," but he insisted that the resumption would depend on the political creation of commercial opportunity.[25]

———

HAWKESBURY and the other British neomercantilists faulted the Americans for a crude, retaliatory mercantilism. The Committee for Trade had resented the States' discrimination against British trade and painstakingly detailed such legislation state-by-state.[26] In 1788 and 1789 the committee had conducted hearings to determine the effect of these measures on British trading and manufactures. The committee noted that whereas numerous state acts had discriminated explicitly against British trade, the tonnage and impost acts of the new federal Congress distinguished only between American and foreign shipping. The committee received a strong representation from Liverpool advis-ing retaliation in the form of equivalent tonnage duties for American vessels. Liverpool merchants warned that American discrimination would increase unless Britain reacted to assert its interests, but they advised against retaliatory duties on imports from America because they would reduce American ability to purchase British goods. They recommended instead that there be an export duty, equivalent to the American remittance of 10 percent, on goods shipped from Britain in American vessels. The committees from other ports advised caution not to provoke more forthright American discrimination, especially because the measures to date had had so little invidious effect. As the committee of Bristol merchants noted, "to make trade between two independent nations mutually convenient the benefits must be reciprocal." Having heard these and other representations from committees of merchants trading to America, the committee concluded that the U.S. legislation imposed affordable costs on British merchants.[27]

The committee considered the federal trade legislation to be less restrictive and arbitrary than that of the individual states. In its report on the impost and tonnage duties, the committee benignly explained how the new Constitution had given the United States a creditable commercial "system," which provided a reasonable basis for commercial negotiations. The Committee for Trade paid close attention to the threat of American retaliation against British trade policy, but it shunned recommendations for Britain to use retaliation. The committee consistently forbore American political resentment and impulsiveness.[28]

The committee's informants in American ports reported that the republican mercantilism identified with Jefferson and Madison posed the chief menace to the mutual advantages of Anglo-American commerce, because it linked questions of navigation with those of commerce. The committee's report on the American acts sharply distinguished between their effects on commerce and on navigation and blandly contemplated that "if all the colonies belonging to European nations in America and the West Indies were to become independent, Great Britain would undoubtedly have the greatest share of the commerce carried on with them." The committee called for an elimination of American privileges in British commerce, not in order to undercut American economic potential, but in order to have a freer market in such staples as tobacco and rice, and thereby encourage Britain's role as an entrepôt. The committee confined its concern with navigation exclusively to the colonial trade, which it equated "with the freight from one American state to another." It advised against the imposition of countervailing tonnage duties on American vessels, because Britain partially depended on American shipping to carry its American imports. Because most American imports were destined for manufacturing or reexport, and British shipping only adequately supplied British home consumption, the support of British navigation should not burden foreign trade excessively.[29]

Hamilton's Report on Manufactures and
The Wealth of Nations

In the *Federalist Papers* Alexander Hamilton had consistently subordinated commercial questions to considerations of power. His Report on Manufactures provided an opportunity to develop the tactics for his apparently mercantilist strategy in political economy. To determine how to encourage manufactures, Hamilton looked to the means used by other countries and provided a checklist of mercantilist possibilities: "protecting duties," "prohibitions of rival articles," "prohibitions of the exportation of the materials of manufactures," "drawbacks," "pecuniary bounties," and "premiums." He considered the negative regulations to be generally inadvisable for the United States because they inadequately balanced constraints on competition with considerations of revenue and supply. He favored positive measures such as premiums and bounties to encourage manufactures because they could directly "stimulate and uphold new enterprises, increasing the chances of profit, and diminishing the risks of loss, in the first attempts," without at the same time raising prices for domestic consumers. Unlike protective duties, bounties did not augment domestic demand through scarcity, and they often provided an "expedient for uniting the encouragement of a new object of agriculture with that of a new object of manufacturing."[30]

Congress's original injunction to the secretary of the treasury, on 15 January 1790, to prepare a report on manufactures had emphasized the strategic need "to render the United States, independent on foreign nations for military and other essential supplies."[31] Hamilton went beyond this narrow concern with strategic autarky to consider the possible role of manufactures in developing the American economy, and he canvassed widely for information on this problem. He appointed Tench Coxe, the most prominent American advocate and authority on manufactures, as assistant secretary of the treasury to assist him with the report. Coxe presented his interim views as "A Brief Examination of Lord Sheffield's Observations on the Commerce of the United States," and it appeared widely in magazines, newspapers, and as a pamphlet. Coxe argued that the United States need not depend on British manufactures and that therefore the nation ought to adopt a policy of encouragement for manufactures in order to achieve national economic self-sufficiency. To compound his contradiction, he concluded that such a policy would force Britain to lift its restrictions on Anglo-American trade. Coxe could disregard such apparent contradictions because he ignored questions of relative costs and benefits with respect to supply and demand.[32]

Coxe's preliminary draft of the report was only a few pages long, whereas Hamilton's first draft was several dozen pages. Coxe's took the desirability of manufactures for granted: he simply listed eight "considerations, which have produced more favorable opinions concerning" "the expediency of encouraging manufactures in the United States":

The advantages of the landholder in furnishing raw materials, subsistence, fuel and other supplies to the workmen—the support which the fisheries derive from them by their consumption of articles drawn from the ocean—the assistance given to external commerce by promoting the importation of raw materials and furnishing manufactured commodities for exportation—their favorable effects on population by inducing the emigration of foreign artists and laborers—the introduction of money by offering a new & promising field to capitalists of other nations—the promotion of individual industry and oeconomy which naturally result from manufactures and particularly when engrafted upon an extensive agriculture—their encreasing and rendering more certain the means of defence and other articles of prime necessity and lastly the Reduction of the prices of convenient & essential supplies for public & private use, which has already taken place on the appearance of competition from the American manufacturer.[33]

The remainder of Coxe's draft dealt with the various means available to encourage manufactures: protective duties, bounties, patents for imported technology, drawbacks, and free importation of raw materials.

Hamilton took little exception to Coxe's recommendations on the various means to encourage manufactures, but he immediately raised liberal criticisms of any policy involving economic privileges, including the encouragement of manufactures. This concern with alternatives to Coxe's unquestioning protectionism appeared in the first of Hamilton's redraftings of the report, and he elaborated on it in subsequent drafts until it took final form as a fabricated quotation paraphrasing Smith.[34]

The Report on Manufactures simultaneously presented the most forthright American expression of a *metropolitan* mercantilist economic policy *and* the most elaborate and best informed American reading of Smith's liberal political economy. Although Hamilton's privileging of manufactures usually strikes commentators as mercantilist, Smith's discussion of the efficiency of market relations determined Hamilton's argument for the encouragement of manufactures. Exactly like the British neomercantilists, Hamilton took Smith to be generally authoritative in political economy, and therefore, just as they had, he conscientiously and self-consciously attended to the inconsistencies between his own recommendations of policies and the principles, argument, and theory of *The Wealth of Nations*. Both Hamilton and the British neomercantilists presented their inconsistencies with Smith as such particular exceptions—navigation for the British neomercantilists, public credit for Hamilton—as to validate the broader lessons of Smith's political economy. As critical strategic considerations for the respective countries, both navigation and public credit justified exceptions to liberal political economy. The United States needed public credit for its sheer survival; besides defense, the national government provided no costly services. The country's fiscal strategy gave priority to the capability to secure "loans in times of public danger, especially from foreign war."[35] In large part Hamilton recommended the encouragement of infant industries as a crucial tactic in his strategy for public credit.

Hamilton self-consciously lapsed as an economic liberal in his confidence in people's psychological readiness to seize economic advantage. Against Smith's assumption of a fundamental economic rationality implicit in the "propensity in human nature . . . to truck, barter, and exchange one thing for another," Hamilton argued the Humean point that "habit and the spirit of imitation—the fear of want of success in untried enterprises" made economic development "more tardy than might consist with the interest either of individuals or of the Society."[36] This entrepreneurial inertia critically concerned Hamilton because he wrote the Report on Manufactures during a period of exceptionally large foreign investment in response to the issue of securities to fund the public debt. These investments might "merely . . . give a temporary spring to foreign commerce," rather than "produce solid and permanent improvements." Hamilton's fiscal purposes in the encouragement of manufactures narrowly focused on getting holders of public securities to invest them in the Society for Establishing Useful Manufactures and thereby moderate speculation.[37] Such fiscal priority complemented Hamilton's broader framework of liberal political economy, which condoned the encouragement of infant industries only as an exception to the efficiency of free markets. A liberal political economy could check both the republicans' policy of commercial discrimination and Congress's inchoate protectionism.

Most of Hamilton's rationale for the encouragement of manufactures derived from liberal political economy. He disavowed protectionism for established industries and would grant privileges only to infant industries. Hamilton's infant industries sought domestic, not overseas, markets. The division of labor between farmers and manufacturers made it possible for "the Produce and Revenue of the Society" to be "greater than they could possibly be, without such establishments [manufactures]." The progressive division of labor encouraged "greater skill and dexterity" as people made "constant and undivided application to a single object." This specialization made greater "oeconomy of time" possible: "A man occupied on a single object will have it more in his power, and will be more naturally led to exert his imagination in devising methods to facilitate and abridge labour, than if he were perplexed by a variety of independent and dissimilar operations." By definition, manufacturing increased the sheer diversity of employment and thereby increased the "fund of national Industry" as people responded to the "greater scope for the diversity of talents and dispositions, which discriminate men from each other." Manufacturing increased the demand for different kinds of labor, for subsistence and raw materials, and for entrepreneurship.[38]

Unlike most of his contemporaries in political economy, who made overseas commerce the privileged concern, Hamilton had none of the typically mercantilist anxiety about shortcomings of domestic demand for manufactures. On the contrary, he wanted the growth of manufactures to increase domestic demand for agricultural production so that it be "steady" and "vigorous" rather than "fluctuating" and "feeble." External markets for agricultural production were unreliable for political and economic reasons. All nations sought "to supply themselves with subsistence from their own soils," just as they sought "to procure from the source, the raw materials necessary for their own fabrics." This "spirit of monopoly" had the irrational goal of "selling everything and buying nothing," and it ignored the fact of commercial life that "the foreign demand for the products of Agricultural Countries is, in a great degree, rather casual and occasional, than certain and constant." An increasing agricultural surplus posed a liability for American economic growth because it depended on inefficient and unreliable markets overseas to absorb it. Manufactures might draw off laborers from agriculture and slow the taking up of land, but the "more certain demand for the surplus produce of the soil" would "cause the lands which were in cultivation to be better improved and more productive."[39] Hamilton would use political means to shape the market, but he intended to encourage innovative entrepreneurship rather than to achieve some ideal balance of supply and demand in staple trades or to protect existing but inefficient industries. His preoccupations with questions of efficiency and relative advantage made it possible to consider the domestic market as the most promising for economic development.

Hamilton gave lip service to agriculture's intrinsically "strong claim to pre-eminence over every kind of industry," "as the primary and most certain source of national supply—as the immediate and chief source of subsistence to man—as the principle source of those materials which constitute the nutriment of other kinds of labor—as including a state most favourable to the freedom and independence of the human mind—one, perhaps, most conducive to the multiplication of the human species." But he would not concede that agriculture had "a title to anything like an exclusive predilection" as "the only productive species of industry." To make these qualifications, Hamilton summarized Smith's analysis of "Agricultural Systems" of political economy in order to show that such ideas depended on "subtile and paradoxical" "general arguments" that were impossible to verify "by any accurate detail of facts and calculations." Paraphrasing Smith, Hamilton insisted that increases of capital "depend upon the savings made out of the revenues of those, who furnish or manage that which is at any time employed, whether in Agriculture, or in Manufactures, or in any other way." The revenues of society could only increase through "some improvement in the productive powers of the useful labour, which actually exists within it, or by some increase in the quantity of such labour."[40]

Hamilton disavowed arguing for the productive superiority of manufacturing over agriculture, but he pointed out several ways in which it had greater potential to contribute to the increase of national wealth. Its capability "of greater subdivision and simplicity of operation than that of Cultivators" provided greater opportunity for "improvement of its productive powers, whether to be derived from an accession of Skill, or from the application of ingenious machinery." Manufactures, with their "constant and regular" labor, allowed fuller realization of productive capability than the inherently "periodical and occasional" character of agricultural labor. The ineluctability of natural processes in agriculture allowed "more examples of remissness" among farmers than among "artificers," who could not thrive at their employments without "ingenuity." But Hamilton raised these considerations, which he admitted to be "so vague and general, as well as so abstract," only to "counterbalance" the comparably vague, general, and abstract arguments for the superior productivity of agriculture. The question of relative productivity for the conventionally denominated sectors of agriculture, manufacturing, and commerce was weak in theory and empirically unanswerable. Measurement applied to the profitable outcomes of individual applications of capital, labor, and technology. Such measures showed that both agriculture and manufacturing provided opportunities for "profitable employment."[41] Because he had argued that neither agriculture nor manufacturing had a privileged place in the theory of political economy, Hamilton could recommend public encouragement of manufactures.

The troublesome question for Hamilton was encouragement, not manufactures. The report started with a lengthy paraphrase of *The Wealth of Nations* to explain how "the extraordinary patronage of Government, to accelerate the growth of manufactures, is, in fact, to endeavor, by force and art, to transfer the natural current of industry from a more, to a less beneficial channel . . . the quicksighted guidance of private interest, will, if left to itself, infallibly find its own way to the most profitable employment: and 'tis by such employment, that the public prosperity will be most effectually promoted." He appreciated that his argument for the encouragement of manufactures as a way to stimulate domestic demand for agricultural production could be construed as an inefficient division of labor for the United States:

> However true it might be, that a state, which possessing large tracts of vacant and fertile territory, was at the same time secluded from foreign commerce, would find its interest and the interest of Agriculture, in diverting a part of its population from tillage to Manufactures, yet it will not follow, that the same is true of a state which having such vacant and fertile territory, has at the same time, ample opportunity of procuring from abroad, on good terms, all the fabrics of which it stands in need, for the supply of its inhabitants. The power of doing this, at least secures the great advantage of a division of labour, leaving the farmer free to pursue exclusively the culture of his land, and enabling him to procure with its products the manufactured supplies requisite either to his wants or to his enjoyments. And though it should be true that, in settled countries, the diversification of Industry is conducive to an increase in the productive powers of labour, and to an augmentation of revenue and capital, yet it is scarcely conceivable that there can be any thing of so solid and permanent advantage to an uncultivated and unpeopled country as to convert its wastes into cultivated and inhabited districts. If the Revenue, in the meantime, should be less, the Capital, in the event, must be greater.

In this liberal argument with himself, Hamilton conceded that "if the system of perfect liberty to industry and commerce were the prevailing system of nations," "a free exchange, mutually beneficial of the commodities which each [country] was able to supply, on the best terms, might be carried on between them, supporting in full vigour the industry of each." He also grudgingly conceded that freely operating markets would eventually produce the results he hoped to achieve through intervention. Hamilton accepted the postulate "that Industry, if left to itself, will naturally find its way to the most useful and profitable employment." Despite the relative lack of development in American manufactures thus far, he repeatedly presented liberal arguments against his own policy. He conceded that "every measure, which obstructs the free competition of foreign commodities," imposed questionable costs on consumers. The encouragement of manufactures had a "tendency to give a monopoly of advantages to particular classes" and thereby denied others the alternative "to procure the requisite supplies of manufactured articles on better terms from foreigners, than from their own Citizens."[42]

Presented with such hypothetical objections to his proposed economic strategy, Hamilton might have resorted to a conventional mercantilist restatement of economic nationalism: because a nation's wealth was finite, it should be spent at home rather than enrich the people of other nations. Hamilton repudiated such arguments in favor of a developmental strategy. He could only justify the encouragement of manufactures if it initiated new ways to produce wealth eventually sustainable without governmental privilege. In contrast to congressional protectionists, he never advocated privileges for established industries needing protection from more efficient foreign competition.[43]

Hamilton presented the Report on Manufactures as a self-conscious exception to an otherwise liberal political economy. Smith was the only author quoted in the report. Hamilton also paraphrased him for paragraphs at a time, and a large proportion of the order of argument in the report had close parallels with sections of *The Wealth of Nations*.[44] Because he held Smith to be so authoritative—on the potential of the domestic economy for development, on the complement of agricultural and manufacturing interests, and on the efficiency of the division of labor—Hamilton compromised his conviction that a free market for demand and supply guaranteed economic efficiency and hence increased wealth.

Hamilton was the preeminent neomercantilist in the United States and therefore its most committed liberal political economist as well. In the Report on Public Credit, he had shown just how much autonomy he would grant market relations to determine the relations between buyer and seller. One of the ancillary benefits of funding the public debt would be a "stock" that "passes current as specie." This reliable medium of exchange would allow the extension of trade because it enlarged the capital on which merchants could draw while allowing them to "trade for smaller profits" because the stock earned interest from the government "when unemployed." This increased enterprise on the part of merchants would in turn increase demand for the products of agriculture and manufacturing. To provide these monetary benefits, the public debt needed "an *adequate* and *stable* value." Otherwise the debt was "a mere commodity, and a precarious one," which would distract capital from commerce, agriculture, and manufactures rather than mobilize it for economic development.[45] For the stock issued on the public debt to provide a "*substitute* for money," there had to be a free market to establish its value.

Although well aware of the counterarguments based on supposed justice, Hamilton insisted that such a market depended on an absence of privileges among public creditors. The argument for discrimination found injustice in the profits that the buyer had eventually after a series of purchases originating from a presumedly needy seller: "It would be hard to aggravate the misfortune of the first owner, who, probably through necessity, parted with his property at so great a loss, by obliging him to contribute to the profit of the person, who had speculated on his distresses." In response, Hamilton insisted that the market gave no privilege to sequence of purchase. At every stage of transactions on the public debt, people calculated the likelihood of the government's meeting its contractual obligation: "Every buyer therefore stands exactly in the place of the seller, has the same rights with him to the identical sum expressed in the security . . . Whatever necessity the seller may have been under, was occasioned by the government, in not making a proper provision for its debts." Discrimination in favor of "primitive proprietors" would give them "an advantage, to which they had no equitable pretension," while doing "real injury" to "purchasers" by "breach of contract." Both original holders and subsequent purchasers, in deciding respectively to sell and to buy, had made the same kind of calculations, assumed the same kinds of opportunity costs, and realized the same kinds of advantages and disadvantages. In ways too various to generalize, members of both groups had made both more and less money than they might have by hypothetically different market behavior.[46]

Hamilton's fiscal system hinged on the continuation of a large overseas commerce because virtually all of the federal government's revenue came from duties on imports. Yet Hamilton never wrote a Report on Commerce.[47] He implicitly agreed with Sheffield that the relatively open trade between the United States and Great Britain allowed something close to a maximization of mutual benefit in foreign trade. Like Sheffield, though with quite different inferences for commercial policy, he had taken Smith's lesson that navigation was the least productive form of investment.[48] Although he approved of protective tariffs for particular infant industries, Hamilton emphasized the fiscal need for British trade: large-scale imports meant large revenues from duties. The priority of this fiscal consideration, with its premium on a robust commerce, may account for the repetition throughout the report of a liberal counterargument *against* the encouragement of manufactures.

———

IN HIS FIRST recorded reference to Smith, in 1790, Jefferson recommended *The Wealth of Nations* as the "best book extant" in political economy. But Jefferson characteristically neglected Smith's economic analysis of commercial relations and emphasized its political implications. He associated Smith as readily with Locke, Montesquieu, and Beccaria as with Malthus and Say.[49] Jefferson's only expression of serious engagement with Smith's thought dealt with the highly politicized questions of money and banking. On the whole he found *The Wealth of Nations* "prolix and tedious"; decades later he would rejoice that the "principles" of Smith's once "novel" system were eventually "assented to as soon as proposed." Then, instead of *The Wealth of Nations*, he could recommend the generalities of his translation of Destutt de Tracy's *Treatise on Political Economy*, with its much more cursory analysis of price mechanisms and of the accumulation of capital and its infrequent use of quantification to make a point.[50]

It was not commerce so much as *markets* to which republicans—preeminently Madison and Jefferson—had a conceptually blocking aversion. Whenever they affirmed their allegiance to principles of free trade, it was to introduce proposals for the imposition of economic regulation, not to recommend the liberalization of markets. These regulations invariably took the form of commercial discrimination against Great Britain in order to displace British shipping and to encourage American trade with France. Jefferson's analysis of American commercial opportunities dealt with political questions of reciprocal *regulations* of commercial advantage and disadvantage, not relative market advantages. His model of "free" commerce was identical with Madison's "natural" commerce—bilateral exchange between manufacturing metropole and staple producing colony. He had a simplistic notion of the division of labor on the basis of the natural endowments of whole nations for the production of staples. He emphasized the promise of introducing new crops, rather than improving the efficiency of existing production. His mercantilist analysis sought to identify underdeveloped natural resources having a highly elastic demand in Europe. Hence his advocacy, after a stay of several weeks in Provence, of the conversion of southern agriculture to the growing of olive trees. He observed that olive oil had a limitless market in Europe and predicted that the trees' cultivation would be less destructive of slave life than the growing of rice. Jefferson seldom wrote extensively on the economic and social relations of agricultural life, though some of his brief passages on the topic have provided shibboleths for American social and political thought. The industry on whose commerce Jefferson expressed himself most fully was the archetypically mercantilist one of the fisheries.[51]

Hamiltonian Liberalism and the Jay Treaty

O N 16 DECEMBER 1793, as "his last major act as Secretary of State," Jefferson presented the House of Representatives his Report on the Privileges and Restrictions on the Commerce of the United States in Foreign Countries. The House had requested the report, now long delayed, as an alternative to adoption of Madison's renewed proposal for a discriminatory tonnage duty, after Washington informed Congress in February 1791 of Gouverneur Morris's unsuccessful efforts to initiate commercial diplomacy with Great Britain. The House had also asked Jefferson to recommend "measures which he should think proper to be adopted for the improvement of the commerce and navigation" of the United States. Jefferson had completed an initial draft of the report during the recess of Congress in the summer of 1791, but a series of diplomatic and political considerations—Britain's sending George Hammond to investigate outstanding issues from the Treaty of Paris, then Genêt's arrival with proposals for a commercial treaty with the new French republic, and, finally, the prospect of a strengthened Republican majority in the Third Congress—resulted in his deferral and redrafting of the report.[1] In the meantime, the outbreak of war between France and Britain on 1 February 1793 jeopardized the neutrality of American shipping in fact as well as principle. Britain aggressively rejected American claims to neutrality in its trade with France, and France used the United States as a base for its privateers.

Jefferson's report on commercial discrimination against the United States largely ignored the ramifications of contemporaneous international politics. Even though it made his report a year and a half out of date, and anachronistic in relation to the French republic, he used the summer of 1792 as his cutoff point for commercial statistics. (The republic had adopted a more mercantilist commercial policy than that of the liberal monarchy—one less tolerant of privileges for American trade. It had also repudiated the Eden Treaty of 1786.)[2] The report identified the United States' major exports by order of value: breadstuffs, tobacco, rice, wood, salted fish, pot and pearl ash, foreign goods, salted meats, indigo, horses and mules, whale oil, flax seed, tar products, and live provisions. Britain, France, Spain, the United Netherlands, and Portugal, in that order with their respective colonies, took nearly all of the United States' exports, with Britain taking almost half and France almost one-quarter. However, Britain reexported most of what it imported from the United States. By definition the report dealt at length only with the export trade of the United States, but it also listed importations to the United States by country of origin—and showed that Great Britain and its colonies accounted for almost 80 percent. Yet American tonnage coming from France and its dominions nearly tripled that coming from Great Britain.

Having introduced his report with these gross commercial data, Jefferson then surveyed the applicability of commercial regulations, country-by-country, to the trade of the United States. The report showed which items each country admitted duty-free, the relative discouragement of other goods by duties, and the prohibitions of still others. Most of these regulations applied generally to each country's foreign trade, but the report also identified privileges for American trade in particular countries—such as exclusive permission to sell whale oil in France, or the preferential admission of American pot and pearl ashes, bar iron, wood, and naval stores to Britain. With respect to navigation, the report generalized about each country's reexport of American goods, as well as its policy toward receiving non-American goods in American ships, and its policy toward the admission of foreign ships, both in the metropole and in its colonies.

The summation of this survey presented a patchwork of restrictions. Britain's Corn Laws usually excluded breadstuffs from Britain but not from its West Indian colonies, whereas metropolitan France admitted them but its West Indian colonies did not. Portugal prohibited the importation of rice, but Britain only duted it. France and Britain effectively prohibited salted provisions, but France allowed some of them into its islands. Britain and Portugal virtually prohibited whale products, but France admitted them preferentially. France and England applied import duties to tobacco, while Spain and Portugal prohibited its importation.

Britain's commercial policy stood out in the report for its restrictiveness on American navigation. American ships, once purchased by Britons, could not trade with the United States. American ships could only carry U.S. products to Great Britain, and the Navigation Act still prohibited U.S. ships from carrying manufactures to Britain. Executive order, rather than legislation, regulated the rest of Anglo-American trade. American ships could not trade at all with the British West Indies, and only British ships could carry goods between the British West Indies and the United States. No legal trade, either in goods or in shipping, could pass between the United States and Britain's North American colonies. Britain's restrictions on American commerce had "already lost us in our commerce with that country and its possessions, between eight and nine hundred vessels of near 40,000 tons burden."[3]

The report dealt with commercial privileges as well as discrimination—apparently the two alternatives in commercial policy. The report wishfully proposed that commercial restrictions might be lessened by "friendly arrangements":

> Instead of embarrassing commerce under piles of regulating laws, duties and prohibitions, could it be relieved from all its shackles in all parts of the world, could every country be employed in producing that which nature has best fitted it to produce, and each be free to exchange with others mutual surpluses for mutual wants, the greatest mass possible would then be produced of those things which contribute to human life and human happiness.

Free trade was only wishful thinking, but the reduction of restrictions through reciprocity in privileges had some likelihood. The United States "could reasonably expect welcome and friendly treatment in every market" because its products met needs rather than offered competition: "The commodities we offer are either necessaries of life, or materials for manufacture, or convenient subjects of revenue; and we take in exchange, either manufactures, when they have received the last finish of art and industry, or mere luxuries." However, if a country continued in "its system of prohibitions, duties and regulations," then the United States must "protect our citizens, their commerce and navigation, by counter prohibitions, duties and regulations, also. Free commerce and navigation are not to be given in exchange for restrictions and vexations; nor are they likely to produce a relaxation in them."[4]

In the name of "reciprocity" Jefferson proposed a strategy to reduce restrictions on American commerce and navigation by exactly matching those of other nations. "Where a nation imposes high duties on our productions, or prohibits them altogether," the United States should exclude those goods for which there was already American competition, and gradually raise duties on other goods to encourage the substitution of American production and foreign supplies. However, having suggested such tactics as means to reduce restrictions on foreign commerce, Jefferson further recommended them as part of a domestic program to encourage manufactures. Jefferson apparently distanced himself from the Report on Manufactures by calling for the states, not the federal government, to provide direct encouragement for "house-hold" manufactures, but the economic rationale closely resembled Hamilton's. Jefferson conceded that there might be "some inconvenience" during the transition to this policy of strict reciprocity in discrimination, but "these inconveniences are nothing when weighed against the loss of wealth and loss of force, which will follow our perseverance in the plan of indiscrimination."

Navigation demanded forthright public support.[5] If American ships could not import non-American goods into a particular country, then the ships from that country should not be allowed to bring foreign goods into U.S. ports. If a particular nation prohibited American ships from trading with its colonies, then that nation's ships should not be allowed to trade between the United States and those colonies, either. Viewed this way, the priority of navigation in commercial policy inextricably linked political and economic questions, and it implied that commercial relations *resulted* from political decisions. Jefferson had subtly implied this linkage in the sheer organization of his report. By presenting a statistical overview of American commerce before he surveyed the foreign restrictions on it, Jefferson implied that the measurable commercial patterns *resulted* from those restrictions.

Immediately after the House went into Committee of the Whole to discuss Jefferson's report, Madison proposed a series of resolutions "to narrow the sphere of our commerce with those nations who see proper not to meet us on terms of reciprocity." Madison equated such restrictions with effective "regulation of commerce," which, he reminded Congress, was the most important reason for the adoption of the Constitution. Madison's proposals closely followed the recommendations of Jefferson's report: additional duties should be placed on the manufactures of nations not in commercial treaty with the United States; additional tonnage duties should be levied on their vessels as well; if a nation would not allow American goods to be imported in foreign vessels, then ships from other foreign nations should not be able to carry that nation's products to the United States. However, rather than reciprocate the prohibition of American vessels from trade with the British West Indies, Madison proposed an "extraordinary" tonnage duty. The resolutions had the threefold intent to encourage competition among foreign suppliers, to increase the substitution of American products, and to "obtain an equitable share in carrying our own produce." Madison expected that a policy of reciprocal commercial restrictions would became a "contest of self-denial," for which the United States enjoyed economic advantages. It exported goods indispensable abroad for subsistence and livelihoods, and it largely imported luxuries, by definition dispensable.[6]

The immediate response to Madison's proposals came from William Loughton Smith of South Carolina, who delivered an extraordinarily devastating daylong attack on the substantiation, rationale, and policy of Jefferson's report. Hamilton provided Smith with much of his commercial information and almost certainly worked with him on the speech itself, which amounted to the Report on Commerce he never formally presented. Smith's speech insisted that if the issue were the regulation of commerce, then the discussion should be strictly commercial, "disengaging the inquiry from all topics of a political nature."[7]

It simply was not true that, while Britain had an "unfriendly, illiberal, and persecuting policy," France had a "generous policy" toward commerce with the United States. France allowed American trade special treatment only with regard to whale products, while Britain allowed the United States a number of exceptional privileges with respect to import and export trade with its West Indian colonies and with respect to exports and navigation to Great Britain. At least six staples entered Britain from the United States with lower duties than from elsewhere; some other goods were simply exempt from the duties applied to trade from other countries. American ships carrying American goods entered Britain on nearly the same terms as British ships, rather than bear all the usual charges on foreign vessels. The British West Indian colonies admitted several products from the United States though prohibited from any other foreign country, and several British West Indian products could be exported to the United States but to no other foreign destination.[8]

These criticisms met Jefferson on his own ground of formal commercial discriminations. However, most of Smith's speech introduced an economic calculation of relative (and hypothetically alternative) costs and benefits utterly lacking in Jefferson's report. Jefferson had mapped trade on the basis of its regulations, but he had not analyzed the marketability of goods or shown how foreign regulations affected their actual exchange.[9] Smith looked at prices and the likelihood of sales regardless of the intent of regulations to make them more or less likely. For example, in the case of breadstuffs the Corn Laws kept foreign grains out of Britain except when the domestic price reached a high level, but France allowed the free importation of grain. Yet, Smith argued, "the result of both systems [is] the same to us. In neither country is our flour saleable with advantage but in times of particular scarcity." Using prices of grain on the Philadelphia market and adding the costs of shipment to France, Smith could show that most of the time French supplies kept demand for American grain below a profitable price. Conversely, the Committee for Trade's own figures forecast a shortfall in British grain supplies, which promised a better market for

American grains there. Meanwhile, France prohibited the importation of any foreign grain into its West Indian colonies, while Britain allowed the entry of American grain exclusively.[10]

Where commercial regulations allowed trade at all, the opportunities for profit, Smith argued, not the formalities of regulation, determined the conduct of commerce. Duties on products only partially affected their marketability. For example, in the case of rice, the duties of France and Britain were not the major constraints on American sales. In Western Europe rice was a food of the well-to-do, and it was a principle of business that "the addition which is made to the price of a luxury of the wealthier classes is no great obstacle to its consumption by them."[11]

Rather than follow Jefferson and Madison in veering from a wistful desire for universal free trade to a mechanical policy of reciprocal discrimination, Smith urged the calculation of real economic opportunities in a commercial world where governments took for granted the desirability of monopoly. For example, in the case of the fisheries, "the principle upon which each [France and Britain] proceeds is the monopoly of her own market to the productions of her own fisheries." Their differences in commercial regulations regarding the fisheries resulted from differences in their economic, territorial, and political resources, which required different tactics to execute the same monopolistic strategy. Because Britain could meet its own demand, it prohibited the importation of salted fish to either the metropole or its colonies. France allowed the importation of fish on payment of a duty, but it intended to use the proceeds of that duty in conjunction with a bounty on French fish to secure eventually a French monopoly of its own supply. France granted privileged admission to American whale oil only in order to prevent the migration of American whalers to Britain while France used bounties "to erect her own whale fishery on the ruins of that of the United States."[12]

The crucial commercial fact was that "Great Britain is a more important customer to us than France." Smith's speech chided Jefferson with heavy irony for using Sheffield's *Observations* to show "'that the greatest part of what she receives from us is re-exported to other countries, under the useless charges of an intermediate deposit and double voyage.'" Sheffield's information related to when Britain *had* political control over America, which it used to maintain a commercial monopoly. Jefferson tried to have it both ways: he presented it as a grievance that Britain now imported less tobacco and rice than before the Revolution (when they were enumerated), and he complained that too many of America's exports still passed through their former imperial entrepôt. With American trade free, more of it went directly to Europe.

Worse than the inapplicable information on reexports in the report were its "false principles" in explaining their significance. What continued to pass through the British entrepôt was the calculated result of relative economic advantage. Because American merchants had access to the same countries to which British merchants reexported American goods, it was a reasonable inference that "we shall carry them there ourselves, in every case in which it is our interest to do so." However, to make it worthwhile for a merchant to conduct such direct trade, there had to be a basis of exchange, a desirable supply abroad, not just a need there for American goods. Otherwise, the direct trade would be a waste of shipping resources and an inefficient use of capital. If markets worked at all, then presumably the British entrepôt provided crucial mechanisms, particularly in its scale of capital, for the sale of American goods. Britain acted as "intermediary" in American trade as a "result of the natural course of trade." By "extending, instead of abridging our commerce," this "intervention" was "no less beneficial to us, than if she were herself the consumer of the commodities."[13]

Smith's speech brought this same liberal perspective to bear on the supposed "grievance" of Britain's predominance as the supplier of three-quarters of American imports. "Every effort to turn the tide of trade from Great Britain" amounted to a public program for the encouragement of *foreign* manufactures. With presumable irony, Smith noted the lack of sufficient support in the United States for "an efficacious system of encouragement of home manufactures," so "every effort to turn the tide of trade from Great Britain to other countries, will amount to a premium upon the manufactures and productions of those countries, at the expense of the people of the United States." Economic, not political, reasons explained the large scale of Britain's exports to the United States: British manufacturers made the widest range of goods, at the most affordable prices, and the large capital of British merchants enabled them to extend credit on the most attractive terms. It might be hypothetically desirable to have more suppliers in American markets, because the competition would presumably improve the terms of credit, as well as the quality and variety of goods. But American markets had already been open to foreign suppliers for a decade and a half, and "as trade has been hitherto left to find its own channels, the presumption is, that it has flowed into those where its natural relations and its best interests have led."[14]

Even a policy of discrimination, Smith reminded Congress, had to take markets into account. If Congress legislated new markets, they would have a new set of relative costs and advantages. Jefferson's proposals "to lessen the importation of the commodities of Great Britain" would require "recourse to prohibitions or to duties, so much higher

than those paid by other countries on the like articles, as to counterbalance the disadvantages they labor under, in the competition for our
market." Prohibitions or protectionist duties "will operate as a bounty
upon the commodities of certain foreign nations, to the prejudice of
others, which bounty will be paid at the expense of our citizens"
through higher prices for inferior goods. Prices would be higher because the new suppliers would be less efficient and because credit
would be less readily available. Jefferson's report had implied that
British credit "is pernicious, by inducing us to run into debt." But
credit per se was benign and necessary for almost any enterprise:
"Credit, though liable to abuse, is the substitute for capital in all trades,
and . . . it serves to foster them, and increase the mass of industry,
though the slothful and extravagant suffer by it."[15]

The notion of relative advantage applied to navigation as well.
Jefferson's report referred "discriminations" to treatment of the
United States, with the implication that such policies were particularly
invidious toward the new republic. British regulation did not subject
the ships of the United States to particular negative discriminations:
they simply bore the constraints that Britain applied to all foreign
trade. France might have a less stringent navigation policy on American shipping, but American ships simply benefited from French regulations for its "most favored nations." Britain had the more protective
navigation policy, but it applied equally to all foreign trade—except for
the United States, which enjoyed unique privileges in order to maintain
certain mercantilist priorities in the postcolonial context.

Smith insisted that *commerce* with France and Britain, not their policies, mattered for the American economy. A comparison of "the principles and motives of their respective systems" left "as little room for
eulogium on the one as censure on the other . . . Both, like other nations, have aimed at securing the greatest portion of benefit to themselves, with no greater concession to our interests than was supposed to
coincide with their own." Both aimed to monopolize their colonial
trade, "a predominant feature in the system of almost every country in
Europe." Such monopolies had "foundation in reason": the monopoly
of trade made the expenses of colonial defense economically rational.
"This was thought reasonable by the United States, while colonies,"
Smith mildly reminded Congress, "even after their disputes on the
point of taxation had begun." Once independent, the United States
could not consistently object to being so treated by Great Britain's trade
regulations. After all, the United States now had its "own system with a
number of exclusions and restrictions similar to those of which we
complain." By all means undertake negotiations for commercial advantage, but do not embark on the "quixotism of an attempt by vio-

lence, on the part of this young country, to break through the fetters which the universal policy of nations imposes on their intercourse with each other."[16]

In reply to Smith, Madison "professed himself to be a friend to the theory which gives to industry a free course, under the impulse of individual interest and the guidance of individual sagacity." He made this profession in order to absolve himself from applying it: "The rule itself required what did not exist—that it should be general." In a commercial world of Navigation Laws and protectionist legislation for manufactures, the United States had to reciprocate in kind: "To allow trade to regulate itself is not, therefore, to be admitted as a maxim universally sound." U.S. strategy in the regulation of commerce should be to reduce dependence on Great Britain by the encouragement of navigation and the protection of manufactures and by cultivation of trade with France.[17]

After the initial speeches of Madison and Smith, the debate became repetitive on economic issues, but supporters of Madison complained about the prolixity in political economy, which "was very well for merchants to calculate in their counting houses, but . . . the Legislature should determine the question upon political considerations." These obscurantists on political economy increasingly introduced noneconomic grievances regarding Britain. Because of American "acquiescence" to "commercial bondage," Britain had gained an "irresistible influence" "upon the internal Government" of the United States. The political effects of this "commercial influence" made the patriotism and commitment to republicanism of Madison's opponents questionable, because they would not support proposals for commercial discrimination against Britain or for commercial privileges toward France.[18]

Late in the debate Madison began to use similar political slanders to refute commercial arguments against his resolutions. Arguments that "trade ought to be free to find its proper channels, under the conduct of merchants," proposed "that every species of business ought to be left to the sagacity and interest of those carrying it on, without any interference whatever of the public authority." Although "the mercantile class of citizens was certainly an enlightened and a respectable one," "it did not follow that their opinions, even on questions of trade, ought to be consulted as an oracle by those who are equally bound to watch over the interests of every class of citizens, and over the joint concerns of the whole":

> If in any country the mercantile opinion ought not to be implicitly followed, there were the strongest reasons why it ought not in this. The body of merchants who carry on the American commerce is well known to be

composed of so great a proportion of individuals, who are either British subjects, or trading on British capital, or enjoying the profits of British consignments, that the mercantile opinion here might not be an American opinion; nay, it might be the opinion of the very country of which, in the present instance at least, we ought not to take counsel.[19]

In response, Smith asked why, if commercial relations with Great Britain were intrinsically so threatening, did Madison advocate a commercial strategy that, if successful, would result in a commercial treaty with Great Britain?[20]

Madison's resolution to apply discriminatory import and tonnage duties to trade from countries not in commercial treaty with the United States passed initial reading in the House on 3 February 1794. Madison then acceded to postponement of further debate until early March, in order to accommodate "several of the Eastern members friendly to the object" who wanted reassurance that opinion at home had not changed to disapproval of the resolutions.[21] Debate renewed six weeks later in the context of a crisis with Great Britain arising from newly disputed rights of neutral trade. Word had just reached the United States of massive seizures of American vessels in the West Indies, as a consequence of an Order-in-Council issued 6 November 1793 that directed British naval commanders to seize ships carrying products of the French West Indies.[22] Madison's resolutions, which had earlier presented the liability of commercial warfare, now seemed inappropriate for the likelihood of actual war. Congress imposed a thirty-day embargo on ships sailing abroad. When the embargo ended, a motion to halt trade with Britain passed the House but not the Senate. Shortly thereafter, Washington sent John Jay to Britain. Madison viewed Jay's mission as a ploy to prevent commercial retaliation against Great Britain. He considered his resolutions to be appropriate to the new crisis, and he (unsuccessfully) opposed legislation for naval armaments. Apparently he wanted discriminatory commercial legislation against Great Britain more than he wanted an end to its supposed commercial discrimination against the United States.[23] This implication became explicit in his response to the Jay Treaty.

The Jay Treaty was one of "Amity," "Commerce," and "Navigation." The most complicated negotiations involved issues unresolved by the 1783 Treaty of Paris—neutral trade, prewar debts, sequestered property, western boundaries and garrisons. The commercial clauses went far toward reciprocity and involved little disagreement.[24] Despite all the grievances voiced by Americans regarding their denial of "rights" in trade with Britain, the Jay Treaty for the first time established *British* rights in American trade, while the United States lost all the *privileges* that had been legacies from the prerevolutionary acts of trade and navigation. Between Great Britain and the United States there would be "a reciprocal and perfect liberty of commerce and navigation." People from each country could bring "their ships and cargoes" to any place in the other country and live there indefinitely. The treaty disavowed discrimination: the ships and cargoes of each country could enter the other with duties no higher than on those from any other country. Exports were similarly free of restrictions. Britain could impose tonnage duties equal to those payable by British ships entering the United States, and the United States agreed not to increase British liability to tonnage duties or duties on imports.

Trade in North America and the Caribbean tempered reciprocity with recognition of privileges of navigation to Britain's colonies. British subjects and American citizens could trade freely over land and on inland waters in North America (except in territory of the Hudson's Bay Company), but American ships could not enter ports in Britain's North American colonies. All goods not entirely prohibited in the respective territories could be traded freely within North America, and they would be not be liable to discriminatory duties on the basis on nationality. Trade on the Mississippi would be free for both countries.

The treaty's momentous change involved navigation in the Caribbean. American ships could bring into the British West Indies any American goods that British ships could bring, and on the same terms regarding charges and duties. American ships could carry from the West Indies to the United States any goods that British ships could carry there. British ships would be able to engage in the U.S.–West Indian trade as though they were American. This exception to the navigation system had two major qualifications. American vessels were limited in size to burdens of under seventy tons, and "the United States will prohibit and restrain the carrying any molasses, sugar [but not rum], coffee, cocoa or cotton in American vessels, either from His Majesty's islands or from the United States to any part of the world except the United States." This "Article Twelve" soon became notorious as the chief American objection to the treaty. Although seldom emphasized then, or since, the article was explicitly a wartime expedient with the implicit purpose to co-opt American commercial interests in support of British strategic concerns in the Caribbean. The article would become inapplicable two years after conclusion of the current war, at which point negotiations would begin "with a view to such arrangements as may best conduce to the mutual advantage and extension of commerce." At that same time the two countries would "treat for the more exact equalization of the duties on the respective navigation of their subjects and people, in such manner as may be most beneficial to the two countries."[25] If renegotiation of Article 12 failed, then all the commercial clauses of the treaty would "cease and expire together."

Contrary to charges then and since of Hamilton's "acquiescence in British maritime dominion,"[26] in his conversations with British envoys he had repeatedly expressed support for the American diplomatic goal of direct American trade with the British West Indies. He drafted Jay's instructions that made the continued prohibition of American navigation to the British West Indies a deal breaker for an Anglo-American commercial treaty.[27] For Britain to admit non-British vessels of even limited tonnage to its West Indian colonies—a proposal that was initially Hamilton's—represented a dramatic departure from British policy on navigation. On the basis of Beckworth's reports of conversations with Hamilton, Foreign Secretary Lord Grenville had instructed Hammond to entertain the subject of American shipping to the West Indies as part of a broader discussion of commercial reciprocity. At that point, Grenville hoped the hypothetical concession would forestall Madison's strategy of commercial discrimination; by the time of Jay's mission, he made it a real term for negotiation because he wanted to prevent a war with the United States. When the matter inevitably arose during the Jay-Grenville negotiations, Hawkesbury insisted on its inappropriateness for negotiation in a commercial treaty, and he fought the proposal by every bureaucratic and political means at his disposal. Once defeated, he refused to attend cabinet meetings on the treaty, though he approved of its other contents.[28]

Hamilton judged Article 12 to be "exceptionable" and "inadmissible" because it restricted non–Anglo-American trade, namely, the export from the United States of tropical products regardless of whether they were British in origin (including cotton, which the United States produced). He willingly risked the treaty rather than accede to the article. The Senate followed Hamilton's suggestion that it withhold approval of Article 12 but approve the rest of the treaty while calling for renewed negotiations regarding American trade in the British West Indies. As a result of this tactic, the Republicans lost their chief basis of objection to the treaty, and the treaty passed after several futile obstructionist efforts by Republicans.[29]

Now Madison repudiated reciprocity: its place in the treaty became yet another manifestation of Britain's monopolization of American trade. The treaty prevented the United States from reciprocating a privilege from any other country without extending the same privilege to Great Britain: "This extraordinary feature would monopolize us to G.B. by precluding any material improvement of our existing Treaties, or the hope of any new ones that would be of much advantage to us." In addition to preventing the United States from bargaining bilaterally for privileges, the treaty also prevented it from encouraging its shipping by preferential tonnage and import duties. Now the treaty licensed the retaliatory tonnage duties that Britain had previously been too reluctant to enact. Only treasonable bad faith could explain the actions of Jay and the dictates of his party: "The Treaty from one end to the other must be regarded as a demonstration that the Party to which the Envoy belongs & of which he has been more the Organ than of the U. S. is a British party, systematically aiming at an exclusive connection with the British Govern̈t. & ready to sacrifice to that object as well the dearest interests of our Commerce, as the most sacred dictates of national honor." Jefferson also saw it as disastrous that the House should be prevented "from ever restraining the commerce of their patron-nation," but he read in awe Hamilton's apologies for the treaty—"a colossus of the antirepublican party"—and pleaded with Madison to write a pamphlet in response to Hamilton's Camillus.[30]

The Jay Treaty put a twelve-year moratorium on the priority of commercial policy in national politics. It sanctioned the Hamiltonian view that the patterns of Anglo-American trade largely resulted from market relations rather than policy, and it repudiated commercial discrimination. Madison's obsession with Great Britain's control of American commerce did not abate, but the focus of his grievances shifted from Britain's denial of reciprocity to its calculated violation of neutral trading rights in order to maintain a monopoly over the West Indies carrying trade. His conviction of Britain's dependence on American trade remained unchanged, and he remained convinced of the necessity for a policy of coercive commercial discrimination in order to establish Anglo-American trade on its natural basis. In the Republican administrations of the next decade, the Embargo, the Non Intercourse Law, and congressional authorization for the president to impose nonintercourse on nations revoking rights of neutrals provided him the opportunity to test his strategy. Lord Sheffield, with delicious Smithian irony, would observe how the Republicans' commercial discrimination reinforced British encouragement of navigation by forcing American trade through Upper Canada, Lower Canada, New Brunswick, and Nova Scotia to supply the West Indies—while incidentally confirming the neomercantilist strategy he had advocated three decades earlier.[31] Eventually Madison had no alternative but to invade Canada in order to restore Britain's economic dependence on the United States and thereby restore American commercial privileges in the British empire.

NOTES

1. Gordon C. Bjork, "The Weaning of the American Economy: Independence, Market Changes, and Economic Development," *Journal of Economic History* 24 (1964): 550–51, 564–65; Gordon C. Bjork, *Stagnation and Growth in the American Economy, 1784–1792* (New York: Garland, 1985); Robert Bruce Bittner, "The Definition of Economic Independence and the New Nation," Ph.D. diss., University of Wisconsin, 1970; James F. Shepherd and Gary M. Walton, "Economic Change after the American Revolution: Pre- and Post-War Comparisons of Maritime Shipping and Trade," *Explorations in Economic History* 13 (1976): 397–422; Robert H. Wiebe, *The Opening of American Society: From the Adoption of the Constitution to the Eve of Disunion* (New York: Knopf, 1984), pp. 18–20, 67–89, 147–52; and Morrell Heald and Lawrence S. Kaplan, *Culture and Diplomacy: The American Experience* (Westport, Conn.: Greenwood, 1977), chap. 3.

2. Jacob Viner, *Studies in the Theory of International Trade* (New York: Harper & Brothers, 1937), pp. 3, 14, 59, 92–103, 107, 109, 112; William Letwin, *The Origins of Scientific Economics: English Economic Thought, 1660–1760* (London: Methuen, 1963), pp. 214–16; Gerald Stourzh, *Benjamin Franklin and American Foreign Policy*, 2d ed. (Chicago: University of Chicago Press, 1969), pp. 34–40; Drew R. McCoy, *The Elusive Republic: Political Economy in Jeffersonian America* (Chapel Hill: University of North Carolina Press, 1980); Cathy Diane Matson, "Fair Trade, Free Trade: Economic Ideas and Opportunities in Eighteenth-Century New York City Commerce," Ph.D. diss., Columbia University, 1985, p. 2n; and Gordon S. Wood, *The Radicalism of the American Revolution* (New York: Knopf, 1992), pp. 65, 315, 337.

3. Adam Smith, *An Inquiry into the Nature and Causes of the Wealth of Nations*, ed. R. H. Campbell and A. S. Skinner, 2 vols. (Oxford: Clarendon, 1976), IV.ii.9. Richard Pares, "American versus Continental Warfare," *English Historical Review* 51 (1936): 438, 441–42; Albert O. Hirschman, *Rival Views of Market Society and Other Recent Essays* (New York: Viking, 1986), pp. 39, 44; and cf. J. Ronnie Davis, "Adam Smith on the Providential Reconciliation of Individual and Social Interests: Is Man Led by an Invisible Hand or Misled by a Sleight of Hand?" *History of Political Economy* 22 (1990): 350.

4. Drew R. McCoy, "Republicanism and American Foreign Policy: James Madison and the Political Economy of Commercial Discrimination, 1789 to 1794," *William and Mary Quarterly*, 3rd ser., 31 (1974): 636–38, 640, 645.

5. Smith, *Wealth of Nations*, iv, introduction; Terence Hutchison, *Before Adam Smith: The Emergence of Political Economy, 1662–1776* (Oxford: Basil Blackwell, 1988), pp. 4–7; and John R. Nelson, *Liberty and Property: Political Economy and Policymaking in the New Nation, 1789–1812* (Baltimore: Johns Hopkins University Press, 1987), pp. xi, xiii.

6. Cf. McCoy, *The Elusive Republic*, p. 91.

INTRODUCTION
Mercantilism in the Enlightenment

1. Terence Hutchison, *Before Adam Smith: The Emergence of Political Economy, 1662−1776* (Oxford: Basil Blackwell, 1988), pp. 175−78; and Anthony Brewer, "Cantillon and Mercantilism," *History of Political Economy* 20 (1988): 447−60.

2. Richard Cantillon, *Essai sur la nature du commerce en général,* ed. and trans. Henry Higgs (1755; reprint, New York: Augustus M. Kelley, 1964), p. 243; see also pp. 75, 185, 225, 239. The *Essai* was written ca. 1730−34.

3. V.D.F., "Colonie," in *Encyclopédie ou dictionnaire raisonné des sciences des arts et des metiers* (facsimile of 1751−80 ed.; Stuttgart: Friedrich Frommann, 1966).

4. Charles Secondat, Baron de Montesquieu, *The Spirit of the Laws,* ed. Franz Neumann and trans. Thomas Nugent, 2 vols. in 1 (1748; reprint, New York: Hafner Publishing, 1962), pp. 316, 318−19, 321, 367−69, 372 (italics added); and Albert O. Hirschman, *The Passions and the Interests: Political Arguments for Capitalism before Its Triumph* (Princeton: Princeton University Press, 1977), pp. 78−81.

5. *Quesnay's "Tableau Economique,"* ed. Marguerite Kuczynski and Ronald L. Meek (London: MacMillan, 1972), pp. 4, 8n, 9n.

6. Marquis de Mirabeau and François Quesnay, "An Extract from 'Rural Philosophy,'" in *Precursors of Adam Smith, 1750−1775,* ed. Ronald L. Meek (London: J. M. Dent, 1973), pp. 111−13.

7. Aside from his authorship and his desire to institutionalize the study of commerce (presumably to secure patronage for himself), little is known about Postlethwayt. Without acknowledgment, he used the most important contemporary work of economic theory, Richard Cantillon's *Essai sur la nature du commerce en général,* throughout his *Universal Dictionary of Trade and Commerce* (1751−55), which had started simply as a translation of Savary des Brulons's *Dictionnaire universel* (1741). Hutchison, *Before Adam Smith,* pp. 241−34; and E. A. J. Johnson, *Predecessors of Adam Smith: The Growth of British Economic Thought* (1937; reprint, New York: A. M. Kelley, 1960), pp. 185−205, 402−8.

8. Such priorities were repeatedly acknowledged, even by advocates of lessened fundamentalism regarding the Navigation Acts; namely, Thomas Pownall, *The Administration of the Colonies, Wherein Their Rights and Constitution Are Discussed and Stated,* 4th ed. (London, 1768), pp. 38−42, 282−83.

9. Malachy Postlethwayt, *Britain's Commercial Interest Explained and Improved in a Series of Dissertations on Several Important Branches of Her Trade and Police: Containing a Candid Enquiry into the Secret Causes of the Present Misfortunes of the Nation. With Proposals for Their Remedy. Also the Great Advantages Which Would Accrue to This Kingdom from an Union with Ireland,* 2 vols. (London, 1757; reprint, New York: Augustus M. Kelley, 1968), 1:483−89.

10. Ibid., 1:149−50, 153−54, 177, 181, 246, 427; 2:378. Postlethwayt borrowed the analogy from Charles Davenant; Klaus Eugen Knorr, *British Colonial Theories* (Toronto: University of Toronto Press, 1944), p. 106.

11. Postlethwayt, *Britain's Commercial Interest,* 1:153−54.

12. Ibid., 1:181.

13. Ibid., 1:21−24.

14. Kathleen Wilson, "Empire, Trade and Popular Politics in Mid-Hanoverian Britain: The Case of Admiral Vernon," *Past and Present* 121 (1988): 77; see also John Brewer, *The Sinews of Power: War, Money and the English State, 1688−1783* (New York: Knopf, 1989), pp. 167−75. For a discussion of the fiscal priorities in English commercial legislation after the Glorious Revolution, and of the initial absence of "de-

liberate industrial protection," see Ralph Davis, "The Rise of Protection in England, 1689–1786," *Economic History Review,* 2d ser., 19 (1966): 306–17. However, Davis notes that the effect of this heavier tariff legislation was protectionist. In response to lobbying by particular interests aggrieved by higher customs rates, commercial legislation came into closer agreement with seventeenth-century mercantilist principles regarding issues such as duties on exports, duties on imported raw materials, drawbacks on reexports, and the advantages given British manufactures in the colonial trade.

15. Wilson, "Empire, Trade and Popular Politics," pp. 97–100, 106–7; Richard Pares, "American versus Continental Warfare," *English Historical Review* 51 (1936): 441–42; and Jacob M. Price, "Colonial Trade and British Economic Development, 1660–1775," *Lex et Scientia* 14 (July-September 1978): 106–26.

16. For Hume's relevance to American political economy, see Gerald Strouzh, *Alexander Hamilton and the Idea of Republican Government* (Stanford: Stanford University Press, 1970), pp. 71–75; see also Cathy Diane Matson, "Fair Trade, Free Trade: Economic Ideas and Opportunities in Eighteenth-Century New York City Commerce," Ph.D. diss., Columbia University, 1985, pp. 90–110; and Drew R. McCoy, *The Elusive Republic: Political Economy in Jeffersonian America* (Chapel Hill: University of North Carolina Press, 1980), pp. 17–85.

17. David Hume, "Of Refinement in the Arts" [1752], in *Essays, Moral, Political, and Literary,* ed. Eugene F. Miller, rev. ed. (Indianapolis: Liberty Classics, 1987), pp. 268, 277, 279–80; Hume criticized the lessons about the corruption of virtue by luxury that "severe moralists" had drawn from the history of ancient Rome in ibid., p. 275.

18. David Hume, "Of Commerce" [1752], in ibid., pp. 263–65.

19. David Hume, "Of the Balance of Trade" [1752], pp. 324, 312; and David Hume, "Of the Jealousy of Trade" [ca. 1759], in ibid., pp. 328–29.

20. Benjamin Franklin, "Observations concerning the Increase of Mankind, Peopling of Countries, Etc." [1751], in *The Papers of Benjamin Franklin,* ed. Leonard W. Labaree et al., 29 vols. to date (New Haven: Yale University Press, 1961), 4:229, 227–34.

21. Benjamin Franklin, "The Interest of Great Britain Considered, with Regard to Her Colonies, and the Acquisitions of Canada and Guadaloupe" [1763], in ibid., 9:89. An exceptionally balanced view of the place of mercantilism in Franklin's thought is Gerald Stourzh, *Benjamin Franklin and American Foreign Policy,* 2d ed. (Chicago: University of Chicago Press, 1969), pp. 104–10.

22. Franklin, "The Interest of Great Britain," pp. 73, 80, 90.

23. Franklin, "Marginalia in a Pamphlet by Josiah Tucker" [n.d], in *Papers of Benjamin Franklin,* 17:364–69, 373–74, 379, esp. 367.

24. Robert Livingston Schuyler, "The Rise of Anti-Imperialism in England," *Political Science Quarterly* 37 (1922): 440–51.

25. Walter Ernest Clark, *Josiah Tucker, Economist: A Study in the History of Economics* (New York, 1903; reprint, New York: AMS, 1968); and W. George Shelton, *Dean Tucker and Eighteenth-Century Economic and Political Thought* (New York: St. Martin's, 1981).

26. "The Elements of Commerce and Theory of Taxes" [1755], in *Josiah Tucker: A Selection from His Economic and Political Writings,* ed. Robert Livingston Schuyler (New York: Columbia University Press, 1931), p. 126.

27. Ibid., pp. 130–31.

28. Ibid., pp. 127, 146, 158–59, 205.

29. Ibid., p. 181.

30. "The Case of Going to War," in ibid., pp. 283, 295, 302.

31. "A Letter from a Merchant in London to His Nephew in America" [1766], in ibid.

CHAPTER ONE
The Prosperity of Colonial Dependence

1. For numerous citations of these views, see Jack P. Greene, "The Seven Years' War and the American Revolution: The Causal Relationship Reconsidered," in *The British Atlantic Empire before the American Revolution*, ed. Peter Marshall and Glyn Williams (London: Cass, 1980), p. 86.

2. Malachy Postlethwayt, *Britain's Commercial Interest Explained and Improved in a Series of Dissertations on Several Important Branches of Her Trade and Police: Containing a Candid Enquiry into the Secret Causes of the Present Misfortunes of the Nation. With Proposals for Their Remedy. Also the Great Advantages Which Would Accrue to This Kingdom from an Union with Ireland*, 2 vols. (London, 1757; reprint, New York: Augustus M. Kelley, 1968), 1:482, 485, 488.

3. Thomas C. Barrow, "Background to the Grenville Program, 1757–1763," *William and Mary Quarterly*, 3rd ser., 22 (1965): 93–104. See also Jack P. Greene, "'A Posture of Hostility': A Reconsideration of Some Aspects of the Origins of the American Revolution," *Proceedings of the American Antiquarian Society* 87, pt. 1 (1977): 27–68; and J. M. Bumsted, "'Things in the Womb of Time': Ideas of American Independence, 1633–1763," *William and Mary Quarterly*, 3rd ser., 31 (1974): 533–64.

4. Treasury to Privy Council, 4 October 1763, quoted in Barrow, "Background to the Grenville Program," p. 102.

5. An important exception is Thomas Pownall, who wrote *The Administration of the Colonies, Wherein Their Rights and Constitution Are Discussed and Stated*, 4th ed. (London, 1768), to deal with the "crisis" in commercial policy at the end of the Seven Years' War. He was much more tolerant of British colonists' trading directly in foreign ports and colonies. As long as it expanded "a grand marine dominion," such trade was mutually advantageous to Great Britain and the colonies. His test of the appropriateness of such a new commercial strategy was whether the colonists continued to consume British manufactures, even though they traded directly with foreign nations. If they did so, then such trade was comparable to the trading factories established in the Levant, the East Indies, and elsewhere; pp. 4–11, 164. Historians usually cite Pownall's book in reference to the political dimension of the imperial crisis, but his actual priorities for the reform of imperial government were commercial.

6. "Considerations upon the Act of Parliament" [Boston, 1764], in *Pamphlets of the American Revolution, 1750–1776*, ed. Bernard Bailyn (Cambridge, Mass.: Harvard University Press, 1965), 1:366, 370–71, passim. See also the "State of Trade [December 1763]," circulated by the Society for Encouraging Trade and Commerce, which formed in Boston in April 1763 for the specific purpose of opposing renewal of the Molasses Act; *Publications of the Colonial Society of Massachusetts* (Boston, 1917), 19:382–90.

7. Edward Countryman, *The American Revolution* (New York: Hill & Wang, 1985), p. 59.

8. Stephen Hopkins, *Essay on the Trade of the Northern Colonies* (Philadelphia, 1764), pp. 2–3, 6, 8.

9. Ibid., pp. 3–4.

10. Hopkins, *Essay on the Trade of the Northern Colonies*, p. 9.

11. On British North American colonists' resentment of West Indian political advantages, see Michael Kammen, *Empire and Interest: The American Colonies and the Politics of Mercantilism* (Philadelphia: Lippincott, 1970), pp. 125–28.

12. Hopkins, *Essay on the Trade of the Northern Colonies*, pp. 18–19.

13. Ibid., pp. 16–17.

14. *Consideration upon the Act of Parliament* (Boston, 1764), pp. 21, 23, 26–27, 33.

15. 4 George III, chap. 15 (5 April 1764); *The Statutes at Large, from the Twenty-sixth Year of the Reign of King George the Second, to the Sixth Year of the Reign of King George the Third*, 14 vols. (London, 1786), 7:457.

16. John Bullion, *A Great and Necessary Measure: George Grenville and the Genesis of the Stamp Act, 1763–1765* (Columbia: University of Missouri Press, 1982), pp. 44, 52–58; and Ian R. Christie and Benjamin W. Labaree, *Empire or Independence, 1760–1776: A British-American Dialogue on the Coming of the American Revolution* (New York: Norton, 1976), pp. 20–24, 34–38.

17. Thomas Whately, *The Regulations Lately Made Concerning the Colonies, and the Taxes Imposed upon Them, Considered* (London, 1765), p. 6; cf. the hardline analysis of "Charles Jenkinson's Memorandum [1765]," in Bullion, *A Great and Necessary Measure*, pp. 224–29.

18. Whately, *The Regulations Lately Made Concerning the Colonies*, pp. 39, 63.

19. Ibid., pp. 39–53.

20. Ibid., pp. 78–81.

21. Ibid., p. 88; see also Pownall, *Administration of the Colonies*, pp. 282–83, 298–305, 314–15.

22. Jack P. Greene, *Peripheries and Center: Constitutional Development in the Extended Polities of the British Empire and the United States, 1607–1788* (New York: Norton, 1990), pp. 90–91, 115; cf. 135–36.

23. Robert W. Tucker and David C. Hendrickson, *The Fall of the First British Empire: Origins of the War of American Independence* (Baltimore: Johns Hopkins University Press, 1982), pp. 137–44, view this petition as "the most explicit statement of the principle that Parliament's right to regulate trade had to be tempered by the equity of the results."

24. "The New York Petition to the House of Commons, October 18, 1764," in *Prologue to Revolution: Sources and Documents on the Stamp Act Crisis, 1764–1766*, ed. Edmund S. Morgan (Chapel Hill: University of North Carolina Press, 1959), pp. 8–14.

25. On colonial acceptance of Parliament's regulation of commerce, see Edmund S. Morgan and Helen M. Morgan, *The Stamp Act Crisis: Prologue to Revolution* (New York: Macmillan, 1953), pp. 272–74; see also Greene, *Peripheries and Center*, pp. 61–62, 88–97, 120–21, 129, 139, 148.

26. Daniel Dulany, "Considerations of the Propriety of Imposing Taxes in the British Colonies, for the Purpose of Raising a Revenue, by Act of Parliament" [1765], in *Pamphlets of the American Revolution*, 1:638.

27. Ibid., 1:619, 638.

28. Ibid., 1:648, 652–56.

29. Ibid., 1:647–49; and C. Robert Haywood, "Economic Sanctions: Use of the Threat of Manufacturing by the Southern Colonies," *Journal of Southern History* 25 (1959): 207–19.

30. Richard Bland, "An Inquiry into the Rights of the British Colonies" [1966], in *Tracts of the American Revolution, 1763–1776*, ed. Merrill Jensen (Indianapolis: Bobbs-Merrill, 1967), p. 122; cf. p. 120, where Bland dealt with the initial Naviga-

tion Act. See also Henry Laurens, "Extracts from the Proceedings of the Court of Vice-Admiralty" [1769], in ibid., in which Laurens described the restrictions on the colonists' buying and selling as "hard" and virtually "a much greater tax than any person of equal fortune on the other side of the Atlantic" paid, but then conceded that he might abide by these constraints if he were sure he would "enjoy the pittance left him" (pp. 203–4).

31. William Hicks, "The Nature and Extent of Parliamentary Power" [1768], in ibid., pp. 171–72, 175–76, 180.

32. Stephen Hopkins, *The Rights of the Colonies Examined* (Providence, 1765), pp. 10, 22–23; and Paul A. Varg, "The Advent of Nationalism, 1758–1776," *American Quarterly* 16 (1964): 174–76.

33. *Pamphlets of the American Revolution*, 1:409–17; and cf. James R. Ferguson, "Reason in Madness: The Political Thought of James Otis," *William and Mary Quarterly*, 3rd ser., 36 (1979): 194–214.

34. James Otis, "Considerations on Behalf of the Colonists in a Letter to a Noble Lord" [London, 1765], in *Some Political Writings of James Otis*, ed. Charles F. Mullett, University of Missouri Studies, 4, 2 vols. (Columbia, October 1929): 116.

35. "John Hampden to William Pym," *Boston Gazette*, 9 December 1765; the reference is from John W. Tyler, *Smugglers and Patriots: Boston Merchants and the Advent of the American Revolution* (Boston: Northeastern University Press, 1986), but the interpretation is different.

36. Tyler, *Smugglers and Patriots*, p. 92.

37. Otis, "Considerations on Behalf of the Colonists in a Letter to a Noble Lord," pp. 118–19. Otis bitterly condemned New Englanders' smuggling; see Otis, "Brief Remarks on the Defence of the Halifax Libel," in *Some Political Writings of James Otis*, p. 170.

38. "John Hampden to William Pym," *Boston Gazette*, 16 December 1765.

39. John Dickinson, "Letters from a Farmer in Pennsylvania" [17676–8], in *Empire and Nation*, ed. Forrest McDonald (Englewood Cliffs, N.J.: Prentice-Hall, 1962), Letter 2, pp. 7–8, 13–14. Similarly, when Dickinson assessed the British government's exploitation of Ireland, he criticized the imposition of taxes and pensions, but not the limitations on Irish trade; Letter 10, pp. 60–63.

40. In the colonial period "free trade" was also a euphemism for justifiable smuggling; Cathy Matson, "Fair Trade, Free Trade: Economic Ideas and Opportunities in Eighteenth-Century New York City," Ph.D. diss., Columbia University, 1985.

41. Dickinson, "Letters from a Farmer in Pennsylvania," Letter 3, p. 19; Letter 5, pp. 27–33; and Letter 6, p. 37.

42. On the metropolitan orientation prevailing in colonial political economy, see Matson, "Fair Trade, Free Trade," pp. 9–13, 35, 42–47, 67–68, 73, 81–82.

43. Tyler, *Smugglers and Patriots*, pp. 4, 13, 19, 22, 86–87, 90, 99, 231, 249.

44. Cathy D. Matson and Peter S. Onuf, *A Union of Interests: Political and Economic Thought in Revolutionary America* (Lawrence: University of Kansas, 1990), pp. 21–30; Cathy D. Matson, "American Political Economy in the Constitutional Decade," in *The United States Constitution: The First Two Hundred Years*, ed. R. C. Simmons (Manchester: Manchester University Press, 1989), pp. 17–21; Matson, "Fair Trade, Free Trade," pp. 13–18, 34, 68, 87–88; and Tyler, *Smugglers and Patriots*, pp. 167–69.

45. Whately, *The Regulations Lately Made*, p. 104; and Paul Langford, "The British Business Community and the Later Nonimportation Movements, 1768–1776," in *Resistance, Politics, and the American Struggle for Independence, 1765–1775*, ed. Walter H. Conser, Jr., et al. (Boulder: Lynne Rienner, 1986), pp. 312–14.

46. Lord Lyttelton, 3 February 1766, in *Proceedings and Debates of the British Parlia-*

ments Respecting North America, 1754–1783 [hereafter *Proceedings and Debates*], ed. R. C. Simmons and P. D. G. Thomas, 6 vols. (Millwood, N.Y.: Kraus, 1982–86), 2:127.

47. Dissent to Lords Proceedings on the Stamp Act, 11 March 1766, [quoting letter from Commander in Chief of His Majesty's Forces in North America to Mr. Secretary Conway, 7 November 1765], in ibid., 2:333; see also Lord Mansfield, 17 December 1765, in ibid., 2:565.

48. Isaac Barré, 3 February 1766, in ibid., 2:144; see also Charles Yorke, 21 February 1766, in ibid., 2:283.

49. Earl of Chatham, 21 February 1766, in ibid., 2:285.

50. On "the fundamental authoritarianism of the Rockinghams in their imperial attitudes," see Paul Langford, "The Rockingham Whigs and America, 1767–1773," in *Statesmen, Scholars and Merchants: Essays in Eighteenth-Century History Presented to Dame Lucy Sutherland,* ed. Anne Whiteman et al. (Oxford: Clarendon, 1973), pp. 147–48; quotation from Burke, p. 149. The Rockinghams also stood out among parliamentarians in their utter unwillingness to go to war to enforce imperial authority, however legitimate; ibid., pp. 149–50.

51. Josiah Tucker, "A Letter from a Merchant in London to His Nephew in America" [1766], in *Josiah Tucker: A Selection from His Economic and Political Writings,* ed. Robert Livingston Schuyler (New York: Columbia University Press, 1931), p. 322.

52. Josiah Tucker, "The True Interest of Great Britain Set Forth in Regard to the Colonies; and the Only Means of Living in Peace and Harmony with Them" [1774], in ibid., pp. 333, 338.

53. Josiah Tucker, "A Letter from a Merchant in London," in ibid., p. 325.

54. Josiah Tucker, "The True Interest of Great Britain," in ibid., pp. 364–65.

55. Ibid., pp. 358–60.

56. John Shy, "Thomas Pownall, Henry Ellis, and the Spectrum of Possibilities, 1763–1775," in *Anglo-American Political Relations, 1675–1775,* ed. Alison Gilbert Olson and Richard Maxwell Brown (New Brunswick, N.J.: Rutgers University Press, 1970), pp. 165, 181–85.

CHAPTER TWO

Commercial Monopoly and Parliamentary Sovereignty

1. Bernard Donoughue, *British Politics and the American Revolution: The Path to War, 1773–75* (London: MacMillan, 1964), pp. 48–49.

2. *Proceedings and Debates of the British Parliaments Respecting North America, 1754–1783* [hereafter *Proceedings and Debates*], ed. R. C. Simmons and P. D. G. Thomas, 6 vols. (Millwood, N.Y.: Kraus, 1982–86), 4:31, 37.

3. Lord North, 14 March 1774, in ibid., 4:56–57.

4. Lord North, in ibid., 4:63.

5. John Rushout, 14 March 1774, in ibid., 4:64; and Ira D. Gruber, "The American Revolution as a Conspiracy: The British View," *William and Mary Quarterly,* 3rd ser., 26 (1969): 360–72.

6. Edmund Burke, 14 March 1774, in *Proceedings and Debates,* 4:70.

7. Edmund Burke, 19 April 1774, in ibid., 4:209.

8. Edmund Burke, 19 April 1774, in ibid., 4:210–13, 230.

9. Alexander Wedderburn, 15 April 1774, in ibid., 4:172.

10. Wedderburn, 19 April 1774, in ibid., 4:188–89.

11. Merrill Jensen, *The Founding of a Nation: A History of the American Revolution, 1763–1776* (New York: Oxford University Press, 1968), pp. 456, 483; and Jack Rakove, *The Beginnings of National Politics: An Interpretive History of the Continental Congress* (New York: Knopf, 1979), pp. 22–27.

12. John Adams recorded that Congress split evenly on the issue of whether Parliament had the "Power of Regulating Trade"; *Diary and Autobiography of John Adams*, vol. 2, *Diary, 1771–1781*, ed. L. H. Butterfield et al., 4 vols. (Cambridge, Mass.: Harvard University Press, 1961), 13 October 1774, p. 151.

13. Helen Hill Miller, *George Mason: Gentleman Revolutionary* (Chapel Hill: University of North Carolina Press, 1975), pp. 102–8; David L. Ammerman, "The Continental Association: Economic Resistance and Government by Committee," in *Resistance, Politics and the American Struggle for Independence, 1765–1775*, ed. Walter H. Conser, Jr., et al. (Boulder: Lynne Rienner, 1986), p. 234; and "Fairfax County Resolves" [18 July 1774], in *The Papers of George Mason, 1725–1792*, vol. 1, *1749–1778*, ed. Robert A. Rutland, 3 vols. to date (Chapel Hill: University of North Carolina Press, 1970), 1:202.

14. Thomas Jefferson, "Draft of Instructions of the Virginia Delegates to the Continental Congress" [July 1774; manuscript of "A Summary View of the Rights of British America"], in *The Papers of Thomas Jefferson*, ed. Julian P. Boyd et al., 27 vols. to date (Princeton: Princeton University Press, 1950), 1:125.

15. Ibid., pp. 121–25, 135. Dumas Malone, *Jefferson and His Time: Jefferson the Virginian* (Boston: Little, Brown, 1948), pp. 180–88. On the economics of the *Summary View*, see William D. Grampp, "A Re-examination of Jeffersonian Economics," *Southern Economic Journal* 12 (1946): 166–71. In his criticism of *The Wealth of Nations*, Thomas Pownall would use similar distinctions between "circuitous" and "roundabout" trade to identify the acceptability of a commercial monopoly of colonial trade. *A Letter from Governor Pownall to Adam Smith, L.L.D., F.R.S. being an Examination of Several Points of Doctrine Laid Down in His "Inquiry into the Nature and Causes of the Wealth of Nations"* (London, 1776), pp. 7, 24–27. Cf. Adam Smith's medical analogies for Britain's dangerously concentrated colonial trade, *An Inquiry into the Nature and Causes of the Wealth of Nations*, ed. R. H. Campbell and A. S. Skinner, 2 vols. (Oxford: Clarendon, 1976), IV.vii.c.43.

16. Cf. Jack P. Greene, *Peripheries and Center: Constitutional Development in the Extended Polities of the British Empire and the United States, 1607–1788* (New York: Norton, 1990), p. 135.

17. James Wilson, "Considerations on the Nature and Extent of the Legislative Authority of the British Parliament" [1774], in *The Works of James Wilson*, ed. Robert Green McCloskey, 2 vols. (Cambridge, Mass.: Harvard University Press, 1967), 2:745–46.

18. Jerrilyn Greene Marston, *King and Congress: The Transfer of Political Legitimacy, 1774–1776* (Princeton: Princeton University Press, 1987), pp. 115–16.

19. John Dickinson, *A New Essay on the Constitutional Power of Great Britain*, quoted in Oliver Morton Dickerson, *The Navigation Acts and the American Revolution* (Philadelphia, 1951; reprint, New York: A. S. Barnes, 1963), pp. 116–17.

20. "Continental Association October 1774," in *Resistance, Politics, and the American Struggle*, Appendix F, pp. 550–53.

21. Ammerman, "The Continental Association," pp. 243–45.

22. *Journals of the Continental Congress, 1774–1789*, vol. 1, 1774, ed. Worthington Chauncey Ford, 34 vols. (Washington, D.C.: Government Printing Office, 1904), 1:75–80; and *Diary and Autobiography of John Adams*, pp. 137–44, 147–49. See Jensen, *Founding of a Nation*, pp. 505–7, esp. 515–28, 530–34, on the local politics of the Association.

23. *Journals of the Continental Congress*, 1:84, 89.
24. Donoughue, *British Politics and the American Revolution*, pp. 173–75, 208–9.
25. Lord North, 10 February 1775, in *Proceedings and Debates*, 5:412.
26. Lord North, 8 March 1775, in ibid., 5:513.
27. Lord Townshend, 20 January 1775, in ibid., 5:274.
28. Lord Mansfield, 7 February 1775, in ibid., 5:402; Lord Lyttelton, 30 November 1774, in ibid., 5:238.
29. Lord Lyttelton, 30 November 1774 and 20 January 1775, in ibid., 5:238, 272.
30. Earl of Chatham, 20 January 1775, in ibid., 5:273–78.
31. John Wilkes, 6 February 1775, in ibid., 5:367; cf. Lord Mansfield, 7 February 1775, in ibid., 5:389.
32. 23 January 1775, in ibid., 5:287–89. There were also pro-administration petitions from Birmingham and Nottingham, urging that the government maintain a policy of firm "Execution of the Laws respecting the Colonies of *Great Britain*," but they did not elaborate on reasons to do so; Birmingham petition, 25 January 1775, in ibid., 5:303; Nottingham petition, 27 February 1775, in ibid., 5:461–62. Rather than refer such petitions to the committee dealing with American papers presented to Lord North, the Commons referred them to a separate committee (termed the "Coventry Committee" by Burke); in ibid., 5:297.
    British mercantile lobbying on behalf of the colonists weakened in the early 1770s. Americans seemed to be conspiring to repudiate the colonial monopoly; American colonial trade was becoming relatively and absolutely less important in British overseas trade, as commerce with Europe increased; and the tactics of lobbying were becoming divisive among the merchants themselves. Donoughue, *British Politics and the American Revolution*, pp. 152–56, 238; Michael Kammen, *Empire and Interest: The American Colonies and the Politics of Mercantilism* (Philadelphia: Lippincott, 1970), pp. 128–35; Alison G. Olson, "The London Mercantile Lobby and the Coming of the American Revolution," *Journal of American History* 69 (1982): 21–41; Paul Langford, "The British Business Community and the Later Nonimportation Movements, 1768–1776," in *Resistance, Politics, and the American Struggle*, pp. 314–18; and Jacob M. Price, "Who Cared about the Colonies? The Impact of the Thirteen Colonies on British Society and Politics, Circa 1714–1775," in *Strangers within the Realm: Cultural Margins of the First British Empire*, ed. Bernard Bailyn and Philip D. Morgan (Chapel Hill: University of North Carolina Press, 1991), pp. 413–16.
33. Lord Clare, 23 January 1775, in *Proceedings and Debates*, 5:23, 298.
34. Hans Stanley, 26 January 1775, in ibid., 5:311.
35. Wedderburn, 2 February 1775, in ibid., 5:353; Lord Mansfield, 7 February 1775, in ibid., 5:389. Progovernment petitions began to adopt an appropriate stance of patriotic self-sacrifice; Huddersfield petition, 9 March 1775, in ibid., 5:517.
36. Fox, 6 March 1775, in ibid., 5:503.
37. Sir William Meredith, 10 February 1775, in ibid., 5:415.
38. Burgoyne, 27 February 1775, in ibid., 5:477.
39. John E. Crowley, "Empire versus Truck: The Official Interpretation of Debt and Labour in the Eighteenth-Century Newfoundland Fishery," *Canadian Historical Review* 70 (1989): 311–36.
40. Poole petition, 28 February 1775, in *Proceedings and Debates*, 5:480.
41. Bridport petition, 15 February 1775, in ibid., 5:425–6.
42. London petition, 24 February 1775, in ibid., 5:455.
43. Brook Watson, 28 February 1775, in ibid., 5:481–89.
44. Benjamin Lister, 6 March 1775, in ibid., 5:501–3.
45. Henry Dundas, 6 March 1775, in ibid., 5:504; cf. Lord Camden, 16 March

1775, in ibid., 5:541–42. By November 1775, West Country merchants petitioned Parliament for modification of the Corn Laws in order to ease exports of grain products for the resident Newfoundland fishery; Dartmouth merchants, 2 November 1775, in ibid., 6:165.

46. Brook Watson, 28 February 1775, in ibid., 5:489.

47. Lord Shelburne, 16 March 1775, in ibid., 5:547–48.

48. Molyneux Shuldham and Hugh Palliser, 15 March 1775, in ibid., 5:526, 529, 533.

49. Commons Proceedings, 11 April 1775, in ibid., 6:19.

50. Lord North, 27 April 1775, in ibid., 6:24.

51. 15 George III, chap. 31; *The Statutes at Large from the Seventh Year of the Reign of King George the Third, to the Eighteenth Year of the Reign of George the Third, Inclusive,* 14 vols. (London, 1786), 8:436–43.

52. 17 and 26 May 1775, *Proceedings and Debates,* 6:58.

53. George Walker, John Ellis, 16 March 1775, in ibid., 5:556–58, 565–67.

54. George Walker, 16 March 1775, in ibid., 5:558, 560.

55. John Ellis, 16 March 1775, in ibid., 5:566–67.

56. George Walker, 16 March 1775, in ibid., 5:562–63. On the Revolution's "traumatic and permanently devastating" effect on the British West Indies, see Selwyn H. H. Carrington, "The American Revolution and the British West Indies' Economy," *Journal of Interdisciplinary History* 17 (1987): 823–50.

57. John Glover, 16 March 1775, in ibid., 5:571.

58. 21 March 1775, in ibid., 5:582.

59. Edmund Burke, "Speech on American Taxation, 19 April 1774," in *The Writings and Speeches of Edmund Burke,* vol. 2, *Party, Parliament, and the American Crisis, 1766–1774,* ed. Paul Langford, 8 vols. (Oxford: Clarendon, 1981), pp. 426, 428; Edmund Burke, "Speech on Moving Resolutions for Conciliation with the Colonies, March 22, 1775," in *The Works of Edmund Burke,* 9 vols. (Boston: C. C. Little & J. Brown, 1839), 1:27, 50–51; and Bernard Semmel, *The Rise of Free Trade Imperialism: Classical Political Economy and the Empire of Free Trade and Imperialism, 1750–1850* (Cambridge: Cambridge University Press, 1970), pp. 20–24.

60. Edmund Burke, 22 March 1775, *Proceedings and Debates,* 5:601–3.

61. Reginald Coupland, *The American Revolution and the British Empire* (1930; reprint, New York: Russell & Russell, 1965), pp. 69–76.

62. Andrew S. Skinner, "Adam Smith and the American Economic Community: An Essay in Applied Economics," *Journal of the History of Ideas* 37 (1976): 59–63.

63. Donoughue, *British Politics and the American Revolution,* pp. 148–51; and Benjamin W. Labaree, "The Idea of American Independence: The British View, 1774–1776," *Proceedings of the Massachusetts Historical Society* 82 (1970): 16. Cf. John Sainsbury, *Disaffected Patriots: London Supporters of Revolutionary America, 1769–1782* (Kingston and Montreal: McGill-Queen's University Press, 1987), pp. 54–88, 127–28, which largely ignores views on trade.

64. [John Cartwright], *American Independence the Interest and Glory of Great Britain* (London, 1774), pp. 8, 13, 20, 25, 63, 66, 69, 71. Cartwright readily conceded the legitimacy of claims to independence on the part of the West Indian islands, but he did not expect them to seek it, because "their soil itself points out to them dependency, supplying only the means of effeminacy, luxury, and intoxication, while for *bread,* and the *necessaries of life,* its inhabitants must depend upon other countries"; in ibid., p. 23.

65. Colin C. Bonwick, *English Radicals and the American Revolution* (Chapel Hill: University of North Carolina Press, 1977), p. 97. See also Thomas Pownall, *The*

Administration of the Colonies, wherein Their Rights and Constitution Are Discussed and Stated, 4th ed. (London, 1768), pp. 165–72.

66. Price, "Observations on the Nature of Civil Liberty, the Principles of Government, and the Justice and Policy of the War with America" [1776], in *Two Tracts on Civil Liberty, the War with America, and the Debts and Finances of the Kingdom: With a General Introduction and Supplement* (London, 1778; reprint, New York: Da Capo, 1972), pp. 105, 111; and D. O. Thomas, *The Honest Mind: The Thought and Work of Richard Price* (Oxford: Clarendon, 1977), pp. 152n, 154, 208, 210.

67. Shelburne, 15 December 1775, *Proceedings and Debates*, 6:367.

CHAPTER THREE

Commercial Diplomacy during the Revolution

1. Quoted in Oliver M. Dickerson, *The Navigation Acts and the American Revolution* (Philadelphia, 1951; reprint, New York: A. S. Barnes, 1963), p. 132.

2. "Report on Lord North's Conciliatory Resolution," quoted in ibid., p. 132 (italics added); and Weldon A. Brown, *Empire or Independence: A Study in the Failure of Reconciliation, 1774–1783* (1941; 2d ed., Port Washington, N.Y.: Kennikat, 1966), pp. 30–31.

3. Vernon G. Setser, *The Commercial Reciprocity Policy of the United States, 1774–1829* (Philadelphia: University of Pennsylvania Press, 1937), pp. 6–12.

4. *Journals of the Continental Congress, 1774–1789*, ed. Worthington Chauncey Ford, 34 vols. (Washington, D.C.: Government Printing Office, 1905), 2:200–201.

5. Benjamin Franklin, "Resolutions on Trade Submitted to Congress" [ca. 21 July 1775], in *The Papers of Benjamin Franklin*, ed. William B. Wilcox, 29 vols. to date (New Haven: Yale University Press, 1982), 22:127.

6. Dickerson, *Navigation Acts*, pp. 103–11.

7. "The Second Petition to the King (8 July 1775)," in *American Colonial Documents to 1776*, ed. Merrill Jensen (London: Eyre & Spottiswoode, 1955), pp. 848–49.

8. Benjamin Franklin, "Intended Vindication and Offer from Congress to Parliament, in 1775," in *Papers of Benjamin Franklin*, 22:119.

9. Felix Gilbert, *To the Farewell Address: Ideas of Early American Foreign Policy* (Princeton: Princeton University Press, 1961), pp. 39–40.

10. R. Livingston, 4 October 1775, Zubly, 5 and 12 October 1775, Jay, 12 October 1775, in *Journals of the Continental Congress*, 3:41, 477n, 491–92.

11. E. Rutledge, 4 October 1775, Johnson, 4 October 1775, Chase, 12 and 20 October 1775, in ibid., 3:476.

12. Gadsden, 5 October 1775, Randolph, 20 October 1775, Chase, 12 and 20 October 1775, debate, 13 and 20 October, in ibid., 3:480, 494, 496.

13. Ibid., 3:268–69, 291–93.

14. John Adams to Abigail Adams, 23 July 1775, John Adams to James Warren, 24 July 1775, in *Letters of Members of the Continental Congress*, ed. Edmund C. Burnett, 7 vols. (1921; reprint, Gloucester, Mass.: Peter Smith, 1963), 1:174–77.

15. John Adams to James Warren, 23 July 1775, in *Letters of Delegates to Congress, 1774–1789*, ed. Paul H. Smith et al., 17 vols. to date (Washington, D.C.: Library of Congress, 1976-), 1:652–53.

16. John Adams to James Warren, 7 October 1775, in *Letters of Members of the Continental Congress*, 1:218–20.

17. Ibid.

18. John Adams to James Warren, 7 October 1775 and 21 March 1776, in ibid., 1:219–20, 403.

19. On the influence of *Common Sense* on American diplomacy, see Gilbert, *To the Farewell Address*, pp. 44, 55; and Janet Ann Riesman, "The Origins of American Political Economy, 1690–1781," Ph.D. diss., Brown University, 1983, pp. 278–79.

20. Thomas Paine, "Common Sense" [1776], in *The Writings of Thomas Paine*, ed. Moncure Daniel Conway, 4 vols. in 2 (New York: Burt Franklin, 1982), 1:83, 85, 86, 88, 103, 106–8.

21. Charles M. Andrews, *The Colonial Period of American History: England's Commercial and Colonial Policy*, 4 vols. (1938; reprint, New Haven: Yale University Press, 1964), 4:427.

22. Setser, *The Commercial Reciprocity Policy*, pp. 7, 10–11.

23. Benjamin Franklin et al. [Committee of Secret Correspondence] to Silas Deane, 3 March 1776, Deane to the Committee of Secret Correspondence, 18 August 1776, Deane to Charles Dumas, 6 October 1776, in *The Revolutionary Diplomatic Correspondence of the United States*, ed. Francis Wharton, 6 vols. (Washington, D.C.: Government Printing Office, 1889), 2:78–79, 114–15, 166.

24. It was a message Vergennes and other European ministers easily understood; Jonathan R. Dull, "France and the American Revolution Seen as Tragedy," in *Diplomacy and Revolution: The Franco-American Alliance of 1778*, ed. Ronald Hoffman and Peter J. Albert (Charlottesville: University Press of Virginia, 1981), pp. 87–88. Vergennes's chief mercantilist concerns were with the balance of power, not privileges in trade; Orville T. Murphy, "The View from Versailles: Charles Gravier Comte de Vergenne's Perceptions of the American Revolution," in ibid., pp. 116–17.

25. Gilbert, *To the Farewell Address*, pp. 45–46, 49–50; Lawrence S. Kaplan, *Colonies into Nation: American Diplomacy, 1763–1801* (New York: Macmillan, 1972), pp. 90–92; William C. Stinchcombe, "John Adams and the Model Treaty," in *The American Revolution and "A Candid World,"* ed. Lawrence S. Kaplan (Kent, Ohio: Kent State University Press, 1977), pp. 69–70; William C. Stinchcombe, *The American Revolution and the French Alliance* (Syracuse: Syracuse University Press, 1969), pp. 8–9; and Gerald Stourzh, *Benjamin Franklin and American Foreign Policy*, 2d ed. (Chicago: University of Chicago Press, 1969), pp. 125, 130–31, 140–41. Stinchcombe cautions against exaggerating the importance of the model treaty in American diplomacy. Adams drafted the model treaty, but he did not serve on the Committee of Secret Correspondence, which actually conducted American foreign affairs.

26. Deane's mission had already made Congress well aware of the elaborate privileges in French domestic and foreign trade; *Journals of the Continental Congress*, 5:768.

27. Stinchcombe, "Model Treaty," pp. 79, 81.

28. Gregg L. Lint, "The Law of Nations and the American Revolution," in *American Revolution and "A Candid World,"* pp. 111–14; cf. 121–22. On the place of neutral rights in postrevolutionary American diplomacy, see Robert W. Tucker and David C. Hendrickson, *Empire of Liberty: The Statecraft of Thomas Jefferson* (New York: Oxford University Press, 1990), pp. 48–62.

29. Gilbert, *To the Farewell Address*, p. 48.

30. A minority of members of Congress argued that France should be given exclusive trading privileges for all American trade if such a guarantee would secure an alliance; Setser, *The Commercial Reciprocity Policy*, p. 18; *Journals of the Continental Congress*, 5:815.

31. September 1776, *Journals of the Continental Congress*, 5:768–71, 813–15,

NOTES TO PAGES 59–62

6:1055; and Silas Deane to Charles Dumas, 11 September 1776, in *Revolutionary Diplomatic Correspondence*, 2:138.

32. In the spring and early summer of 1776 there was a counterpoint between confidence regarding France and fear of a partition treaty among Britain, France, and Spain. James H. Hutson, *John Adams and the Diplomacy of the American Revolution* (Lexington: University Press of Kentucky, 1980), pp. 18, 23, 27; and James H. Hutson, "The Partition Treaty and the Declaration of American Independence," *Journal of American History* 58 (1972): 887–96.

33. Benjamin Harrison et al. [Committee of Secret Correspondence] to Benjamin Franklin, Silas Deane, and Arthur Lee, 21 December 1776, in *Revolutionary Diplomatic Correspondence*, 2:229.

34. Robert Morris to the Commissioners at Paris, 21 December 1776, in ibid., 2:235.

35. Gilbert, *To the Farewell Address*, pp. 17–18, 20–21; cf. 28, 43; and Hutson, *John Adams*, pp. 28–30.

36. All of the North ministry's conciliatory plans involved explicit commitments to refrain from colonial taxation; Alan S. Brown, "The Impossible Dream: The North Ministry, the Structure of Politics, and Conciliation," in *The American Revolution and "A Candid World,"* p. 29.

37. Report of the Committee Appointed to Confer with Lord Howe, 17 September 1776, in *Revolutionary Diplomatic Correspondence*, 2:142–3 (italics added); and Weldon Brown, *Empire or Independence*, pp. 78, 83, 125.

38. Stinchcombe, *American Revolution*, p. 9; and Setser, *The Commercial Reciprocity Policy*, pp. 14–15.

39. Silas Deane to the Committee of Secret Correspondence, 18 August 1776, in *Revolutionary Diplomatic Correspondence*, 2:114.

40. Stinchcombe, "Model Treaty," p. 72; and Lint, "The Law of Nations," pp. 125–26.

41. Treaty of Amity and Commerce, 4 May 1778, in *Journals of the Continental Congress*, 11:422, 428. Arthur Lee waged a campaign of correspondence against this "twelfth article," which denied American export duties on provisions bound for the French islands. He objected that the treaty benefited only those Americans who imported molasses, whereas all provisions shipped to the French islands would be free of export duty. Lee to Vergennes, 14 June 1778, in *Revolutionary Diplomatic Correspondence*, 2:611. In October 1778, Congress asked the commissioners to eliminate the terms regarding the exclusion of export duties, "as inconsistent with that equality and reciprocity which form the best surety to perpetuate the whole"; *Journals of the Continental Congress*, 12:1040.

42. Stinchcombe, *American Revolution*, p. 21.

43. And strategic—troops raised by the colonies would be under the command of royal appointees, and the colonists were denied warships.

44. "Royal Instructions to the Peace Commission of 1778," 12 April 1778, in *Sources and Documents Illustrating the American Revolution, 1764–1788, and the Formation of the Federal Constitution*, ed. S. E. Morison, 2d ed. (Oxford: Clarendon, 1929), pp. 188, 198, 199, 201; and Brown, *Empire or Independence*, pp. 216–19.

45. Setser, *The Commercial Reciprocity Policy*, pp. 35, 37–38; and Jack N. Rakove, *The Beginnings of National Politics: An Interpretive History of the Continental Congress* (New York: Knopf, 1979), p. 243.

46. Resentments lingering from the Deane-Lee affair reinforced this potential for conflict because Arthur Lee had been unsuccessful as a candidate for peace

commissioner; Edmund Cody Burnett, *The Continental Congress* (New York: Macmillan, 1941), p. 432.

47. Rakove, *Beginnings of National Politics*, p. 248.

48. Samuel Adams to James Warren, 2/3 November 1778, in *Letters of Members of the Continental Congress*, 3:476; quoted by Stinchcombe, *American Revolution*, pp. 24–25.

49. John Adams to Congress, 8 December 1778, in *Revolutionary Diplomatic Correspondence*, 2:857; quoted by Stinchcombe, *American Revolution*, p. 25.

50. "Americanus," quoted in Thomas Paine, "Peace and the Newfoundland Fisheries," [*Pennsylvania Gazette*, 30 June, 14 July, 21 July, 1779], in *Writings of Thomas Paine*, 2:2–3.

51. Ibid., pp. 3–4, 10–11, 14.

52. Ibid., pp. 18–19.

53. Ibid., pp. 14–16.

54. Samuel Adams to Thomas McKean, 29 August 1781; quoted in Stinchcombe, *American Revolution*, pp. 17–18.

55. "Peace and the Newfoundland Fisheries," in *Writings of Thomas Paine*, 2:17.

56. Rakove, *Beginnings of National Politics*, pp. 254–58, 262.

57. February 1779, in *Journals of the Continental Congress*, 13:241.

58. June 1779, in ibid., 14:680–83.

59. *Journals of the Continental Congress*, 14:897.

60. 14 August 1779, in *Journals of the Continental Congress*, 14:961 (italics added); and Richard Brandon Morris, *The Peacemakers: The Great Powers and American Independence* (New York: Harper & Row, 1965), p. 194.

61. Setser, *The Commercial Reciprocity Policy*, pp. 36–37.

62. James Madison, seconded by John Mathews of South Carolina, made the motion for these changes; only Massachusetts and Connecticut voted against it; 12 July 1781, in *Journals of the Continental Congress*, 20:746.

CHAPTER FOUR

The Recolonization of Anglo-American Trade

1. Vernon G. Setser, *The Commercial Reciprocity Policy of the United States, 1774–1829* (Philadelphia: University of Pennsylvania Press, 1937), p. 40.

2. Samuel Flagg Bemis, *The Diplomacy of the American Revolution* (1935; reprint, Bloomington: Indiana University Press, 1957), pp. 191–93, 204–6; and Richard Brandon Morris, *The Peacemakers: The Great Powers and American Independence* (New York: Harper & Row, 1965), pp. 257, 261, 267–68, 284–86.

3. Gerald Stourzh, *Benjamin Franklin and American Foreign Policy*, 2d ed. (Chicago: University of Chicago Press, 1969), pp. 238–34; Bemis, *The Diplomacy of the American Revolution*, pp. 207–8, 225–26, citing *Correspondence of King George the Third*, 6:131; and Morris, *The Peacemakers*, pp. 290, 294–96, 307, 317.

4. Quoted in Bemis, *The Diplomacy of the American Revolution*, pp. 228–29 (his italics); and Morris, *The Peacemakers*, pp. 344–48.

5. John Jay to Robert R. Livingston [with enclosures], 17 November 1782, in *The Correspondence and Public Papers of John Jay, 1763–1826*, ed. Henry P. Johnston, 4 vols. (New York, 1890–93; reprint, New York: Da Capo, 1971), pp. 406–7; Bemis, *The Diplomacy of the American Revolution*, pp. 229–31; and Morris, *The Peacemakers*, p. 349.

6. "Text of the Preliminary and Conditional Articles of Peace," [30 November

1782], in Bemis, *The Diplomacy of the American Revolution*, pp. 259, 261. As preliminaries for the negotiation of peace became more intense during the summer of 1782, it had become apparent to American negotiators that it was the French ministry, not the British, who resisted the American claim to fishing rights on the Newfoundland banks. The British ministry only denied American claims to use the coasts of Newfoundland for drying, and it knew Americans were not insistent on the issue. From the French view, however, even the American claim to the banks fishery compromised interests in the Newfoundland fishery that the French had been asserting on the basis of the treaties of Utrecht and of Paris. Rather than view the enhancement of American fisheries as a way to reduce Britain's naval resources, France identified the continuation of this British interest with a greater security for its own. Vergennes held that Americans had given up their right to the British part of the Newfoundland fisheries when they declared independence. Therefore France could attempt to negotiate an exclusive right to fish on the part of the Newfoundland coast where its fishermen at least already had treaty rights to use the coast for drying; Morris, *The Peacemakers*, pp. 317–18, 324–26, 333, 349–503.

7. Vincent Todd Harlow, *The Founding of the Second British Empire, 1763–1793*, 2 vols. (London: Longmans, Green, 1952), 1:307, 300–310, 435–40, 448–51; Jerald A. Coombs, *The Jay Treaty: Political Battleground of the Founding Fathers* (Berkeley: University of California Press, 1970), pp. 3–6; John Aston Cannon, *The Fox-North Coalition: Crisis of the Constitution, 1782–1784* (Cambridge: Cambridge University Press, 1969), pp. 6, 14n, 52; and Morris, *The Peacemakers*, pp. 411–17, 421–22.

8. "Observations of London Merchants on American Trade, 1783," ed. Edmund C. Burnett, *American Historical Review* 18 (1912–13): 770.

9. Ibid., pp. 773–80.

10. Quoted in Reginald Coupland, *The American Revolution and the British Empire* (London: Longmans, Green, 1930), p. 168n; Morris, *The Peacemakers*, p. 430; and Lawrence S. Kaplan, *Colonies into Nation: American Diplomacy, 1763–1801* (New York: Macmillan, 1972), pp. 159–60.

11. Morris, *The Peacemakers*, pp. 430–33 (Hartley quoted on p. 432); Kaplan, *Colonies into Nation*, pp. 158–59; Thomas Jefferson to Edmund Pendleton, 16 December 1783, in *The Papers of Thomas Jefferson*, ed. Julian P. Boyd et al., 27 vols. to date (Princeton: Princeton University Press, 1952), 6:386–87; and Setser, *The Commercial Reciprocity Policy*, pp. 46–47. In order to assure the reopening of American markets to British manufactures, however, Fox would have allowed American ships to bring American goods to Britain and the West Indies; in ibid., p. 49.

12. For William Knox the orders were the heart of British commercial policy. He was an unreconstructed mercantilist, who sought a commercial strategy that would create a self-sufficient empire and retard the economic growth of the United States. [William Knox], *Extra-official State Papers Addressed to the Right Honorable Lord Rawdon and the Other Members of the Two Houses of Parliament, Associated for the Preservation of the Constitution and Promoting the Prosperity of the British Empire*, 2 vols. (London, 1789), 2:8, 23, 53. Knox was initially exceptional in thinking that the policy represented by the 2 July orders in council would be permanent; see Robert Bruce Bittner, "The Definition of Economic Independence and the New Nation," Ph.D. diss., University of Wisconsin, 1970, p. 36. In its own terms, the policy proved to be largely effective; Herbert C. Bell, "British Commercial Policy in the West Indies, 1783–93," *English Historical Review* 31 (1916): 429–41. As predicted, the policy contributed to the undernourishment and morbidity of slaves; Richard B. Sheridan, "The Crisis of Slave Subsistence in the British West Indies during and after the American Revolution," *William and Mary Quarterly*, 3rd ser., 33 (1976): 615–41.

13. Virginia Delegates to Benjamin Harrison, 12 March 1783, in *The Papers of James Madison*, ed. William T. Hutchinson and William M. E. Rachal, 16 vols. to date (Chicago: University of Chicago Press, 1969), 6:334 (italics added); Edmund Pendleton to James Madison, 23 June 1783, in *The Letters and Papers of Edmund Pendleton, 1734–1803*, ed. David John Mays, 2 vols. (Charlottesville: University Press of Virginia, 1967), 2:453.

14. Stephen Higginson to Theophilus Parsons, Sr., 7 April 1783, in *Letters of Members of the Continental Congress*, ed. Edmund C. Burnett, 7 vols. (1921; reprint, Gloucester, Mass.: Peter Smith, 1963), 7:123; and Setser, *The Commercial Reciprocity Policy*, p. 65.

15. John Francis Mercer to George Weedon, 20 September 1783, in *Letters of Members of the Continental Congress*, 7:303.

16. Report of the Committee for Dispatches from Foreign Ministers, 25 September 1783, in ibid., 7:304–5. Much of the fall-off (and increase) in trade was attributable to the end of the peculiarities of wartime commerce, namely, French and British spending on their forces in America and differentials of access depending on alliance or hostility; see John F. Stover, "French-American Trade during the Confederation, 1781–1789," *North Carolina Historical Review* 35 (1958): 399–414. See also Setser, *The Commercial Reciprocity Policy*, pp. 52–54; and Roy F. Nichols, "Trade Relations and the Establishment of the United States Consulates in Spanish America, 1779–1809," *Hispanic American Historical Review* 13 (1933): 289–92. On the spectrum of policies under consideration in France after the war, see Frederick L. Nussbaum, "The French Colonial Arrêt of 1784," *South Atlantic Quarterly* 27 (1928): 62–78. The predominant pressure on the government from French merchants was for further restrictions on American trade to the French West Indies, but on the whole Franco-American trade remained more open than before the Revolution.

17. "Report on Letters from the American Ministers in Europe" [20 December 1783], in *Papers of Thomas Jefferson*, 6:393–94; "Draft of a Model Treaty" [1784], in ibid., 479–80; Kaplan, *Colonies into Nation*, pp. 154–55; and Stourzh, *Benjamin Franklin and American Foreign Policy*, p. 125.

18. Reginald Horsman, *The Diplomacy of the New Republic, 1776–1815* (Arlington Heights, Ill.: Harlan Davidson, 1985), pp. 30–31, 34–35; Kaplan, *Colonies into Nation*, pp. 162, 166–77; and Merrill D. Peterson, "Thomas Jefferson and Commercial Policy, 1783–1793," *William and Mary Quarterly*, 3rd ser., 22 (1965): 587–600, esp. 593.

19. Sir Lewis Namier and John Brooke, *The House of Commons, 1754–1790*, 3 vols. (London: Her Majesty's Stationery Office, 1964), 2:674–79; Frank O'Gorman, *The Rise of Party in England: The Rockingham Whigs, 1760–1782* (London: Allen & Unwin, 1975), pp. 405–6, 618; Philip Lawson, *George Grenville: A Political Life* (Oxford: Clarendon, 1984), pp. 193, 251n; *The Jenkinson Papers*, ed. Ninetta S. Jucker (London: MacMillan, 1949), pp. vi–xxiii; and *The Historical and Posthumous Memoirs of Sir Nathaniel William Wraxall, 1772–1784*, ed. Henry B. Wheatley, 5 vols. (London: Bicker & Son, 1884), 1:419.

20. Namier and Brooke, *House of Commons*, 2:43.

21. Grace Amelia Cockroft, *The Public Life of George Chalmers* (New York: Columbia University Press, 1939), pp. 48, 54–56, 65, 74, 90–91.

22. Tucker particularly influenced Pitt and Shelburne, especially regarding Ireland. Bernard Semmell, "The Hume-Tucker Debate and Pitt's Trade Proposals," *Economic Journal* 75 (1965): 760–66, 769.

23. Adam Smith, *An Inquiry into the Nature and Causes of the Wealth of Nations*, ed.

R. H. Campbell and A. S. Skinner, 2 vols. (Oxford: Clarendon, 1976), IV.viii.49, 53, and 54; and Michael Kammen, *Empire and Interest: The American Colonies and the Politics of Mercantilism* (Philadelphia: Lippincott, 1970), p. 141.

24. John Ehrman, *The Younger Pitt: The Years of Acclaim* (London: Constable, 1969), pp. 330, 336, 346–48, 394–95; Bernard Semmel, *The Rise of Free Trade Imperialism: Classical Political Economy and the Empire of Free Trade and Imperialism, 1750–1850* (Cambridge: Cambridge University, 1970), pp. 14–33; and Peter Marshall, *Problems of Empire: Britain and India, 1757–1813* (London: Allen & Unwin, 1968), pp. 97–98.

25. George Chalmers, *Additional Observations on the Nature and Value of Civil Liberty, and the War with America* (Dublin, 1777), pp. 69, 94.

26. George Chalmers, *An Estimate of the Comparative Strength of Britain during the Present and Four Preceding Reigns; and of the Losses of Her Trade from Every War since the Revolution* (London, 1782), pp. iv, 75–76, 164n; and George Chalmers, *An Estimate of the Comparative Strength of Britain during the Present and Four Preceding Reigns; and of the Losses of Her Trade from Every War since the Revolution* (London, 1786), pp. 22, 30, 32.

27. John Baker Holroyd, Lord Sheffield, *Observations on the Commerce of the United States with Europe and the West Indies*, 6th ed. (London, 1784), pp. 279, 284; and Smith, *Wealth of Nations*, IV.i.10 and 31.

28. Chalmers, *Estimate* (1786), pp. 41–42; and Chalmers, *Estimate* (1782), pp. 75–76. See Smith, *Wealth of Nations*, IV.vii.b.7 and 56; IV.vii.c.48.

29. Smith, *Wealth of Nations*, IV.vii.c.63.

30. On medical analogies for Britain's dangerously concentrated colonial trade, see ibid., IV.vii.c.43.

31. Chalmers, *Estimate* (1782), pp. 76–77; and Sheffield, *Observations,* pp. 300, 227. See Smith, *Wealth of Nations*, IV.ii.3–9, which refers to an "invisible hand" giving preference to the support of domestic industry.

32. Chalmers, *Estimate* (1782), pp. 48, 60; and Sheffield, *Observations,* pp. xxxv, 226. See Smith, *Wealth of Nations*, IV.ii.30.

33. Sheffield, *Observations,* pp. xxxvii, 157, 184–87, 286–87, 295–96; and Smith, *Wealth of Nations*, IV.ii.6.

34. Smith, *Wealth of Nations*, IV.ii.30. Edward Mead Earle, "Adam Smith, Alexander Hamilton, Friedrich List: The Economic Foundations of Military Power," in *Makers of Modern Strategy: Military Thought from Machiavelli to Hitler,* ed. Edward Mead Earle (Princeton: Princeton University Press, 1948), pp. 121–24.

35. Chalmers, *Additional Observations,* pp. 265–67, 295–96.

36. Draft of Four Resolutions of the Committee, 31 May 1784, P.R.O., BT 5/1, fol. 123; and Smith, *Wealth of Nations*, IV.vii.b.24 and 39; cf. ibid., 40 and 63.

37. Sheffield, *Observations,* p. 284; Harlow, *The Founding of the Second British Empire,* 2:266–67; and Anna Lane Lingelbach, "The Inception of the British Board of Trade," *American Historical Review* 30 (1925): 703.

38. Brian Edwards, *Thoughts on the Late Proceedings of Government Respecting the Trade of the West India Islands with the United States of North America* (London, 1783), pp. 2, 12, 29–30; W. Bingham, *A Letter from an American, Now Resident in London, to a Member of Parliament, on the Subject of the Restraining Proclamation; and Containing Strictures on Lord Sheffield's Pamphlet on the Commerce of the American States,* 2d ed. (London, 1784), pp. 22–23; [Richard Champion], *Considerations on the Present Situation of Great Britain and the United States of America, with a View to Their Future Commercial Connexions* (London, 1784), pp. 9–10, 26–82, 200–201, 204–5; and Charles R. Ritcheson, *Aftermath of Revolution: British Policy toward the United States, 1783–1795*

(1969; reprint, New York: Norton, 1971), pp. 9–13. Cf. Smith, *Wealth of Nations*, IV.i.10; IV.vii.b.4.

39. Edwards, *Thoughts*, p. 7; *A Free and Candid Review of a Tract, Entitled, "Observations on the Commerce of the American States"; Shewing the Pernicious Consequences, Both to Great Britain, and to the British Sugar Islands, of the Systems Recommended in That Tract* (London, 1784), p. 58; Observations of the Committee of London Merchants Trading to America before the Late War, on Regulations to Recover That Commerce, 16 July 1783, Public Record Office (P.R.O.), BT 6/20, fols. 408–13; and Bingham, *A Letter from an American, Now Resident in London*, p. 14.

40. Sheffield, *Observations*, pp. xxx, xxxv, 1–3, 223–24, 226, 284.

41. Ibid., pp. xxx, 1–3, 223–24.

42. Interview of George Chalmers, 6 April 1784, P.R.O., BT 5/1, fols. 70–72.

43. Adam Smith to William Eden, 15 December 1783, in *The Journal and Correspondence of William, Lord Auckland, with a Preface and Introduction by the Bishop of Bath and Wells*, 4 vols. (London, 1861), 1:64–66.

44. Willard Clark Fisher, "American Trade Regulations before 1789," *Papers of the American Historical Association* 3 (1888–89): 467–93; Merrill Jensen, *The New Nation: A History of the United States during the Confederation, 1781–1789* (New York: Vintage, 1950), pp. 282–301; Richard B. Morris, *The Forging of the Union, 1781–1789* (New York: Harper & Row, 1987), pp. 148–52; Cathy D. Matson and Peter S. Onuf, *A Union of Interests: Political and Economic Thought in Revolutionary America* (Lawrence: University Press of Kansas, 1990), pp. 31–49; Cathy Matson, "American Political Economy in the Constitutional Decade," in *The United States Constitution: The First Two Hundred Years*, ed. R. C. Simmons (Manchester: Manchester University Press, 1989), pp. 22–26; William F. Zornow, "The Tariff Policies of Virginia, 1775–1789," *Virginia Magazine of History and Biography* 62 (1954): 307–19; William F. Zornow, "New York Tariff Policies, 1775–1789," *New York History* 37 (1956): 40–63; William F. Zornow, "Massachusetts Tariff Policies, 1775–1789," *Essex Institute Historical Collections* 90 (1954): 194–215; William F. Zornow, "New Hampshire Tariff Policies, 1775 to 1789," *Social Studies* 45 (1954): 252–56; William F. Zornow, "North Carolina Tariff Policies, 1775–1789," *North Carolina Historical Review* 32 (1955): 151–64; and William F. Zornow, "Georgia's Tariff Policies, 1775–1789," *Georgia Historical Quarterly* 38 (1954): 1–10.

45. Pitt denied the Committee for Trade a comparable role in Anglo-Irish trade policy. In January 1785, after he had decided on his response to the Irish Resolutions, Pitt directed the committee to hold hearings on particular aspects of Anglo-Irish trade. He excluded the Navigation Acts from the terms of reference, and he allowed Parliament to resume debate before the committee had completed its report on the matter. See Ehrman, *Younger Pitt*, pp. 205–9. Sheffield, in alliance with William Eden against Pitt's Irish policy, published a typically influential pamphlet. In these *Observations on the Manufactures, Trade, and Present State of Ireland*, 2d ed. (London, 1785), pp. viii, 3, 7, 22, 38, 86–88, he again distinguished between a protectionist policy regarding the Navigation Laws and a liberal policy toward the equalization of duties and the elimination of bounties.

46. W. O. Henderson, "The Anglo-French Commercial Treaty of 1786," *Economic History Review*, 2d ser., 10 (1957): 104–14; and Ehrman, *British Government*, pp. 28–69. British Library (B.L.), Add. MS 38395, Jenkinson to Mr. Liston, 12 September 1786, fols. 13–14; Commerce with France. Observations on. Office, [n.d.], fol. 13, P.R.O., BT 6/111 (reference from Ehrman, *British Government*, p. 12n); and Smith, *Wealth of Nations*, IV.vii.c.17. Smith counseled moderation when lowering import duties on goods whose domestic manufacturers had not previously been subject to

competition, lest "cheaper foreign goods of the same kind might be poured so fast into the home market, as to deprive all at once many thousands of our people of their ordinary employment and means of subsistence"; ibid., IV.ii.38. Silks and linens were the trades he identified particularly in this regard, as did the Committee for Trade.

47. On the opposition to free trade, even among those manufacturers favoring the French treaty, see Ehrman, *British Government,* p. 47. Adam Smith had predicted inevitable opposition to free trade: "To expect, indeed, that the freedom of trade should ever be entirely restored in Great Britain, is as absurd as to expect that an Oceana or Utopia should ever be established in it. Not only the prejudices of the public, but what is much more unconquerable, the private interests of many individuals, irresistibly oppose it"; Smith, *Wealth of Nations,* IV.ii.43.

48. Minutes of the Committee for Trade, 25 August 1786, P.R.O., BT 5/4, fol. 8.

49. Sheffield to Eden, 9 October 1786, B.L., Add. MS 34422, fols. 427–28 (reference from Ehrman, *British Government*); Sheffield to Eden, 4 October 1786, in *Journal and Correspondence of William Lord Auckland* 1:163; and see also Sheffield to Eden, 25 October 1786, in ibid., 1:393.

50. The immediate issue was response to the French government's appeal for British grain exports during the Great Fear in the summer of 1789, when the Corn Laws precluded them because of high domestic prices. With a view toward the likelihood of the British harvest falling short of domestic demand, Pitt regretfully concluded that concern for public order at home prevented approval. He came to this conclusion in early July 1789, eight months before the Committee for Trade presented its report; Ehrman, *The Younger Pitt,* pp. 44–50.

51. C. R. Fay, *The Corn Laws and Social England* (Cambridge: Cambridge University Press, 1932), pp. 28–37.

52. Smith, *Wealth of Nations,* IV.v.b.28–29 and 43–52.

53. Draft Representation on the Present State of the Corn Laws, 8 March 1790, P.R.O. BT 5/6, fol. 45.

54. Hawkesbury to Sir Joseph Banks, 19 May 1790, B.L. Add. MS 38310, fol. 53.

55. *Representation of the Lords of the Committee of Council, Appointed for the Consideration of All Matters Relating to Trade and Foreign Plantations, upon the Present State of the Laws for Regulating the Importation and Exportation of Corn* (London, 1790), p. 20.

56. Adam Smith assigned a similarly paternalistic function to dealers' efforts of sell at the highest price. He compared their decisions with those of a ship's captain dispensing provisions; *Wealth of Nations,* IV.v.b.3.

57. Smith, *Wealth of Nations,* IV.v.b.22.

58. John Baker Holroyd, Lord Sheffield, *Observations on the Corn Bill now depending in Parliament,* 2d ed. (London, 1791), pp. 3, 10, 15n, 16, 20, 24, 27, 43, 45–46, 73. See Smith, *Wealth of Nations,* IV.v.b.5.

59. Sheffield, *Observations on the Corn Bill,* p. 27. See Smith, *Wealth of Nations,* IV.v.b.4.

60. Liverpool to Sir Joseph Banks, 20 August 1795, B.L. Add. MS 38310, fol. 139.

61. Smith, *Wealth of Nations,* IV.v.b.40 and 53.

62. Chalmers, *Estimate* (London, 1794), pp. 269–79.

63. Andrew S. Skinner, "Adam Smith and the American Economic Community: An Essay in Applied Economics," *Journal of the History of Ideas* 37 (1976): 59–78.

64. Smith, *Wealth of Nations,* IV.vii.c.44.

65. Jacob Viner, "Adam Smith and Laissez-Faire," in *The Long View and the Short: Studies in Economic Theory and Policy* (Glencoe, Ill.: Free Press, 1958), pp. 244–45;

and Donald Winch, "Science and the Legislator: Adam Smith and After," *Economic Journal* 93 (1983): 501-11.

66. Donald Winch, *Adam Smith's Politics: An Essay in Historiographic Revision* (Cambridge: Cambridge University Press, 1978), pp. 87-98, 148-60, 169-77; and A. W. Coats, "Adam Smith and the Mercantile System," in *Essays on Adam Smith*, ed. Andrew S. Skinner and Thomas Wilson (Oxford: Clarendon, 1975), pp. 221, 225-26.

CHAPTER FIVE

The Madisonian Definition of National Economic Interests

1. Madison to Edmund Randolph, 30 August 1783, in *The Writings of James Madison*, ed. Gaillard Hunt, 9 vols. (New York: Putnam's, 1903), 2:11-12.

2. Madison to Edmund Randolph, 13 September 1783, in *The Papers of James Madison*, ed. William T. Hutchinson and William M. E. Rachal, 16 vols. to date (Chicago: University of Chicago Press, 1971), 7:14-15; and Madison to Thomas Jefferson, 20 August 1785, in *Writings of James Madison*, 2:162. For an economically liberal and exceptionally analytical critique of the privileging of navigation in British neomercantilism, see "Abstracts of Gouverneur Morris' Letters on Commerce" [May 1784], in *The Papers of Thomas Jefferson*, ed. Julian P. Boyd et al., 27 vols. to date (Princeton: Princeton University Press, 1953), 7:350-51.

3. James Madison to Thomas Jefferson, 13 May 1783, in *Letters of Members of the Continental Congress*, ed. Edmund C. Burnett, 7 vols. (1921; reprint, Gloucester, Mass.: Peter Smith, 1963), 7:163.

4. Madison to Edmund Randolph, 20 May 1783, in *Papers of James Madison*, 7:61.

5. Madison to Edmund Randolph, 20 May 1783, in ibid., 7:59-61.

6. Ibid., 7:62; Madison to Edmund Randolph, 10 June 1783, in ibid., 7:134.

7. [Madison], Report on the Address to the States by Congress, 25 April 1783, in ibid., 6:489, 494.

8. Ralph Louis Ketcham, *James Madison, a Biography* (New York: Macmillan, 1971), pp. 95-98, 160, 168-70; and Norman Risjord, *Chesapeake Politics, 1781-1800* (New York: Columbia University Press, 1978), pp. 71-88, 132-37, 255-66.

9. Risjord, *Chesapeake Politics*, pp. 136, 251 (italics added).

10. Madison to James Monroe, 21 June 1785, in *Writings of James Madison*, 2:147; and Madison to Thomas Jefferson, 20 August 1784, in ibid., 2:66.

11. Madison to Thomas Jefferson, 20 August 1785, in *Papers of James Madison*, 8:345; Madison to Monroe, 21 June 1785, in *Writings of James Madison*, 2:148; and Madison to Thomas Jefferson, 20 August 1785, in ibid., p. 162. Drew R. McCoy, "The Virginia Port Bill of 1784," *Virginia Magazine of History and Biography* 38 (1975): 288-303 is exceptional for showing how critically indicative the Port Bill was of Madison's political economy. Conventional treatment is in Irving Brant, *James Madison, the Nationalist, 1780-1787* (New York: Bobbs-Merrill, 1948), pp. 315-16. On changes in the marketing of tobacco, see Gordon C. Bjork, *Stagnation and Growth in the American Economy, 1784-1792* (New York: Garland, 1985), pp. 21-25, 55.

12. Madison to Thomas Jefferson, 18 March 1786, in *Writings of James Madison*, 2:229; and Madison to Thomas Jefferson, 20 August 1784, in ibid., 2:65. Several features of the Port Bill actually enacted differed critically from Madison's intents. To secure passage the bill added ports on each of the major rivers, which undermined the intention to create an entrepôt.

13. Protest by "A Private Citizen" against the Port Bill, [November-December? 1786], in *The Papers of George Mason, 1725-1792*, ed. Robert A. Rutland, 3 vols.

[188]

(Chapel Hill: University of North Carolina Press, 1970), 2:859–61.

14. Madison to Edmund Randolph, 25 February 1783, in *Papers of James Madison*, 6:286–87, 288n; and McCoy, "Virginia Port Bill," p. 297.

15. "Jefferson's Notes on Sheffield's *Observations on the Commerce of the American States*" [1783–84?], in *The Papers of Thomas Jefferson*, 19:127–31; Richard Henry Lee to Samuel Adams, 18 November 1784, in *The Letters of Richard Henry Lee*, ed. James Curtis Ballagh, 2 vols. (New York: Macmillan, 1911), 1:294; Richard Henry Lee to George Washington, 20 November 1784, in ibid., 1:299; see also Richard Henry Lee to James Madison, 20 November 1784, in ibid., 1:294, 299, 301; and James Monroe to Thomas Jefferson, 1 November 1784, in *The Writings of James Monroe*, ed. Stanislaus Murray Hamilton, 7 vols. (New York: G. P. Putnam's, 1898), 1:42–44. With such conspiratorial interpretations of Britain's commercial policy, it was not farfetched for rumors to spread that Silas Deane or anonymous Loyalists had written part of Sheffield's book; Richard Henry Lee to Samuel Adams, 18 November 1784, in *Letters of Richard Henry Lee*, 1:294–95; and Richard Henry Lee to John Adams, 23 October 1785, in ibid., 1:398. Americans seldom noted that theirs was a privileged position in British trade. Nor were their extreme constructions of British policy realized: Britain applied its legislation to the Confederation as a whole, and therefore the ships of one state were allowed to carry the goods of another state to Britain; Vernon G. Setser, *The Commercial Reciprocity Policy of the United States, 1774–1829* (Philadelphia: University of Pennsylvania Press, 1937), p. 64.

16. Benjamin Harrison to the Virginia Delegates in Congress, 14 November 1783, in *Papers of Thomas Jefferson*, 6:354; Richard Henry Lee to Madison, 30 May 1785, 11 August 1785, in *Papers of James Madison*, 8:289, 340; and Virginia Delegates to the Governor of Virginia [Benjamin Harrison], 1 November 1783, in *Letters of Members of the Continental Congress*, 7:367.

17. Report of the Committee for Dispatches from Foreign Ministers, 25 September 1783; see also John Francis Mercer to the Governor of Virginia [Benjamin Harrison], 10 December 1783, in *Letters of Members of the Continental Congress*, 7:305–6, 390.

18. Benjamin Harrison to Virginia Delegates, 3 October 1783, in *Papers of James Madison*, 7:366; and Francis Dana to the Massachusetts Assembly, 22 July 1784, in *Letters of Members of the Continental Congress*, 7:570–71.

19. *Journals of the Continental Congress, 1774–1789*, ed. Gaillard Hunt, 34 vols. (Washington, D.C.: Government Printing Office, 1904–37), 29 September 1783, 22 October 1783, 29 October 1783, 22 April 1784, 30 April 1784, 6 May 1784, 25:629–31, 720, 754, 26:269–71, 318–22, 358; John Adams to John Jay, 19 July 1785, 29 July 1785, in *The Diplomatic Correspondence of the United States of America, from the Signing of the Definitive Treaty of Peace, 10th September, 1783, to the Adoption of the Constitution, March 4, 1780*, 7 vols. (Washington, D.C.: Blair & Rives, 1837), 2:398, 400–401; the Commissioners [John Adams and Thomas Jefferson] to the Marquis of Carmarthen, 4 April 1786, in *Diplomatic Correspondence*, 1:603; and Jefferson to Thomas Pleasants, 8 May 1786, in *Papers of Thomas Jefferson*, 9:472.

20. Madison to Thomas Jefferson, 25 April 1784, in *Writings of James Madison*, 2:48–49; Resolutions to Strengthen Powers of Congress, 19 May 1784, in ibid., 8:38; Madison to Thomas Jefferson, 18 March 1786, in *Papers of Thomas Jefferson*, 9:334; and Jefferson to Thomas Pleasants, 8 May 1786, in ibid., 9:472.

21. Benjamin Harrison to Virginia Delegates, 26 September 1783, in *Papers of James Madison*, 7:358–59; and North Carolina Delegates to the Governor of North Carolina [Alexander Martin], 26 September 1783, in *Letters of Members of the Continental Congress*, 7:309–11.

22. Jefferson to Nathaniel Tracy, 17 August 1785, in *Papers of Thomas Jefferson*, 8:399.

23. Abiel Foster to Josiah Bartlett, 1 May 1784, in ibid., 7:510; and New Hampshire Delegates to the President of New Hampshire [Meshech Weare], 5 May 1784, in ibid., 7:514. For the exceptional view that commercial developments themselves would coerce the British government into a reversal of its policy toward American trade, see North Carolina Delegates to the Governor of North Carolina [Alexander Martin], 19 October 1783, in ibid., 7:343.

24. Report to Grant Congress Power of Regulating Commerce, 28 March 1785, in *Writings of James Monroe*, 1:80–83; and Henry Ammon, *James Monroe: The Quest for National Identity* (New York: McGraw-Hill, 1971), pp. 50–51.

25. Report to Grant Congress Power of Regulating Commerce, 1:80–83.

26. Ibid., 1:82–85. Monroe was a nationalist opponent of the proposed federal Constitution. He wanted a strong, directly elected, executive, and he opposed the equality of states in the Senate. But he did not share the federalists' sense of critical urgency, and his experience with the manipulation of congressional procedure during the Jay-Gardoqui negotiations led him to fear that small quorums in the Senate would allow the ratification of treaties that favored particular sections; Ammon, *James Monroe*, pp. 68–73.

27. Resolution Calling for the Regulation of Commerce by Congress, 14 November 1785, in *Papers of James Madison*, 8:413; Monroe to James Madison, 26 December 1785, in *Writings of James Monroe*, 1:109–11; and Monroe to James Madison, 16 June 1785, in ibid., 1:134. American commercial policy toward Canada demonstrated how insistence on a "liberal" policy from Great Britain with respect to American trade with the West Indies did not depend on a deeply held commitment to free trade. Monroe forthrightly recommended that the United States restrain the Canadian fur trade in order to encourage American trade, and to "weaken it as a British province," so that Canadian traders "will feel their own misfortunes and envy the blessings to be attained under the protection of the federal arm": "While we give those within our bounds great indulgences we must prohibit under high penalties all commerce between the U.S. and Canada." Monroe to Jefferson, 1 November 1784, in ibid., 1:42–44. Monroe later advised against bringing his recommendations to Congress's attention, because any debate on such a policy might compromise negotiation of the British withdrawal from the northwestern posts, which was a precondition for any effective policy against Canada; Monroe to Jefferson, 12 April 1785, in ibid., 1:68. See also Ammon, *James Monroe*, pp. 48–50.

28. Monroe to Thomas Jefferson, 16 June 1785, in *Writings of James Monroe*, 1:84–86; Monroe to James Madison, 26 July 1785, in ibid., 1:97–99; and see also Monroe to Madison, 26 December 1785, in ibid., 1:108–9. Both Madison and Monroe mentioned *The Wealth of Nations* when writing Jefferson in 1785, but there is no record of a relevant response; Madison to Jefferson, 27 April 1785; and Monroe to Jefferson, 16 June 1785, in *Papers of Thomas Jefferson*, 8:110–11, 216.

29. Madison to Monroe, 7 August 1785, in *Writings of James Madison*, 2:159, 160; and Madison to Thomas Jefferson, 20 August 1785, in ibid., 2:161.

30. Madison to James Monroe, 7 August 1785, in ibid., 2:156.

31. Instructions to John Jay: Boundaries and Free Navigation of the Mississippi, 17 October 1780, in ibid., 1:82, 89.

32. Ibid., pp. 89–90.

33. Madison to Lafayette, 20 March 1785, in ibid., 2:121; and James Madison to Jefferson, 9 January 1785, in *Papers of Thomas Jefferson*, 7:588–92. "Internal" improvements is a tricky term to use for canals and roads intended to facilitate export

trades; see Joseph H. Harrison, Jr., *"Sic et Non:* Thomas Jefferson and Internal Improvement," *Journal of the Early Republic* 7 (1987): 335–49, which refers to Jefferson as a "Virginia mercantilist" (p. 336). See also Merrill D. Peterson, "Thomas Jefferson and Commercial Policy, 1783–1793," *William and Mary Quarterly,* 3rd ser., 22 (1965): 590: "Like nearly everyone else, he [Jefferson] regarded inland commerce as an accessory of foreign commerce." On the "remarkably sophisticated, international pattern of consumption" in early Trans-Appalachia, see Elizabeth A. Perkins, "The Consumer Frontier: Household Consumption in Early Kentucky" *Journal of American History* 78 (1991): 486–510.

34. Jefferson to George Washington, 15 March 1784, in *Papers of Thomas Jefferson,* 7:26; and Madison to Lafayette, 20 March 1785, in *Writings of James Madison,* 2:122.

35. Madison to Thomas Jefferson, 25 April 1784, in *Writings of James Madison,* 2:67–69.

36. Ibid., pp. 72–73.

37. Monroe to Thomas Jefferson, 19 August 1786, in *Writings of James Monroe,* 1:156.

38. Madison to Thomas Jefferson, 27 February 1785, in *Writings of James Madison,* 2:138; and Madison to Lafayette, 20 March 1785, in ibid., 2:123–24. Much of the southern opposition in Congress to the Jay-Gardoqui negotiations arose from concern about their negative implications for land prices, and therefore land speculation, in the West; Setser, *The Commercial Reciprocity Policy,* pp. 95–96.

39. Madison to Lafayette, 20 March 1785, in *Writings of James Madison,* 2:122–23.

40. Pendleton to Madison, 9 December 1786, in ibid., 8:202–3; Madison to Pendleton, 9 January 1787, in *Writings of James Madison,* 2:306–7; and Monroe to James Madison, 3 September 1786, in *Writings of James Monroe,* 1:163.

41. Madison to George Washington, 9 December 1785, in *Writings of James Madison,* 2:196; Madison to James Monroe, 22 January 1786, in ibid., 2:223; Madison to Thomas Jefferson, 18 March 1786, in ibid., 2:228–29; editorial note, in *Papers of James Madison,* 8:406–9; and cf. Mervin B. Whealy, "'The Revolution Is Not Over': The Annapolis Convention of 1786," *Maryland Historical Magazine* 81 (1986): 228–40.

CHAPTER SIX

Commerce and the Philadelphia Constitution

1. Madison to Thomas Jefferson, 30 June 1789, in *The Papers of James Madison,* ed. Charles F. Hobson and Robert A. Rutland et al., 16 vols. to date (Charlottesville: University Press of Virginia, 1979), 12:269. The other power was taxation.

2. Randolph, 29 May, Sherman, 6 June; cf. Elsworth, 30 June, in *The Records of the Federal Convention of 1787,* ed. Max Farrand, rev. ed., 4 vols. (New Haven: Yale University Press, 1966), 1:19, 133, 406. Hereafter the references to comments at the convention are simply by speaker and date in the relevant volume and page of *Records,* ed. Farrand.

3. Wilson, 26 June, 1:426; and Pinckney, 25 June, 1:401–3.

4. Committee of Detail, "An Appeal for the Correction of All Errors Both in Law and Fact," 2:157; and Madison, 16 August, 2:306. Gouverneur Morris envisaged a deliberate use of export duties for regulatory purposes; Morris, 16 August, 2:307; see also Sherman, 16 August, 2:308. Suspicions about the potential commercial effects of fiscal legislation frequently focused on the question of which section

would derive disproportionate commercial benefits from a navy; McHenry's notes, 7 August, 2:211–12; Morris, 8 August, 2:222; and Mercer, 16 August, 2:307.

5. Pinckney, 12 July, 1:592; Williamson, 21 August, 2:360; and Clymer, 21 August, 2:363.

6. Morris, 21 August, 2:360; see also Madison, 21 August, 2:361. On Gouverneur Morris's exceptional attentiveness to market relations, see Jennifer Nedelsky, *Private Property and the Limits of American Constitutionalism* (Chicago: University of Chicago Press, 1990), pp. 67–75; the crucial documentation for this interpretation of Morris's liberal political economy dates from well after the convention, but it is consistent with what he said there.

7. Wilson, 21 August, 2:362; Pinckney, 23 July, 2:95; and Cathy D. Matson and Peter S. Onuf, *A Union of Interests: Political and Economic Thought in Revolutionary America* (Lawrence: University of Kansas Press, 1990), pp. 120–23.

8. Rutledge, 21 August, 2:364; and Mason, 22 August, 2:370. Mason also opposed slavery because it corrupted masters and increased the likelihood of rebellion.

9. Elsworth and Pinckney, 22 August, 2:371; Wilson, 22 August, 2:372; King, 22 August, 2:373; and Pinckney and Rutledge, 22 August, 2:373. Paul Finkelman, "Slavery and the Constitutional Convention: Making a Covenant with Death," in *Beyond Confederation: Origins of the Constitution and American National Identity*, ed. Richard Beeman, Stephen Botein, and Edward C. Carter II (Chapel Hill: University of North Carolina Press, 1987), pp. 213–21.

10. Morris, 29 August, 2:450.

11. Pinckney, Williamson, Madison, Rutledge, Butler, Mason, Randolph, 29 August, 2:449–52, 639–40, 651–52.

12. *Federalist* 4, *The Federalist Papers: Alexander Hamilton, James Madison, John Jay*, ed. Clinton Rossiter (New York: New American Library, 1961), p. 46. See also Hamilton in *Federalist* 6, p. 54.

13. Of the *Federalist Papers* that dealt at any length with commerce, Hamilton wrote seven (numbers 6, 7, 11, 12, 17, 22, and 35), Madison wrote two (numbers 41 and 42), and Jay wrote one (number 4).

14. *Federalist* 6, p. 56.

15. Ibid., pp. 57–58; see also *Federalist* 17, p. 118.

16. *Federalist* 6, p. 59.

17. *Federalist* 7, p. 63.

18. *Federalist* 11, pp. 85, 88–89.

19. *Federalist* 4, pp. 48–49; and *Federalist* 11, p. 87.

20. *Federalist* 11, pp. 85–86; see also *Federalist* 22, p. 144.

21. *Federalist* 11, p. 89.

22. *Federalist* 12, pp. 91–92, 94; and Madison, *Federalist* 42, pp. 267–68. Hamilton employed this same model of the domestic economy to argue that duties not be the *sole* source of revenue, lest they have broadly discouraging economic effects. The liability was that duties on imports would be used "to discourage an extravagant consumption to produce a favorable balance of trade and to promote domestic manufactures." Such an excessive readiness to rely on duties would "render other classes of the community tributary in an improper degree to the manufacturing classes, to whom they give a premature monopoly of the markets"; *Federalist* 35, p. 212. Madison also argued against such a restriction because it would eventually be inappropriate to the development of the American economy; *Federalist* 41, p. 262; and *Federalist* 42, pp. 267–68.

23. *Federalist* 42, p. 266; and cf. Hamilton, *Federalist* 21, p. 141.

24. *Federalist* 41, p. 262.

25. *Federalist* 10, p. 79.

26. Cecilia Kenyon, "Men of Little Faith: The Anti-Federalists on the Nature of Representative Government," *William and Mary Quarterly*, 3rd ser., 12 (1955): 3–43; and Stanley M. Elkins and Eric McKitrick, "The Founding Fathers: Young Men of the Revolution," *Political Science Quarterly* 76 (1961): 181–216.

27. Richard E. Ellis, "The Persistence of Antifederalism after 1789," in *Beyond Confederation*, pp. 299–300.

28. Hutson, "Country, Court, and Constitution"; Jackson Turner Main, *Political Parties before the Constitution* (1973; reprint, New York: Norton, 1974), pp. 32–33. "Agrarian-localist" and "commercial-cosmopolitan" correspond to the correlation Main found between residence and political partisanship; ibid., pp. 387–88. The book contains virtually no analysis of evidence on ideology; the ideological implications of residence are imputed.

29. Gordon S. Wood, "Interests and Disinterestedness in the Making of the Constitution," in *Beyond Confederation*, pp. 79, 81; and Janet A. Reisman, "Money, Credit, and Federalist Political Economy," in ibid., pp. 156–61.

30. Hereafter "antifederalist(s)" refers to the views published in opposition to ratification of the Philadelphia Constitution.

31. "The Fallacies of the Farmer Detected by a Farmer," (Philadelphia) *Freeman's Journal*, April 1788, in *Complete Anti-Federalist*, 3:186. See also Samuel Chase, Notes of Speeches Delivered to the Maryland Ratifying Convention [April 1788], in ibid., 5:82–83; and *Letters from the Federal Farmer*, October 1787, in ibid., 2:239.

32. Main, *Political Parties*, chap. 12, esp. p. 359n.

33. "Candidus," 20 December 1787, in (Boston) *Independent Chronicle*, in *Complete Anti-Federalist*, 4:131. For citations of similar sentiments among many antifederalists, see Frederick W. Marks, "Power, Pride, and Purse: Diplomatic Origins of the Constitution," *Diplomatic History* 11 (1987): 307n.

34. "An Old Whig," 6, (Philadelphia) *Independent Gazetter*, October 1787 February 1788, in *Complete Anti-Federalist*, 3:39; *Letters from the Federal Farmer*, in ibid., 2:293; "Address by Cato Uticensis," *Virginia Independent Chronicle*, 17 October 1787, in ibid., 5:121; "Essays by Sidney," (Poughkeepsie) *Country Journal*, 11 March 1788, in ibid., 6:99; and "An Old Whig," in ibid., 3:39.

35. Centinel, "To the People of Pennsylvania," 5 November 1787, (Philadelphia) *Independent Gazetter*, October 1787–April 1788, in *Complete Anti-Federalist*, 2:156, 164.

36. "Address by a Plebeian" (New York, 1788), in *Complete Anti-Federalist*, 6:140; "Candidus," (6 December 1787), in ibid., 4:129–30; and "Address of the Albany Antifederal Committee," *New York Journal*, 26 April 1788, in ibid., 6:125.

37. [James Winthrop], "Letters of Agrippa," *Massachusetts Gazette*, 23 November 1787, in *Complete Anti-Federalist*, 4:74; see also in ibid., p. 81. For other antifederalist expressions of such views, see Norman A. Graebner, "Isolationism and Antifederalism: The Ratification Debates," *Diplomatic History* 11 (1987): 340–46.

38. "Letters of Cato," in *Complete Anti-Federalist*, 2:120–21.

39. "Essays by Sidney," (Poughkeepsie) *Country Journal*, 11 March 1788, in *Complete Anti-Federalist*, 6:99; "Address by a Plebeian," in ibid., 6:140; Centinel, "To the People of Pennsylvania," in ibid., 2:164; and "Letters of Cato," in ibid., 2:121.

40. Centinel, "To the People of Pennsylvania," 29 December 1787, in *Complete Anti-Federalist*, 2:178.

41. [Winthrop], "Letters of Agrippa," 25 January 1788, in *Complete Anti-Federalist*,

4:104–5; and "Candidus," 20 December 1787, (Boston) *Independent Chronicle*, in ibid., 4:135.

42. Wood, "Interests and Disinterestedness," p. 101; quotation from [Winthrop], "Letters of Agrippa," 18 December 1787, in *Complete Anti-Federalist*, 4:82.

43. [Winthrop], "Letters of Agrippa," 23 November 1787, in *Complete Anti-Federalist*, 4:71.

44. Ibid., 28 December 1787, 4:92, 96.

45. Adam Smith, *An Inquiry into the Nature and Causes of the Wealth of Nations*, ed. R. H. Campbell and A. S. Skinner, 2 vols. (Oxford: Clarendon, 1976), I.ii.1.

CHAPTER SEVEN

Commercial Privilege in the New Republic

1. *Annals of Congress: The Debates and Proceedings in the Congress of the United States . . . Volume I, Comprising (with Volume II) the Period from March 3, 1789, to March 3, 1791, Inclusive. Compiled from Authentic Materials by Joseph Gales* (Washington, D.C.: Gales & Seaton, 1834), 1st Cong., pp. 107–8 (8 April 1789); "Editorial Note," in *The Papers of James Madison*, ed. Charles F. Hobson and Robert A. Rutland, 16 vols. to date (Charlottesville: University Press of Virginia, 1979), 12:54; and Roger K. Brown, *Redeeming the Republic: The Federalists, Taxation, and the Origins of the Constitution* (Baltimore: Johns Hopkins University Press, 1993), chap. 2.

2. *Annals of Congress*, 1st Cong., pp. 113–14 (9 April 1789).

3. Ibid., 1st Cong., pp. 110–11 (9 April 1789).

4. Hartley, *Annals of Congress*, 1st Cong., pp. 114–15 (9 April 1789); and Madison, in ibid., 1st Cong., pp. 115–16 (9 April 1789).

5. *Annals of Congress*, 1st Cong., pp. 116–18, 120 (9 April 1789).

6. Goodhue (10 April 1789), Madison (15 April 1789); see also Scott (17 April 1789), Bland (14 April 1789), in ibid., 1st Cong., pp. 121, 154–56, 173, 129.

7. Goodhue, in ibid., 1st Cong., p. 184 (21 April 1789).

8. Fitzsimons, Laurence, Tucker, in ibid., 1st Cong., pp. 184–88 (21 April 1789).

9. Madison, 1st Cong., pp. 189–90 (21 April 1789); see also Fitzsimons and Baldwin, in ibid., 1st Cong., pp. 278, 280 (6 May 1789).

10. "Tonnage Duties," [4 May 1789], "Population and Emigration," [*National Gazette*, 19 November 1791], in *Papers of James Madison*, 11:128, 14:119. Madison confidently seconded Fitzsimons's point that added charges on foreign shipping would have no effect on the real price of American goods abroad because Americans almost monopolized the available supply of commodities such as tobacco and rice; *Annals of Congress*, 1st Cong., p. 190 (21 April 1789).

11. Laurence (21 April 1789), *Annals of Congress*, 1st Cong., pp. 191–92.

12. Madison to Thomas Jefferson, 30 June 1789, *Papers of James Madison*, 12:268–69. In reply to Madison's summary of this debate, Jefferson strongly emphasized that political gratitude provided sufficient imperative and justification for the United States to discriminate in France's favor; Jefferson to James Madison, 28 August 1789, in ibid., 12:362–63.

13. Madison (21, 24 April 1789; 6 May 1789); see also Goodhue (7 May 1789), *Annals of Congress*, 1st Cong., pp. 196–97, 285–86, 281. "Tonnage Duties," [4 May 1789], "Import Duties," [25 April 1789], Madison to Thomas Jefferson, 30 June 1789; see also Madison to James Madison, Sr., 5 July 1789, *Papers of James Madison*, 11:126–27, 269–70, 278–79, 12:112.

14. Hamilton played a crucial role in turning around congressional opinion on

the advisability of discrimination; Jerald A. Coombs, *The Jay Treaty: Political Battleground of the Founding Fathers* (Berkeley: University of California Press, 1970), pp. 32–43, 50–51, 59–62; and Vernon G. Setser, *The Commercial Reciprocity Policy of the United States, 1774–1829* (Philadelphia: University of Pennsylvania Press, 1937), pp. 107–8.

15. "Navigation and Trade," [25 June 1790], in *Papers of James Madison*, 13:255. Sheffield was Madison's main (and largely unacknowledged) authority for information on Anglo-American trade; see "Notes on Navigation and Trade," [ca. 13 May 1790], in ibid., 13:198–204. For Jackson's reference to Smith, see *Annals of Congress*, 1st Cong., p. 1618 (10 May 1790).

16. Preface, in *Papers of James Madison*, 13:xx–xxi; and "Address of the President to Congress," 8 December 1790, in ibid., 13:313.

17. Joseph Charles, *The Origins of the American Party System* (New York: Harper & Row, 1956), pp. 95, 97, 101, 122.

18. Jefferson to Alexander Hamilton, 13 January 1791, in *The Papers of Thomas Jefferson*, ed. Julian P. Boyd et al., 27 vols. to date (Princeton: Princeton University Press, 1971), 18:563–64.

19. Alexander Hamilton to Jefferson, 11 January 1791, in ibid., 18:562–63; Merrill D. Peterson, "Thomas Jefferson and Commercial Policy, 1783–1793," *William and Mary Quarterly*, 3rd ser., 22 (1965): 604; Merrill D. Peterson, *Thomas Jefferson and the New Nation: A Biography* (New York: Oxford University Press, 1970), pp. 423–24; "Representation by France against the Tonnage Acts . . . Editorial Note," in *Papers of Thomas Jefferson*, 18:516–81, 556–58; and Robert W. Tucker and David C. Hendrickson, *Empire of Liberty: The Statecraft of Thomas Jefferson* (New York: Oxford University Press, 1990), pp. 33–47.

20. Alexander Hamilton to Jefferson, 13 January 1791, in *Papers of Thomas Jefferson*, 18:564–65. Hamilton doubted that an American Navigation Act would significantly affect British shipping; "Conversation with George Beckwith," 19–20 January 1791, in *The Papers of Alexander Hamilton*, ed. Harold C. Syrett and Jacob E. Cooke, 27 vols. (New York: Columbia University Press, 1963), 7:441.

21. On the report's political context, see "Report on the Fisheries . . . Editorial Note," in *Papers of Thomas Jefferson*, 19:140–72. France, Great Britain, and the United States jealously sought the skills of the American whale fishery, which before the Revolution had centered on Nantucket. In 1786 Jefferson persuaded the French ministry to eliminate duties on American whale oil, as the most effective way to counter Britain's bounties for its domestic whale fishery, and thereby prevent the migration of the Nantucket fishery to the British isles. However, when British oils continued to dominate the French market, the French government responded by prohibiting the importation of all oils. Jefferson wrote his "Observations on the Whale-Fishery" to protest this prohibition; see "Report on the American Fisheries by the Secretary of State," in ibid., 19:207; "Observations on the Whale-Fishery," in ibid., 14:242–56.

22. "Report on the American Fisheries," 19:207–10, 213–15.

23. Ibid., 19:210–11.

24. "Report on the American Fisheries," 19:209, 218; "Republican Distribution of Citizens," [*National Gazette*, 3 March 1792], in *Papers of James Madison*, 14:245; cf. "Fashion," [*National Gazette*, 20 March 1792], in ibid., 14:257–59. Drew R. McCoy, *The Elusive Republic: Political Economy in Jeffersonian America* (Chapel Hill: University of North Carolina Press, 1980), pp. 156–57, overlooks Madison's invidious distinction between manufacturing and maritime labor.

25. "Report on the American Fisheries," 19:218–19.

26. A Statement of Such Duties and Other Burdens as Have Been Imposed by the American States on British Ships and Goods, 15 March 1788, Public Record Office (P.R.O.), BT 6/20, fols. 148–52. See Adam Smith, *An Inquiry into the Nature and Causes of the Wealth of Nations*, ed. R. H. Campbell and A. S. Skinner, 2 vols. (Oxford: Clarendon Press, 1976), IV.ii.39: "To judge whether such retaliations are likely to produce such an effect ['repeal of high duties or prohibitions'], does not, perhaps, belong so much to the science of a legislator, whose deliberations ought to be governed by general principles which are always the same, as to the skill of that insidious and crafty animal, vulgarly called a statesman or politician."

27. Questions Transmitted to Mr. Payne and Others Relating to the Impost and Tonnage Acts, P.R.O., BT 5/5, fols. 190–91; Answers of the Liverpool Committee of Merchants and Shipowners to Questions about the Commerce and Shipping between Great Britain and the United States of America, 25 November 1789, P.R.O., BT 6/20, fols. 281–84; Henry Wilckens to Hawkesbury, 29 September 1789, in ibid., fols. 242–43; Wilckens to Hawkesbury, 5 October 1789, in ibid., fols. 252–53; and Answers from Bristol to Questions Respecting the Commerce and Shipping between Great Britain and the United States of America, 11 December 1789, P.R.O, BT 6/20, in ibid., fol. 286.

28. Draft of Four Resolutions of the Committee, 31 May 1784, P.R.O., BT 5/1, fol. 125.

29. Report of the Committee for Trade upon Two Bills Passed by the Congress of the United States of America, 28 January 1791, P.R.O., PC 1/19/A 24 (iii) fols. 84, 94, 110, 113, 116, 125. With Smithian deftness, the committee also advised against a bounty on British shipping, because it would simply use British revenue to pay the American surcharge; in ibid., fol. 113. See Smith, *Wealth of Nations*, IV.ii.30: "The act of navigation is not favourable to foreign commerce or to the growth of that opulence that can arise from it."

30. "Report on Manufactures, December 5, 1791," in *The Reports of Alexander Hamilton*, ed. Jacob E. Cooke (New York: Harper & Row, 1964), pp. 167–75. Adam Smith also viewed drawbacks and premiums benignly; see *Papers of Alexander Hamilton*, 10:305–7n.

31. Hamilton, "Report on Manufactures," p. 115.

32. On Coxe's utter incapability to apply theories of political economy to policy, see Jacob E. Cooke, *Tench Coxe and the Early Republic* (Chapel Hill: University of North Carolina Press, 1978), pp. 186–87, 201–3. Madison and Jefferson thought Coxe had refuted Sheffield; in ibid., pp. 206–7.

33. Tench Coxe's Draft of the Report on the Subject of Manufactures, [Fall 1790], in *Papers of Alexander Hamilton*, 10:15–16.

34. Alexander Hamilton's First Draft of the Report on the Subject of Manufactures, in ibid., 10:24.

35. "Report Relative to a Provision for the Support of Public Credit, January 9, 1790," in *Reports of Alexander Hamilton*, p. 2. The most important influences on Hamilton's views on public finance were Smith, *The Wealth of Nations*, and Postlethwayt, *Universal Dictionary;* see also "Second Report on the Further Provision Necessary for Establishing Public Credit (Report on a National Bank), [Introductory Note]," in *Papers of Alexander Hamilton*, 7:236–56. Jacques Necker apparently provided Hamilton with most of his counterarguments to policies of free trade; in ibid., 10:8. Hamilton thought of himself as eclectic in political economy: "Most general theories, however, admit of numerous exceptions, and there are few, if any, of the political kind, which do not blend a considerable portion of error with the truths they inculcate"; "Report on Manufactures," p. 118.

36. Smith, *Wealth of Nations*, I.ii.1; and Hamilton, "Report on Manufactures," pp. 140–41. On similarities with Hume's economic psychology, see *Papers of Alexander Hamilton*, 10:241–42n, 256n, 267n. Hamilton's political cultivation of large-scale merchants and other investors to support his fiscal policies apparently ignored Smith's skepticism regarding their pursuit of economic privilege.

37. Hamilton, "Report on Manufactures," p. 165; see also p. 148. John R. Nelson, "Alexander Hamilton and American Manufacturing: A Reexamination," *Journal of American History* 65 (1979): 971–95.

38. Hamilton, "Report on Manufactures," pp. 127–29, 130–32.

39. Ibid., pp. 134–35. Jefferson also sometimes observed that commercial restrictions overseas might be the major encouragement for the development of manufactures in the United States; Jefferson to David Humphreys, 23 June 1791; quoted in *Papers of Alexander Hamilton*, 10:4–5.

40. Hamilton, "Report on Manufactures," pp. 118–19, 121.

41. Ibid., pp. 120–22, 146–47, 124–25.

42. Ibid., p. 116–17, 136–37, 140, 157. The most sophisticated critic of Hamilton's Report on Manufactures on grounds of political economy was George Logan, an uncompromising physiocrat, who had no ideological tolerance for governmental regulation of commerce. He was just as opposed to Madison's navigation laws as to Hamilton's plans for the Society for Establishing Useful Manufactures, or to Congress's fiscal reliance on import duties. [George Logan], *Letters Addressed to the Yeomanry of the United States* (Philadelphia, 1791), pp. 14, 41–44; and [George Logan], *Five Letters Addressed to the Yeomanry of the United States: Containing Some Observations on the Dangerous Scheme of Governor Duer and Mr. Secretary Hamilton, to Establish Manufactures* (Philadelphia, 1792), pp. 13, 23–27.

43. Hamilton, "Report on Manufactures," p. 158; and Frank Bourgin, *The Great Challenge: The Myth of Laissez-Faire in the Early Republic* (New York: George Braziller, 1989), pp. 101–2. Hamilton largely dismissed the balance of trade as a specific issue for economic policy, and when he addressed the topic he expressed more concern to increase industry than to reduce consumption; "The Second Report on the Further Provision Necessary for Establishing Public Credit (Report on a National Bank), December 13, 1790," in *Reports of Alexander Hamilton*, pp. 58–59.

44. Hamilton, "Report on Manufactures," p. 178.

45. Hamilton, "Report Relative to Public Credit," pp. 5–6; and Nelson, "Alexander Hamilton and American Manufacturing," p. 991.

46. Hamilton, "Report Relative to Public Credit," pp. 7–9. When three of the directors of the Society for Establishing Useful Manufactures embezzled the society's funds in order to purchase stocks in the wave of speculation that the society's charter had encouraged, they contributed to a stock crash, but Hamilton insisted that the market take its course and that the government not intervene either for or against the speculators; John R. Nelson, *Liberty and Property: Political Economy and Policymaking in the New Nation, 1789–1812* (Baltimore: Johns Hopkins University Press, 1987), pp. 48–50.

47. Although the House never raised the Report on Manufactures from the table, many of the new tariffs set in March 1792 were in accordance with Hamilton's proposals; see Gerard Clarfield, "Protecting the Frontier: Defense Policy and the Tariff Question in the First Washington Administration," *William and Mary Quarterly*, 3rd ser., 32 (1975): 458–59.

48. *Papers of Alexander Hamilton*, 10:271n.

49. Jefferson to Thomas Mann Randolph, Jr., 30 May 1790, Jefferson to John Garland Jefferson, 11 June 1790, in *Papers of Thomas Jefferson*, 16:449, 481. Jeffer-

son to Jean Baptiste Say, 1 February 1804, in *The Life and Selected Writings of Thomas Jefferson*, ed. Adrienne Koch and William Peden (New York: Modern Library, 1944), pp. 574–75. When James Madison and James Monroe wrote Jefferson about Smith's book, he did not respond; Madison to Jefferson, 27 April 1785, Monroe to Jefferson, 16 June 1785, in *Papers of Thomas Jefferson*, 8:110–11, 216. On economics as Jefferson's "field of lowest competence," see Robert H. Wiebe, *The Opening of American Society: From the Adoption of the Constitution to the Eve of Disunion* (New York: Knopf, 1984), pp. 53–54.

50. "Prospectus on Political Economy," 6 April 1816, Jefferson to John W. Eppes, 6 November 1813, in *The Complete Jefferson, Containing His Major Writings, Published and Unpublished, Except His Letters*, ed. Saul K. Padover (New York: Duell, Sloan & Pearce, 1943), pp. 369–72; [Antoine Louis Claude] Destutt de Tracy, "First Part of the Treatise on the Will and Its Effects: Of Our Actions," in *A Treatise on Political Economy, to Which is Prefixed a Supplement to a Preceding Work on the Understanding, or, Elements of Ideology*, ed. and trans. Thomas Jefferson ([Georgetown, D.C.,] 1817; reprint, New York: A. M. Kelley, 1970), pp. 6–17, 27–28, 30–32, 40, 45; cf. Joyce Appleby, "What Is Still American in the Political Philosophy of Thomas Jefferson?" *William and Mary Quarterly*, 3rd ser., 39 (1982): 295–309.

51. Compare the section on agriculture in the *Notes on the State of Virginia* with the "Report on Cod and Whale Fisheries" in *Complete Jefferson*, pp. 324–42, 349–51, 678–81.

CONCLUSION

Hamiltonian Liberalism and the Jay Treaty

1. Merrill D. Peterson, "Thomas Jefferson and Commercial Policy, 1783–1793," *William and Mary Quarterly*, 3rd ser., 22 (1965): 587–600; and Charles R. Ritcheson, *Aftermath of Revolution: British Policy toward the United States, 1783–1795* (1969; reprint, New York: Norton, 1971), pp. 94–107, 275–88, 325–28.

2. Morrell Heald and Lawrence S. Kaplan, *Culture and Diplomacy: The American Experience* (Westport, Conn.: Greenwood, 1977), p. 8; and Vernon G. Setser, *The Commercial Reciprocity Policy of the United States, 1774–1829* (Philadelphia: University of Pennsylvania Press, 1937), pp. 121–22.

3. "Report on the Privileges and Restrictions on the Commerce of the United States in Foreign Countries, December 16, 1793," in *The Complete Jefferson, Containing His Major Writings, Published and Unpublished, Except His Letters*, ed. Saul K. Padover (New York: Duell, Sloan & Pearce, 1943), p. 219. The report acknowledged that Spain and Portugal had more restrictive navigation policies than Great Britain toward colonial trade, because they prohibited direct trade from anywhere but the metropoles, even in their own ships. However, France allowed American ships to bring most provisions to its islands.

4. Ibid., pp. 216–17.

5. Ibid., pp. 218–19.

6. *Annals of Congress: The Debates and Proceedings in the Congress of the United States . . . Third Congress: Comprising the Period from December 2, 1793, to March 3, 1795, Inclusive* (Washington, D.C.: Gales & Seaton, 1849), 3rd Cong., pp. 155–57 (3 January 1794).

7. Ibid., 3rd Cong., p. 174 (13 January 1794). Smith's speech was printed as a pamphlet in New York and Philadelphia. Jefferson was sure that Hamilton had written it; see Thomas Jefferson to Madison, 3 April 1794, *The Papers of James*

Madison, ed. Thomas A. Mason et al., 16 vols. to date (Charlottesville: University Press of Virginia, 1985), 15:301. Hamilton had compiled most of the commercial information in late 1791 and early 1792, when he and Jefferson were working together in preparation for possible commercial negotiations with both France and Great Britain. "View of the Commercial Regulations of France and Great Britain in Reference to the United States . . . Introductory Note," in *The Papers of Alexander Hamilton,* ed. Harold C. Syrett and Jacob E. Cooke, 27 vols. (New York: Columbia University Press, 1967), 13:406–11.

8. *Annals of Congress,* 3rd Cong., p. 176. Smith's comparison closely resembled early drafts of the Report on Manufactures; cf. "Alexander Hamilton's Second Draft of the Report on the Subject of Manufactures" with "Alexander Hamilton's Final Version of the Report on the Subject of Manufactures," in *Papers of Alexander Hamilton,* 10:56–62.

9. On Jefferson's aversion to the calculation of market imperatives, see William D. Grampp, "A Re-examination of Jeffersonian Economics," *Southern Economic Journal* 12 (1946): 269, 272, 276. Cf. "Memoranda and Statistics on American Commerce . . . Editorial Note," that no other "public official" was "better grounded, both by habit of mind and by legislative and diplomatic experience, in the art of political arithmetic," *Papers of Thomas Jefferson,* 19:121.

10. *Annals of Congress,* 3rd Cong., pp. 177–78 (13 January 1794).

11. Ibid., 3rd Cong., p. 180 (13 January 1794).

12. Ibid., 3rd Cong., pp. 181–82 (13 January 1794). On the play of interests in French commercial policy, see Frederick L. Nussbaum, "American Tobacco and French Politics, 1783–1789," *Political Science Quarterly* 40 (1925): 497–510.

13. *Annals of Congress,* 3rd Cong., pp. 186–90 (13 January 1794); and Gordon C. Bjork, *Stagnation and Growth in the American Economy, 1784–1792* (New York: Garland, 1985), pp. 103–5. During the period from 1785 to 1787, when Robert Morris had a monopoly to supply the Farmers General with tobacco, the restricted demand lowered prices in Virginia. When his contract ended, British importations of tobacco swiftly grew to be seven times those of France, though much of it would be reexported to France. During the 1780s American exports to France actually tripled, but French exportations to the United States declined to one-sixth of wartime levels. See John F. Stover, "French-American Trade during the Confederation, 1781–1789," *North Carolina Historical Review* 35 (1958): 406–9; and Nussbaum, "American Tobacco and French Politics," 497–510.

14. *Annals of Congress,* 3rd Cong., pp. 189–90 (13 January 1794).

15. Ibid., 3rd Cong., p. 191 (13 January 1794).

16. Ibid., 3rd Cong., pp. 193–94, 196–97 (13 January 1794). However, Smith pointed out that by tabulating tonnage from the number of entries rather than the number of ships, Jefferson had grossly exaggerated (by about 50 percent) the American tonnage trading to French possessions. On the legitimacy of imperial commercial monopolies in the eighteenth century, see Gerald Stourzh, *Alexander Hamilton and the Idea of Republican Government* (Stanford: Stanford University Press, 1970), pp. 252–54.

17. Ibid., 3rd Cong., pp. 209–10, 212–13, 220 (14 January 1794). For Madison's criticism of Smith's quantitative analysis, see ibid., 3rd Cong., pp. 370–74 (29 January 1794).

18. Namely, Abraham Clark (16 January 1794), Andrew Moore (22 January 1794), and William B. Giles (23 January 1794), in ibid., 3rd Cong., pp. 246, 270, 279–82. In sarcastic commentary on this chauvinistic alarmism, Uriah Tracy observed: "The mind is roused by such a group of evils, and then called upon to

consider a statement of duties on goods imported from foreign nations"; ibid., 3rd Cong., p. 294 (24 January 1794).

19. Ibid., 3rd Cong., pp. 389–90 (31 January 1794).

20. Ibid., 3rd Cong., p. 410 (31 January 1794).

21. Madison to Thomas Jefferson, 2 March 1794, in *Papers of James Madison,* 15:269; and Jerald A. Coombs, *The Jay Treaty: Political Battleground of the Founding Fathers* (Berkeley: University of California Press, 1970), p. 120.

22. On the order of 6 November, see Ritcheson, *Aftermath of Revolution* (1969; reprint, New York: Norton, 1971), pp. 300–303. The order was revoked 8 January 1794, with the intention that notification of both orders would reach the United States simultaneously, but news of the 8 January order arrived a month later.

23. Madison to Thomas Jefferson, 2, 9, and 12 March 1794, 11 May 1794, in *Papers of James Madison,* 15:269, 274–75, 278–79, 327–28; editorial notes, in ibid., 15:147, 150–51. On the deliberately and incidentally partisan functions of Jay's mission, see Joseph Charles, *The Origins of the American Party System* (New York: Harper & Row, 1956), pp. 91–140.

24. Samuel Flagg Bemis, *Jay's Treaty: A Study in Commerce and Diplomacy* (New York: Macmillan, 1923), pp. 232–51; and Ritcheson, *Aftermath of Revolution,* pp. 323–53.

25. "Treaty of Amity, Commerce, and Navigation," in Bemis, *Jay's Treaty,* pp. 321–43. The treaty also allowed ships from the United States to trade in the British East Indies on the same terms as British ships, but they could export East Indian goods only to the United States.

26. Peterson, "Thomas Jefferson and Commercial Policy," p. 604.

27. "Conversation with George Beckwith," [25–30 September 1790; 15–20 October 1790], "Points to Be Considered in the Instructions to Mr. Jay, Envoy Extraordinary to GB," [23 April 1794], in *Papers of Alexander Hamilton,* 7:71, 112, 16:327n.

28. "Lord Hawkesbury and the Jay-Grenville Negotiations," ed. Bradford Perkins, *Mississippi Valley Historical Review* 40 (1953–54): 291–304; Charles R. Ritcheson, "Lord Hawkesbury and Article Twelve of Jay's Treaty," *Studies in Burke and His Time* 15 (1973–74): 155–66; and Ritcheson, *Aftermath of Revolution,* pp. 141–44. However, Hawkesbury belied his reputation for being anti-American by being more accommodating than Grenville on neutral rights; ibid., pp. 324, 328.

29. "Remarks [for George Washington] on the Treaty of Amity Commerce and Navigation lately made between the United States and Great Britain" [9–11 July 1795], in *Papers of Alexander Hamilton,* 18:432. Hamilton thought that a renegotiated Article 12 should increase the tonnage for American vessels and limit the prohibition on reexported tropical products to those from the British West Indies; Hamilton to George Washington, 4 September 1795, in ibid., p. 233.

30. Madison to Robert R. Livingston, 10 August 1795, Madison to an unidentified correspondent, 23 August 1795, and Thomas Jefferson to James Madison, in *Papers of James Madison,* 16:47, 57, 88–89. Public opinion was initially vehement in its opposition to the treaty, but eventually the prevailing opinion was favorable or grudgingly accepting; see Coombs, *Jay's Treaty,* pp. 161–86.

31. J. C. A. Stagg, *Mr. Madison's War: Politics, Diplomacy, and Warfare in the Early American Republic, 1783–1830* (Princeton: Princeton University Press, 1983), pp. 3–47. On American trade after the Jay Treaty, see Donald R. Adams, Jr., "American Neutrality and Prosperity, 1793–1808: A Reconsideration," *Journal of Economic History* 40 (1980): 713–35. In 1809 Sheffield published the pamphlet *The Orders in Council and the American Embargo Beneficial to the Political and Commercial Interests of Great Britain.*

HISTORIOGRAPHIC NOTE

HISTORIANS have often identified the American Revolution with liberal political economy and noted its break with the mercantilism of the Old World. For an extreme statement of this view, see Robert E. Shalhope, "Individualism in the Early Republic," in *American Chameleon: Individualism in Trans-National Context*, edited by Richard O. Curry and Lawrence B. Goodheart (Kent, Ohio: Kent State University Press, 1991): "[*The Wealth of Nations*] had an enormous impact upon Republicans ... In this single book, Smith articulated inchoate beliefs that had permeated American society for decades" (p. 79). More tempered versions of this view can be found in Bernard Bailyn, "1776 A Year of Challenge—A World Transformed," *Journal of Law and Economics* 19 (1976); Drew R. McCoy, "Benjamin Franklin's Vision of a Republican Political Economy for America," *William and Mary Quarterly*, 3rd ser., 35 (1978); Drew R. McCoy, *The Elusive Republic: Political Economy in Jeffersonian America* (Chapel Hill: University of North Carolina Press, 1980); Joyce Appleby, "Modernization Theory and the Formation of Modern Social Theories in England and America," *Comparative Studies in Society and History* 20 (1978); Don Higginbotham, "The American Republic in a Wider World," in *The American Revolution: Its Character and Limits*, edited by Jack P. Greene (New York: New York University Press, 1987); and Merrill D. Peterson, "Thomas Jefferson and Commercial Policy, 1783–1793," *William and Mary Quarterly*, 3rd ser., 22 (1965). William D. Grampp, "Adam Smith and the American Revolutionists," *History of Political Economy* 11 (1979), places too much emphasis on Smith's nationalism, and most of the substantiation considerably postdates the Revolution.

These exaggerations of liberal political economy in the early Republic largely ignore a rich revisionist historiography taking its orientation from ideological conflicts of the New Deal era; namely, Frank Bourgin, *The Great Challenge: The Myth of Laissez-Faire in the Early Republic* (New York: Braziller, 1989); Oscar and Mary F. Handlin, *Commonwealth, A Study of the Role of Government in the American Economy: Massachusetts, 1774–1861* (1947; rev. ed. Cambridge, Mass.: Harvard University Press, 1969); William Appleman Williams, "The Age of Mercantilism: An Interpretation of American Political Economy, 1763–1828," *William and Mary Quarterly*, 3rd ser., 15 (1958); William Appleman Williams, *The Contours of American History* (London: Jonathan Cape, 1961); E. A. J. Johnson, *The Foundations of American Freedom: Government and Enterprise in the Age of Washington* (Minneapolis: University of Minnesota Press, 1973); and Arthur M. Schlesinger, Jr., "Affirmative Government and the American Economy," in *The Cycles of American History* (Boston: Houghton Mifflin, 1986). The work of Louis Hartz marked and shaped the subsequent privileging of liberal political economy in accounts of the early Republic. Despite his earlier book *Economic Policy and Democratic Thought: Pennsylvania, 1776–1860* (Cambridge, Mass.: Harvard University Press, 1948), in *The Liberal Tradition in America: An Interpretation of American Political Thought since the Revolution* (New York: Harcourt Brace Jovanovich, 1955), Hartz argued that explicit liberal political economy was slight in early American political culture because it was so deeply implicit.

The connection between republicanism and liberal political economy has grown more explicit and elaborate during the past two decades as the classical republican reinterpretation of early modern Anglo-American political culture, advanced most forcefully by J. G. A. Pocock, has itself been subjected to revision, particularly by Joyce Appleby and Isaac Kramnick. The classical republican interpretation has emphasized how the development of commerce was understood to result in the historical and personal erosion of civic virtue. The liberal interpretation has determined how liberty became increasingly identified with the advancement of individual economic interests as commercial relations became more extensive. On classical republican interpretations of a peculiarly defined "commerce" in early America— oriented as much to finance and patronage as to trade—see Pocock, *The Machiavellian Moment: Florentine Political Thought and the Atlantic Republican Tradition* (Princeton: Princeton University Press, 1975), chaps. 13–15; Lance Banning, *The Jeffersonian Persuasion: Evolution of a Party Ideology* (Ithaca: Cornell University Press, 1978); and McCoy, *The Elusive Republic*.

In a distinguished series of studies, Joyce Appleby has qualified the hegemony of classical republicanism by showing that "as important as the financial and glorious revolutions were in the history of ideology, the commercial revolution was even more important"; "Republicanism and Ideology," *American Quarterly* 37 (1983); "The Social Origins of American Revolutionary Ideology," *Journal of American History* 64 (1978); "What Is Still American in the Political Philosophy of Thomas Jefferson," *William and Mary Quarterly*, 3rd ser., 39 (1982); *Capitalism and a New Economic Order: The Republican Vision of the 1790s* (New York: New York University Press, 1984); and "Republicanism in Old and New Contexts," *William and Mary Quarterly*, 3rd ser., 43 (1986). On the fate of "radical economic liberalism" during the Revolution, see Cathy Matson, "American Political Economy in the Constitutional Decade," in *The United States Constitution: The First Two Hundred Years*, edited by R. C. Simmons (Manchester: Manchester University Press, 1989).

For historiographic considerations of the relative importance of classical republicanism and liberal political culture in the eighteenth century, see Donald Winch, "Economic Liberalism as Ideology: The Appleby Version," *Economic History Review*, 2d ser., 37 (1985); Donald Winch, *Adam Smith's Politics: An Essay in Historiographic Revision* (Cambridge: Cambridge University Press, 1978); Isaac Kramnick, "Republican Revisionism Revisited," *American Historical Review* 87 (1982); Isaac Kramnick, "'The Great National Discussion': The Discourse of Politics in 1787," *William and Mary Quarterly*, 3rd ser., 45 (1988); Lance Banning, "Jeffersonian Ideology Revisited: Liberal and Classical Ideas in the New American Republic," *William and Mary Quarterly*, 3rd ser., 43 (1986); Morton J. Horwitz, "Republicanism and Liberalism in American Constitutional Thought," *William and Mary Law Review* 29 (1987); James T. Kloppenberg, "The Virtues of Liberalism: Christianity, Republicanism, and Ethics in Early American Political Discourse," *Journal of American History* 74 (1987); and Daniel T. Rodgers, "Republicanism: The Career of a Concept," *Journal of American History* 79 (1992).

Both classical and liberal interpretations of early American republicanism have identified the relation of commerce to liberty as the crux of revolutionary ideology. Strikingly absent from either approach are considerations of the most apparent commercial compromise of liberty—the colonial relationship itself—and of the implications for liberty once independence ended that relationship. Exceptions are Appleby, "The Social Origins of American Revolutionary Ideology"; John W. Tyler, *Smugglers and Patriots: Boston Merchants and the Advent of the American Revolution* (Boston: Northeastern University Press, 1986); Cathy Diane Matson, "Fair Trade, Free Trade: Economic Ideas and Opportunities in Eighteenth-Century New York City Commerce," Ph.D. diss., Columbia University, 1985; James H. Hutson, "Intellectual Foundations of Early American Diplomacy," *Diplomatic History* 1 (1977); and James H. Hutson, *John Adams and the Diplomacy of the American Revolution* (Lexington: University Press of Kentucky, 1980). However, Hutson exaggerates American condemnation of foreign trade in general; cf. McCoy, *The Elusive Republic*. McCoy provides a convincing explanation for the critical importance of overseas trade in a republican political economy, but he minimizes the problems raised for this interpretation by the prerevolutionary emphasis on foreign trade in Anglo-American political economy.

On the connection between British commercial policy and the imperial crisis, see Jack P. Greene, "The Seven Years' War and the American Revolution: The Causal Relationship Reconsidered," in *The British Atlantic Empire before the American Revolution,* edited by Peter Marshall and Glyn Williams (London: Cass, 1980); John Bullion, *A Great and Necessary Measure: George Grenville and the Genesis of the Stamp Act, 1763–1765* (Columbia: University of Missouri Press, 1982); and Robert W. Tucker and David C. Hendrickson, *The Fall of the First British Empire: Origins of the War of American Independence* (Baltimore: Johns Hopkins University Press, 1982). For assessments of the actual value of the colonial trade, see Ralph Davis, "English Foreign Trade, 1700–1774," *Economic History Review*, 2d ser., 15 (1962–63); Jacob M. Price, "Colonial Trade and British Economic Development, 1660–1775," *Lex et Scientia* 14 (July-September 1978); Jacob M. Price, "Who Cared about the Colonies? The Impact of the Thirteen Colonies on British Society and Politics, Circa 1714–1775," in *Strangers within the Realm: Cultural Margins of the First British Empire,* edited by Bernard Bailyn and Philip D. Morgan (Chapel Hill: University of North Carolina Press, 1991); and Dorothy Burne Goebel, "The 'New England Trade' and the French West Indies, 1763–1774: A Study in Trade Policies," *William and Mary Quarterly*, 3rd ser., 20 (1963). On the 1760s as a period of "a powerful wave of deliberate protective legislation" for overseas trade generally, see Michael Kammen, *Empire and Interest: The American Colonies and the Politics of Mercantilism* (Philadelphia: Lippincott, 1970). For the classic (anachronistic) discussion of the utter distinction between political and economic purposes in imperial reform after the Seven Years' War, see George Louis Beer, *The Commercial Policy of England toward the American Colonies* (New York, 1893; reprint, New York: P. Smith, 1948).

There is an ample historiography about the economic costs and benefits to the American colonists of commercial regulation. For a review of this literature, see John J. McCusker and Russell R. Menard, *The Economy of British America, 1607–1789* (Chapel Hill: University of North Carolina Press, 1985). In particular, see Thomas C. Barrow, *Trade and Empire: The British Customs Service in Colonial America, 1660–1775* (Cambridge, Mass.: Harvard University Press, 1967); Marc Egnal and Joseph A. Ernst, "An Economic Interpretation of the American Revolution," *William and Mary Quarterly*, 3rd ser., 29 (1972); and Marc Egnal, *A Mighty Empire: The Origins of the American Revolution* (Ithaca: Cornell University Press, 1988). Cf. Oliver M. Dickerson, *The Navigation Acts and the American Revolution* (Philadelphia, 1951; reprint, New York: A. S. Barnes, 1963); Charles M. Andrews, *The Colonial Period of American History: England's Commercial and Colonial Policy,* 4 vols. (New Haven: Yale University Press, 1938; reprint, 1964); and Jack P. Greene, *Peripheries and Center: Constitutional Development in the Extended Polities of the British Empire and the United States, 1607–1788* (New York: Norton, 1990). For a discussion of postrevolutionary objections to the colonial character of the American economy, see Drew R. McCoy, "An Unfinished Revolution: The Quest for Economic Independence in the Early Republic," in *The American Revolution: Its Character and Limits,* edited by Jack P. Greene (New York: New York University Press, 1987). On the economic significance of independence, see Gordon C. Bjork, *Stagnation and Growth in the American Economy, 1784–1792* (New York: Garland, 1985); James F. Shepherd and Gary M. Walton, "Economic Change after the American Revolution: Pre- and Post-War Comparisons of Maritime Shipping and Trade," *Explorations in Economic History* 13 (1976); and Donald R. Adams, Jr., "American Neutrality and Prosperity, 1793–1808: A Reconsideration," *Journal of Economic History* 40 (1980).

On commercial diplomacy during the War for American Independence, see Lawrence S. Kaplan, *Colonies into Nation: American Diplomacy, 1763–1801* (New York: Macmillan, 1972); William C. Stinchcombe, "John Adams and the Model Treaty," in *The American Revolution and "A Candid World,"* edited by Lawrence S. Kaplan (Kent, Ohio: Kent State University Press, 1977); William C. Stinchcombe, *The American Revolution and the French Alliance* (Syracuse: Syracuse University Press, 1969); Gerald Stourzh, *Benjamin Franklin and American Foreign Policy,* 2d ed. (Chicago: University of Chicago Press, 1969); Paul A. Varg, *Foreign Policies of the Founding Fathers* (Baltimore: Penguin, 1963); and Vernon G. Setser, *The Commercial Reciprocity Policy of the United States, 1774–1829* (Philadelphia: University of Pennsylvania Press, 1937).

The topic of trade policy appears as an easily dismissed anomaly in interpretations of the politics of the early Continental Congress—namely, Jack N. Rakove, "The Decision for American Independence," *Perspectives in American History* 10 (1976); and H. James Henderson, *Party Politics in the Continental Congress* (New York: McGraw-Hill, 1974). Although historians have unavoidably noted the privileged importance of the fisheries as an issue in national economic interests, they have found it difficult to take fisheries' policy issues seriously and have therefore been unable to explain their significance to contemporaries—except as a natural sectional concern of New England. For example, Edmund Cody Burnett, *The Continental Congress* (New York: Macmillan, 1941), has a chapter facetiously entitled "The Rights of Cod and Haddock: Fish or Fight?" Despite asserting that "the struggle over the fisheries . . . was probably the most hotly contested parliamentary battle ever waged in Congress," Burnett does little to explain the fisheries as an issue (pp. 428–41). The steadfast support of such non–New Englanders as Richard Henry Lee and Henry Laurens for the priority of the fisheries is attributed to their support of Arthur Lee—begging the same question; namely, Jack N. Rakove, *The Beginnings of National Politics: An Interpretive History of the Continental Congress* (New York: Knopf, 1979).

Lord Sheffield's influence on postwar British commercial policy toward the United States is well known and is usually interpreted as archly mercantilist; namely, Anna Lane Lingelbach, "The Inception of the British Board of Trade," *American Historical Review* 30 (1925); Gerald S. Graham, *Sea Power and British North America, 1783–1820: A Study in British Colonial Policy* (1941; reprint, New York: Greenwood, 1968); Vincent T. Harlow, *The Founding of the Second British Empire, 1763–1793,* 2 vols. (London: Longmans, Green, 1952, 1964); Peter Marshall, "The First and Second British Empires: A Question of Demarcation," *History* 49 (1964); Ronald Hyam, "British Imperial Expansion in the Late Eighteenth Century," *Historical Journal* 10 (1967); John Philip Wise, "British Commercial Policy, 1783–1794: The Aftermath of American Independence," Ph.D. diss., University of London, 1971; D. L. MacKay, "Direction and Purpose in British Imperial Policy, 1783–1801," *Historical Journal* 17 (1974); Peter Marshall, "The British Empire in the Age of the American Revolution," in *The American Revolution: Changing Perspectives,* edited by William M. Fowler, Jr., and Wallace Coyle (Boston: Northeastern University Press, 1979); and David Fieldhouse, "British Imperialism in the Late Eighteenth Century: Defence or Opulence?" in *Essays in Imperial Government Presented to Margery Perham,*

edited by Kenneth Robinson and Frederick Madden (Oxford: B. Blackwell, 1963).
Many influential studies contrast British mercantilism and American liberal political economy in the 1780s. Julian Boyd thought that the conjunction of *The Wealth of Nations* and American independence provided an apparent contrast between the mercantilism soon identified with Lord Sheffield's *Observations on the Commerce of the American States* and the liberalism of Jefferson in his 1784 and 1793 reports on commerce: "*The Observations* . . . was a blueprint for policy, not a systematic formulation of the doctrine of mercantilism . . . the incoherent body of projections and practices known as mercantilism was a folk-doctrine with which the name of no theorist of the first rank was connected until the attacks of Smith and others began" (18:224n); *The Papers of Thomas Jefferson*, edited by Boyd et al., 27 vols. to date (Princeton: Princeton University Press, 1971). Madison's editors also contrast Sheffield, "a persuasive champion of mercantilism," with "the free trade followers of Adam Smith" (7:297n); *The Papers of James Madison*, edited by William Hutchinson and William M. E. Rachal, 16 vols. to date (Chicago: University of Chicago Press, 1971). For other identifications of Madison with liberal political economy, see Drew R. McCoy, "Republicanism and American Foreign Policy: James Madison and the Political Economy of Commercial Discrimination, 1789 to 1794," *William and Mary Quarterly*, 3rd ser., 31 (1974); and J. C. A. Stagg, *Mr. Madison's War: Politics, Diplomacy, and Warfare in the Early American Republic, 1783–1830* (Princeton: Princeton University Press, 1983).

In the vast literature on Adam Smith, the following are particularly relevant to this book: Jacob Viner, "Adam Smith and Laissez-Faire," in *The Long View and the Short: Studies in Economic Theory and Policy* (Glencoe, Ill.: Free Press, 1958); Donald Winch, "Science and the Legislator: Adam Smith and After," *Economic Journal* 93 (1983); Andrew S. Skinner, "Adam Smith and the American Economic Community: An Essay in Applied Economics," *Journal of the History of Ideas* 37 (1976); and A. W. Coats, "Adam Smith and the Mercantile System," in *Essays on Adam Smith*, edited by Andrew S. Skinner and Thomas Wilson (Oxford: Clarendon, 1975). For an argument that Smith was "intensely nationalist," see J. Shield Nicholson, *A Project of Empire: A Critical Study of the Economics of Imperialism, with Special Reference to the Ideas of Adam Smith* (London: MacMillan, 1909).

On the economic importance of overseas commerce in the political economy of the early Republic, see Frederick W. Marks III, *Independence on Trial: Foreign Affairs and the Making of the Constitution* (Baton Rouge: Louisiana State University Press, 1973); Janet Ann Riesman, "The Origins of American Political Economy, 1690–1781," Ph.D. diss., Brown University, 1983; Richard Buel, Jr., "Samson Shorn: The Impact of the Revolutionary War on Estimates of the Republic's Strength," in *Arms and Independence: The Military Character of the American Revolution*, edited by Ronald Hoffman and Peter J. Albert (Charlottesville: University Press of Virginia, 1984); and Lance Banning, "The Hamiltonian Madison: A Reconsideration," *Virginia Magazine of History and Biography* 92 (1984).

On the close association of political and commercial negotiations in eighteenth-century diplomacy, as well as the inability of American negotiators to separate them, see Felix Gilbert, *To the Farewell Address: Ideas of Early American Foreign Policy* (Princeton: Princeton University Press, 1961). These American difficulties bear comparison with British success in strictly commercial diplomacy in the 1780s; see John Ehrman, *The British Government and Commercial Negotiations with Europe, 1783–1793* (Cambridge: Cambridge University Press, 1962).

The best accounts of the policy of commercial discrimination in the 1780s are Marks, *Independence on Trial;* Merrill Jensen, *The New Nation: A History of the United*

States during the Confederation, 1781–1789 (New York: Vintage, 1950); Robert Bruce Bittner, "The Definition of Economic Independence and the New Nation," Ph.D. diss., University of Wisconsin, 1970, chap. 7; and McCoy, "Republicanism and American Foreign Policy." McCoy construes republican advocacy of commerce as ipso facto "free trade"; *The Elusive Republic* (pp. 76, 85–95, 100–103). This association leads to the exaggeration of manufactures and the slighting of commercial regulation as issues in the 1780s. Madison's apparent state particularism regarding commercial regulation is not troubling for most interpretations of his nationalism. An excellent corrective is Lance Banning, "James Madison and the Nationalists, 1780–1783," *William and Mary Quarterly*, 3rd ser., 40 (1983).

Sectionalist interpretations of the Confederation's commercial policy cannot offer convincing explanations for southerners' support of the nationalist program; Merrill Jensen, "The Sovereign States: Their Antagonisms and Rivalries and Some Consequences," in *Sovereign States in an Age of Uncertainty*, edited by Ronald Hoffman and Peter J. Albert (Charlottesville: University Press of Virginia, 1981). Such an interpretation overlooks the priority of retaliatory and coercive diplomacy over more strictly commercial concerns in the nationalists' strategy. An especially helpful discussion of economic sectionalism as an issue on the eve of the Constitutional Convention is Cathy D. Matson and Peter S. Onuf, *A Union of Interests: Political and Economic Thought in Revolutionary America* (Lawrence: University Press of Kansas, 1990). On Madison's advocacy of southern and western regional interests in later federal politics, see Drew R. McCoy, "James Madison and Visions of American Nationality in the Confederation Period: A Regional Perspective," in *Beyond Confederation: Origins of the Constitution and American National Identity*, edited by Richard Beeman, Stephen Botein, and Edward C. Carter II (Chapel Hill: University of North Carolina Press, 1987). On the economic potential of the West, see Peter S. Onuf, "Liberty, Development, and Union: Visions of the West in the 1780s," *William and Mary Quarterly*, 3rd ser., 43 (1986).

On the importance of commercial regulation as an issue at the Constitutional Convention, see Lance Banning, "The Hamiltonian Madison: A Reconsideration"; Marks, *Independence on Trial;* Lance Banning, "Power, Pride, and Purse: Diplomatic Origins of the Constitution," *Diplomatic History* 11 (1987); Lawrence S. Kaplan, "Jefferson and the Constitution: The View from Paris, 1786–1789," *Diplomatic History* 11 (1987); Norman A. Graebner, "Isolationism and Antifederalism: The Ratification Debates," *Diplomatic History* 11 (1987); Jack N. Rakove, "The Road to Philadelphia, 1781–1787," in *The Framing and Ratification of the Constitution,* edited by Leonard W. Levy and Dennis J. Mahoney (New York: Macmillan, 1987); and William Winslow Crosskey, "The Eighteenth Century's Usage of *Commerce* and Its Synonyms," in *Politics and the Constitution in the History of the United States,* vol. 1 (Chicago: University of Chicago Press, 1953; reprint, 1965). The best discussion of Hamilton's mercantilism is Gerald Strouzh, *Alexander Hamilton and the Idea of Republican Government* (Stanford: Stanford University Press, 1970); see also Edward Mead Earle, "Adam Smith, Alexander Hamilton, Friedrich List: The Economic Foundations of Military Power," in *Makers of Modern Strategy: Military Thought from Machiavelli to Hitler,* edited by Edward Mead Earle (Princeton: Princeton University Press, 1948). On federalist criticisms of classical republicanism, see Thomas L. Pangle, "The *Federalist Papers'* Vision of Civic Health and the Tradition Out of Which That Vision Emerges," *Western Political Quarterly* 39 (1986). David F. Epstein, *The Political Theory of "The Federalist"* (Chicago: University of Chicago Press, 1984), explains how Madison discussed the differences of wealth in relation to people's general "faculties," rather than address the Lockean question of the economic processes of acquisition. The best discussion of political economy in Madison's constitutional thought is Jennifer Nedelsky, *Private Property and the Limits of American Constitutionalism* (Chicago: University of Chicago Press, 1990), which shows Madison's priority for economic security and his relative lack of concern for economic opportunity. McCoy, "Republicanism and American Foreign Policy," presents a republican interpretation of Madison's political economy as an alternative to interpretations that Madison was either "a parochial or short-sighted agrarian" or a "mercantilist" who "promoted American manufacturing": "Above all, Madison intended to demonstrate the ability of America's 'natural' economic power to shatter Old World mercantilist restrictions" (pp. 634, 645). It is an argument of this book that Madison's political economy, while harmonious with his republicanism, did not depend on it, and it remained self-consciously mercantilist in the sense of slighting or countermanding the imperatives of market relations in the name of political imperatives.

On the antifederalists' political economy, see James H. Hutson, "County, Court, and Constitution: Anti-Federalism and the Historians," *William and Mary Quarterly*, 3rd ser., 38 (1981); Herbert J. Storing, "What the Anti-Federalists Were *For*," in *The Complete Anti-Federalist*, edited by Herbert J. Storing, 6 vols. (Chicago: University of Chicago Press, 1981); and Gordon S. Wood, "Interests and Disinterestedness in the Making of the Constitution," in *Beyond Confederation*. Wood's concern is primarily with the reaction of the federalists against nascent entrepreneuralism during the Revolution, in particular their determination to devise a government that could define a public good when subject to the political demands of particular interests. In one respect Wood perpetuates the agrarian-cosmopolitan distinction between antifederalists and federalists: he identifies the antifederalists with interests primarily in the domestic economy and the federalists with foreign trade.

On republican political economy, see McCoy, "Republicanism and American Foreign Policy," and Cathy Matson and Peter Onuf, "Toward a Republican Empire: Interest and Ideology in Revolutionary America," *American Quarterly* 37 (1985). On Madison and Jefferson's later readiness to support the development of manufactures as well as agriculture, see John R. Nelson, *Liberty and Property: Political Economy and Policymaking in the New Nation, 1789–1812* (Baltimore: Johns Hopkins University Press, 1987); see also Joseph J. Spengler, "The Political Economy of Jefferson, Madison, and Adams," in *American Studies in Honor of William Kenneth Boyd by Members of the Americana Club of Duke University*, edited by David Kelly Johnson (1940; reprint, Freeport, N.Y.: Books for Libraries, 1968). This latter seldom-cited essay anticipated many of the themes discussed in the recent historiography of American republicanism.

On conflicts over commercial policy as sources of partisanship in national politics, see Peterson, "Thomas Jefferson and Commercial Policy, 1783–1793." See also "Representation by France against the Tonnage Acts . . . Editorial Note," in *Papers of Thomas Jefferson*, where Boyd charges Hamilton with "mere political expediency" for having advocated strong powers of commercial regulation for the proposed federal government and then preventing their use (supposedly) lest they disrupt his fiscal program by antagonizing Britain to further restrictions on American trade. However, Madison and Jefferson's efforts to use the new government's powers of commercial regulation "to achieve commercial reciprocity and to restore the dignity of the national character" did not (in Boyd's eyes) make them "advocate[s] of an American system of mercantilism." Hamilton remained mercantilism's "fountainhead in the new world" (18:519). See also "Report on the Fisheries . . . Editorial Note," in ibid., vol. 19; and Robert W. Tucker and David C. Hendrickson, *Empire of Liberty: The Statecraft of Thomas Jefferson* (New York: Oxford University Press, 1990).

For an excellent corrective to American historians' tendency to adopt at face value the Madisonian-Jeffersonian account of British commercial policy, see Charles R. Ritcheson, *Aftermath of Revolution: British Policy toward the United States, 1783–1795* (1969; reprint, New York: Norton, 1971). The best discussion of Hamilton's commercial policy is Nelson, *Liberty and Property*, chap. 4, though the label "neocolonialism" is arguable.

On Hamilton as mercantilist, see Earle, "Adam Smith, Alexander Hamilton, Friedrich List: The Economic Foundations of Military Power"; John C. Miller, *Alexander Hamilton and the Growth of the New Nation* (New York: Harper Torchbooks, 1964); and Louis M. Hacker, *Alexander Hamilton in the American Tradition* (New York: McGraw-Hill, 1957). The best comparison of the influences on Hamilton's political economy is the editorial commentary in *The Papers of Alexander Hamilton*, vol. 10, edited by Harold C. Syrett and Jacob E. Cooke, 27 vols. (New York: Columbia University Press, 1966), which includes Hamilton's four drafts of the report and finds dozens of close parallels with *The Wealth of Nations*.

INDEX

Adams, John: on American fisheries, 63; commercial diplomacy of, 74–75, 105; commercial policy and, 54–55; commissions of, withdrawn, 66, 95; drafts model plan of treaties, 58; Lord Howe's peace commission and, 59

Adams, Samuel, on American fisheries, 63

Agriculture, encouragement of, 136–37; Hamilton on, 150–51

American Intercourse Bill. *See* Pownall, John

Anglo-American trade, 157; Americans as consumers, 84, 105; expectations of reciprocity in, 68–73, 85; Hamilton's liberalism toward, 154; Madison's opposition to reciprocity in, 98–100; restrictions on, in British empire, 96, 189n.15; as threat to American independence, 164; U.S. wants reciprocity in, 104–5

Anglo-French commercial treaty of 1786 (Eden Treaty), 77, 87–88, 156, 186n.46, 187n.47

Antifederalists: as anticapitalist, 127, 193n.28; on commercial regulation, 126–33

Appleby, Joyce, 202

Articles of Confederation, 94, 107; Congress's regulatory powers, 117

Beard, Charles, 127

Beckworth, George, 167

Bland, Richard, 22

Board of Trade, 14. *See also* Committee for Trade and Plantations

Boston Committee of Correspondence, 32

Boston Port Act, 31–32

Boston Tea Party, 30–31

Boyd, Julian, 205, 207

British West Indies: British economy and, 18, 44–45, 178n.64; commercial

privileges and, 45; lobbying of, by merchants and planters, 43, 82; neomercantilists' view of, 81; provisions from mainland colonies and, 14–16, 43; supplies from U.S. and, 104–5, 110, 140, 165–66

Burgoyne, General John, 40

Burke, Edmund, 31–32, 76; on commercial empire, 45–46; opposition of, to commercial reciprocity, 72

Burke, William, 27

Bute, Earl of (John Stuart), 76

Cantillon, Richard, 1

Carlisle, first Earl of (Frederick Howard), peace commission of, 61–62

Cartwright, John, on Anglo-American trade, 47–48, 178n.64

Chalmers, George, 84; on Britain's postrevolutionary economy, 92; career of, 76; neomercantilism of, 78–80

Chatham, Earl of (William Pitt), 27, 38, 46

Clymer, George, 119

Coercive Acts, 30–32, 37, 50

Commerce, American postrevolutionary, foreign restrictions on, 74

Commerce, colonial: British need for, 13, 38–39, 46–49, 177n.32; British need to regulate, 13–14, 18–19, 30, 62. *See also* Anglo-American trade

Commerce, U.S.: Jefferson's report on foreign privileges and restrictions, 156–59

Commerce as foreign trade, xi–xii, 205

Commercial diplomacy, U.S.: historiography of, 204–5; mercantilism in, 57; most-favored-nation status in, 75; postrevolutionary, 74–75; strategy of coercion in, 55

Commercial discrimination, U.S.: Hamilton's opposition to, 194n.14; historiography of, 205–6; Jefferson

Franco-American Treaty of Amity and
Commerce, 60–61, 75, 142, 181n.41
Franklin, Benjamin, 48; commercial diplomacy of, 74; Lord Howe's peace
commission and, 59–60; mercantilism
of, 8–9; opening American trade and,
50–51; treaty of peace and, 66, 68
French Republic: commercial policy of,
156; revolutionary war, 156
French West Indies, American commerce
with, 58–59, 61, 82

Gadsden, Christopher, 36
Gardoqui, Diego de, 75
Genêt, Edmond Charles, 156
George III, King (of England), 78
Germain, Lord George, 76
Gibbon, Edward, 72, 76, 85
Grenville, George, 18, 32; Charles
Jenkinson and, 76
Grenville, Lord William Wyndham, ne-
gotiations of, with Jay, 167

Hamilton, Alexander: on Anglo-
American trade, 154; British model
for policy, 123–24; on commercial origins of war, 122–23; criticized by
George Logan, 197n.42; disputes privileges for France, 142; historiography
on, 208; influence of *The Wealth of Nations* on, 148–49, 151, 196nn. 35, 36;
on market imperatives, 153–54,
197n.46; navigation policy and, 123–
24; as neomercantilist, 148, 153–54;
opposition of, to commercial discrimination, 194n.14, 195n.20; Report on
Manufactures, 146–53, 197n.47; on
revenue from foreign commerce, 124–
25; Smith, William Loughton, and,
160
Hammond, George, 156
Harrison, Benjamin, 73, 103, 105–6
Hartley, David, 72
Hat Act of 1732, 34
Hawkesbury, Lord (Charles Jenkinson),
75–76, 82, 200n.28; on Corn Laws, 91;
on Eden Treaty, 88; on U.S. commercial policy, 145
Hicks, William, 22
Holroyd, John Baker. *See* Sheffield, Lord

Hopkins, Stephen, as spokesman for colonial merchants, 15–17
Howe, Admiral Viscount Richard, peace
commission of, 59–60
Hudson Bay trade, British monopoly of,
105
Hume, David, 48, 78, 83, 149; liberal political economy of, 6–8

Impost, by Confederation, 86; as legislative model for federal Congress, 134–
35; Madison's recommendations for,
99
Independence, American, as issue in
British politics, 67
Ireland and British West Indies, 43

Jay, John, 52, 95; on commercial jealousy,
121; drafts articles of peace, 66, 68;
negotiates commercial treaty with Britain, 165; negotiates Mississippi navigation, 111; negotiations with Diego de
Gardoqui, 75; as secretary for foreign
affairs, 74
Jay-Gardoqui negotiations, 75, 114–15,
191n.38
Jay-Grenville Treaty, terms of: for British West Indies trade, 166; Hamilton's
influence on, 167; Hamilton's repudiation of Article Twelve, 167, 200n.29;
prohibition of U.S. exportation of
tropical products, 166
Jefferson, Thomas: on American consumption patterns, 106; coached by
Madison on diplomacy, 112–14; commercial diplomacy of, 74–75, 105; on
commercial privileges for France, 142,
158–59; compared with British neomercantilists, 145; on encouragement
of manufactures, 159; on encouragement of navigation, 144–45, 159; on
encouragement of U.S. fisheries, 142–
44, 198n.51; on French trade, 106,
194n.12; on impracticality of free
trade, 158; on market imperatives,
155; mercantilism of, 106–7, 207; orientation of, to staple economies, 155;
as peace commissioner, 66; on privileges for American whale products,
195n.21; Report on the Privileges and
Restrictions on the Commerce of

on retaliatory discrimination, 196n.26. *See also* Smith, Adam
Wedderburn, Alexander, 32, 39
West Indies. *See* British West Indies; French West Indies
Whale products as commodities, 73, 157; U.S. exportations of, to France, 75, 143, 195n.21
Whately, Thomas, 18–19

Wilkes, John, 38
Williamson, Hugh, 119
Wilson, James: on commercial empire, 34–35; at Constitutional Convention, 118
Winthrop, James, "Letters of Agrippa," 132–33
Wood, Gordon S., 127, 132, 207

Designed by Laury A. Egan

Composed by The Composing Room of Michigan, Inc.,
in Baskerville text and display

Printed on 50-lb. Penntech Cream
and bound in Holliston Roxite cloth
by Maple Press